Tanks and other Armored Fighting Vehicles
1942–1945

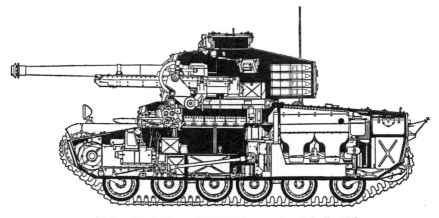

Medium Tank, Type 3 (Chi-Nu), Japan — length (hull) 18′6″

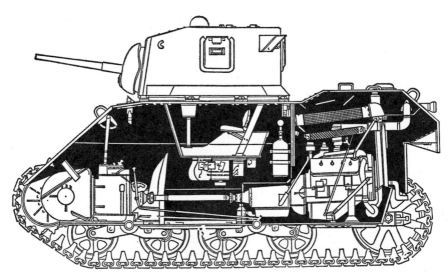

Light Tank, M.5, U.S.A. — length 14′ 2¾″

Mechanized Warfare in Colour

TANKS

and other
Armored Fighting Vehicles
1942–1945

by
B. T. WHITE

Illustrated by
JOHN W. WOOD
B. Hiley
J. Pelling
E. Bruce

NEW ORCHARD EDITIONS

New Orchard Editions Ltd.
Stanley House
3 Fleets Lane
Poole, Dorset BN15 3AJ

This edition published 1988

ISBN 1 85079 039 6

Text printed and bound in Great Britain
by Richard Clay Ltd, Bungay, Suffolk

PREFACE

The period covered by this book is 1942–45, but some tanks and armoured vehicles (notably Japanese and American) developed before this have been included in order that a comparison can be made between them and late vehicles with which they were in combat or served alongside.

The wide variety of armoured vehicles of all kinds appertaining to the period has made it necessary, in many cases, to show illustrations of two different types on one page in order to increase the coverage of representative vehicles. This, in turn, has increased the difficulty of arranging the vehicles in a strict chronological order, even were it possible to reach a satisfactory decision between the relative importance of date of prototype, date of entry into production, date of entry into service, first time in action and so on. Therefore, it has been decided, for this volume, to group vehicles under countries and sub-divided into types—light tanks, medium tanks, heavy tanks, self-propelled guns, special armour, and armoured cars, in approximate chronology, where appropriate, for each type. The sequence of countries follows no particular pattern except that as several Japanese vehicles dating from before 1942 are included, the section on Japan comes first. Commonwealth A.F.V.s are mixed in with corresponding U.K. vehicles, as production and design in the Commonwealth was so closely linked with the U.K. during this period. Specialized armoured vehicles devised and built by the United Kingdom but using American chassis are listed under 'United Kingdom', although the origin

of the basic vehicle is given in the text.

Camouflage colours and vehicle markings applicable to the period covered have been shown as accurately as possible on the strength of the information obtainable. However, readers particularly interested in this subject are referred to the notes in the appendix at the back of this book

Although detailed technical information cannot be provided in a small book of this kind, cross-section side elevations of representative armoured fighting vehicles of several countries are included at the back of this book to give some idea of the internal layout of the various components. Also, to supplement details mentioned in the main text, data tables for some of the leading A.F.V.s are given as an appendix.

Many printed sources, too numerous to acknowledge individually, have been used in the preparation of this book, but two small journals, published for modellers of A.F.V.s but containing the results of a great deal of original work on A.F.V. history deserve special mention—these are *Tankette* (Editor, J. P. Wilkes, 26 Stirling Grove, Whitefield, Manchester, Lancs, M25 6BY, England) and *A.F.V.News* (Editor, George Bradford, R.R. No. 2, Preston, Ontario, Canada).

The author also wishes to thank all the firms, institutions and individuals, including many friends, who have contributed over many years to his general background of knowledge of the subject. In particular, however, should be mentioned Colonel Robert J. Icks (who has an incomparable private collection on the subject of A.F.V.s), Colonel Peter Hordern, Director of the Royal Armoured Corps Tank Museum, Bovington, Dorset, England (where a fine display of A.F.V.s is open to the public) and his predecessors, and the staff of the reference departments of the Imperial War Museum, London.

Finally, for their invaluable help in converting my illegible manuscripts into typescripts, thanks are due to Mrs Betty Scotland and to Janis, my wife.

B. T. WHITE
London, 1975

INTRODUCTION

The war on land 1942-45

The beginning of 1942 was marked by notable success for Japanese arms, following the attack on the United States fleet in Pearl Harbor in December 1941 and the invasion of British, Dutch, French and U.S. overseas territories. The whole area was largely unsuited to the use of armour but, its use nevertheless, was more important than is generally supposed.

Unlike the Far East battles, armour had played the main part in the North African campaign where in April 1942 Axis forces were at the gateway to Cairo; fortunes changed at El Alamein in October and led to the Germans and Italians being expelled from the African continent, the final actions taking place in Tunisia in early 1943, where the British Eighth Army met up with the Anglo-American force that had landed in Morocco and Algeria in November of the previous year. The Mediterranean battles were transferred next to Sicily and then to Italy; much more difficult terrain for the employment of armour.

The great German–Soviet battles on the Eastern Front continued, but the halting of the Germans at Stalingrad in the winter months of 1942 was the turning point. The greatest tank battle of all time took place at Kursk in summer 1943, leading eventually to the Russians fighting their way into Berlin in April 1945.

In the West, the Anglo-Canadian raid on Dieppe in August 1942 showed the need for adequate preparations (including the development of special armoured vehicles) for the full scale invasion of North West Europe so that,

despite Russian demands, D-Day did not take place until June 1944

The land war in the Far East was gradually won by the Allies (before its abrupt termination by the atomic bombs dropped on Japan itself) by the 1944-45 campaign in Burma and the island-hopping amphibious operations in the Pacific.

Armour Developments

The influence of the excellent Soviet medium and heavy tanks and the powerful German tanks developed to counter them was the predominant feature of tank development in 1942 and continued to be so for the greater part of the war. Although the later German tanks—exemplified by the Tiger I, Panther and Tiger II tended to have a slightly better armament/armour combination, the Russian tanks were the more reliable, thanks in part to the longer development history of their excellent diesel engines and, no doubt, to their less complex design. The German PzKpfw III and IV, although greatly improved, were continued in production longer than was desirable, but an earlier change to the new Panther would have left a dangerous shortage of medium tanks at a critical time. Production difficulties also led to the increased emphasis on the well-armed and armoured Sturmgeschütz at the expense of tanks. The turretless Sturmgeschütz was simpler to make but less flexible in use than a tank. An unwanted diversion from German battle-tank production was brought

7

about by the need for anti-aircraft tanks due to Allied air superiority. By contrast, A.A. tanks were largely dropped from British and United States formations after 1944.

British-built tanks were generally out-gunned by German armour to the end of the war, the Comet of 1944 probably being the best all-round answer to enemy medium tanks. The Cromwell was a good fast tank for reconnaissance purposes and the Churchill series were well armoured although both types were under-gunned. The Challenger (built in small numbers) and the British-modified Sherman Firefly, both with the British 17-pr gun, were for a long time the only Allied tanks on the Western front up to tackling the Tiger at all ranges. The U.S. Pershing, equal to the Tiger, arrived in small numbers only in 1945.

The American Sherman and the Russian T-34 were the outstanding tanks of the war on the Allied side. The Sherman, reliable, easy to maintain, and capable of being up-gunned from the original 75-mm. formed the mainstay of American and British armoured formations on many fronts.

Italian armour development during the period under review in essence amounted to the M.15/42 medium, developed from the closely similar M.13/40, and a switch to the production of the Semoventi. These were well-armoured self-propelled mountings, akin to the German Sturmgeschütz and produced to a policy similar to that of the Germans. The only Italian heavy tank was built in small quantities before the Italian armistice.

Japanese tanks were mechanically sound and were the result of a carefully thought out development plan. The lightest tanks ('tankettes') were intended only as infantry carriers and the light and medium tanks were no match for their Allied counterparts. The later better-armed Japanese medium tanks were built in such small numbers as to have no influence on the war. The lack of effective opposition made it possible for the British forces in Burma in 1944–45 to make good use of American-built Lee/Grant tanks, which had made their mark in the 1942 Desert campaigns but were no longer suitable for employment against the Germans.

The most outstanding British contribution to armour in World War II was perhaps in the design and development of specialized armour, such as anti-mine flail tanks, flamethrowers, bridging tanks, armoured searchlight tanks, engineer tanks and amphibious devices. The Japanese also showed ingenuity in producing specialized armour, although apart from amphibians they appear to have made relatively little use of it. The Pacific island battles saw wide use of American tracked landing vehicles in assault, cargo and troop-carrying roles. L.V.T.s were employed by the Allies also in Italy and in major river crossings in Germany.

Self-propelled guns were used in wide variety by Germany, often as a means of putting to good use obsolescent tank chassis to give mobility to field and anti-tank weapons. Lightly armoured compared with the Sturmgeschütz type of vehicle, these self-propelled guns gave good service, despite the logistic problem the many

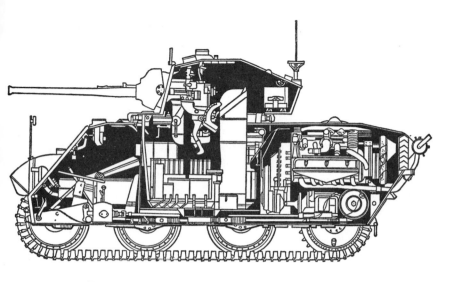

Tank, Light, Mark VIII, Harry Hopkins, U.K. — length 14′3″

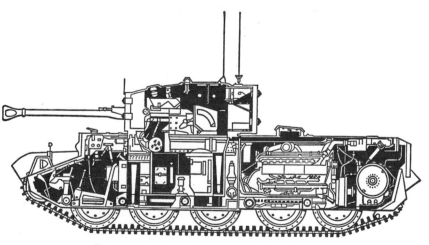

Tank, Cruiser, Cromwell VIII, U.K. — length 20′10″

9

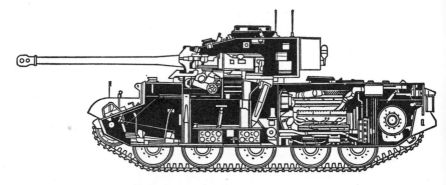

Tank, Cruiser, Comet, U.K. — length 21′6″

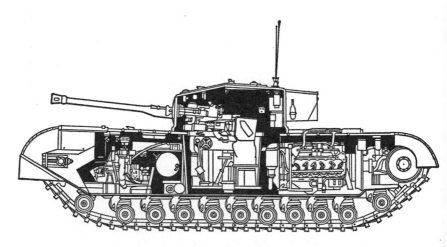

Tank, Infantry, Mark IV, Churchill III, U.K. — length 24′5″

different chassis and weapons must have created. British S.P. weapons were fewer and more standardized, the Canadian 25-pr Sexton being one of the best. American policy, after early efforts on wheeled and half-tracked chassis, was generally to standardize on tank chassis. Some American S.P.s— notably the 105-mm. (Priest) and 3-in. M.10 were also used by British forces. Powerful and well-armoured Soviet S.P. guns were mounted on T-34, KV and JS chassis.

Wheeled armoured vehicles, as in earlier stages of the war, continued to be developed in the greatest variety by the British Commonwealth countries. A version of the useful Daimler Scout Car was built in Canada (and even in prototype form in Italy, where British A.F.V.s were admired) together with light and medium armoured cars. India and South Africa also built in quantity wheeled armoured vehicles using Canadian automotive parts.

The British Daimler armoured car was probably the best Allied armoured car of World War II, being compact and manœuvrable and with a reasonably good cross-country performance as well as being better armoured and

armed than most German armoured cars. The German eight-wheelers were powerful and of excellent mechanical design but clumsy by British standards.

The half-track continued to the end of the war to be a characteristic German vehicle, the armoured 1-ton and 3-ton variants still being used in large numbers, although basically infantry-carrying or support vehicles. Many comparable functions were carried out in British units by small full-tracked armoured vehicles of the Universal Carrier type. Half-tracks were also produced in small numbers by Japan and in large quantities for the Allies by the United States. The U.S. half-tracks, almost all of which were armoured, were relatively straight-forward designs but had one advantage over their German opposite numbers in having a driven front axle

This wide variety of tracked, wheeled and half-tracked armoured vehicles was produced in staggering quantities by the countries at war, production rising (even in Germany under heavy Allied air attack) to a peak in 1944–45, so that, for example, the United States alone had built by the end of the war nearly 89,000 tanks.

A description of each of the following coloured plates commences on page 93 and ends on page 154.

1
Tankette, Type 97 (Te-Ke) (*above*) and Light Tank, Type
95 (Ha-Go)

2
Medium Tank, Type 97 (Shinhoto Chi-Ha) (*above*) and
Medium Tank, Type 3 (Chi-Nu)

3
Medium Tank, Type 4 (Chi-To) (*above*) and Medium Tank, Type 5 (Chi-Ri)

4
Gun Tank, Type 1 (Ho-Ni I) (*above*) and 15-cm. S.P.
Howitzer, Type 4 (Ho-Ro)

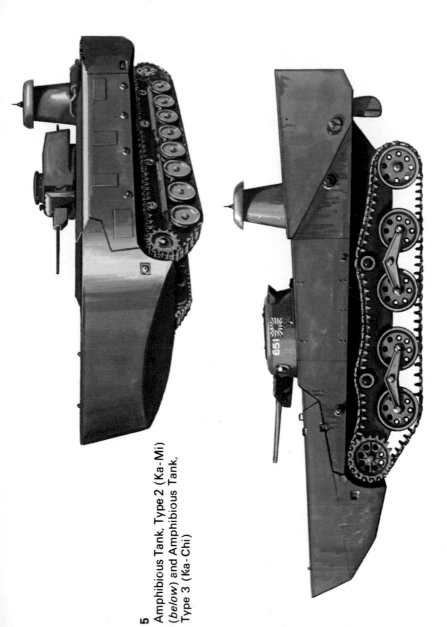

5 Amphibious Tank, Type 2 (Ka-Mi) (*below*) and Amphibious Tank, Type 3 (Ka-Chi)

6

Flail Tank (*above*), and Engineer Vehicle—Jungle Cutter (Ho-K)

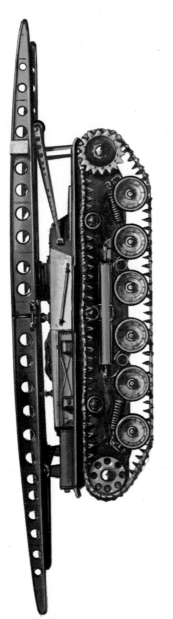

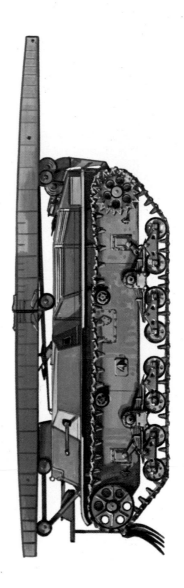

7
Tank Recovery Vehicle, Type E (*below*) and Tank Bridge-layer (Medium Type 97 chassis)

Japan

8
Armoured Personnel Carrier, Half-tracked, Type 1 (Ho-Ha)
(*below*) and Armoured Personnel Carrier, Tracked, Type 1
(Ho-Ki)

9
Light Tank M.5A1 (*below*) and 75-mm. Howitzer Motor
Carriage, M.8

10
Light Tank, M.22 (Locust) (*below*) and Light Tank, M.24
(Chaffee)

11
Medium Tank, M.3 (Lee) (*above*) and Tank, Medium,
Grant

12
Medium Tank, M.4 (typical) (*below*) and Sherman Vc

13
Medium Tank, M.26 (Pershing)

14
Heavy Tanks, M.6 (*above*) and M.6A1

15
105-mm. Howitzer Motor Carriage, M.7 (*above*), and as 'S.P. 105-mm. Priest' (*below*)

16

3-in. Gun Motor Carriage, M.10 (*above*) and 76-mm. Gun Motor Carriage, M.18

17
Landing Vehicle, Tracked (Unarmored) Mark IV (LVT4)
(*below*) and Landing Vehicle, Tracked (Armored), Mark
IV (LVT[A]4)

18
Car, Half-Track M.2A1 (*below*) and 75-mm. Gun Motor
Carriage, M.3

19
Armored Car, Staghound I
(T.17E1) (*below*) and
Armored Car, Boarhound (T.18E2)

U.S.A.

20
Light Armored Car, M.8 (*above*)
and Armored Utility Car, M.20

21
Tank, Light, Mark VII, Tetrarch (*below*)
and Tank, Light, Mark VIII, Harry Hopkins

22
Tanks, Cruiser, Mark VI, Crusader I (*above*) and Crusader III

23
Tanks, Cruiser, Centaur IV (*below*) and Cromwell

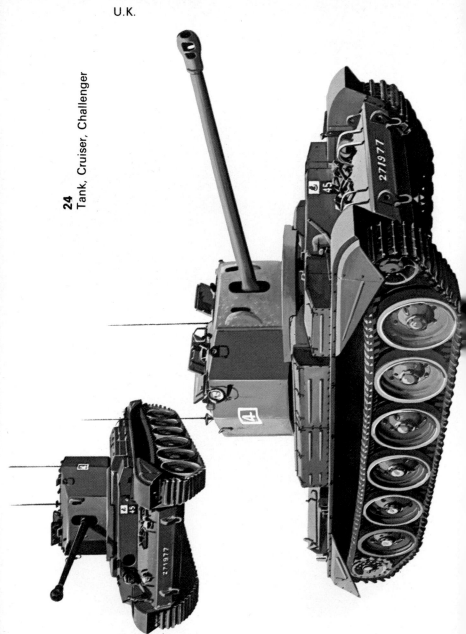

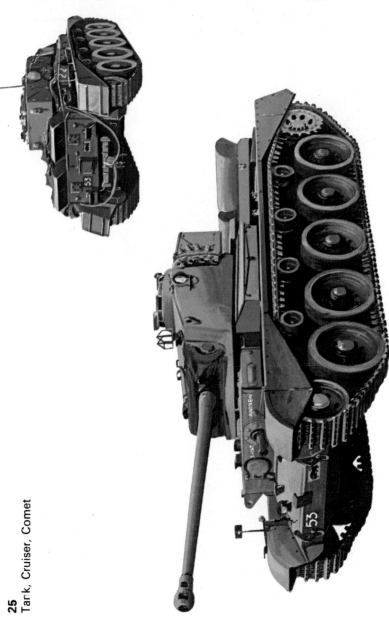

25
Tank, Cruiser, Comet

Canada

26
Tank, Cruiser, Ram II (*above*) and Armoured Personnel
Carrier, Ram Kangaroo

27
Australian Cruiser Tanks, Mark I (*above*) and Mark III

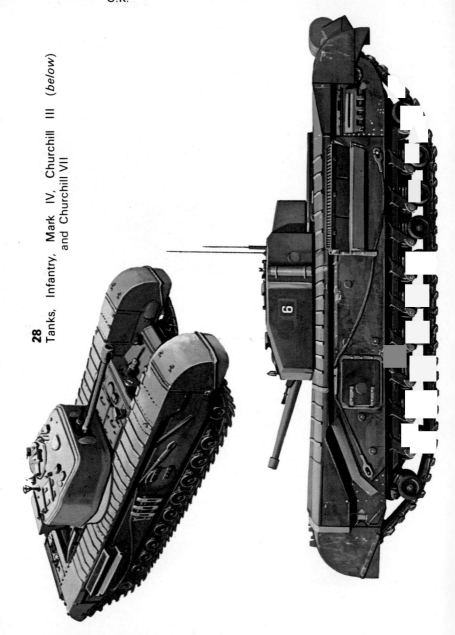

28
Tanks, Infantry, Mark IV, Churchill III (*below*)
and Churchill VII

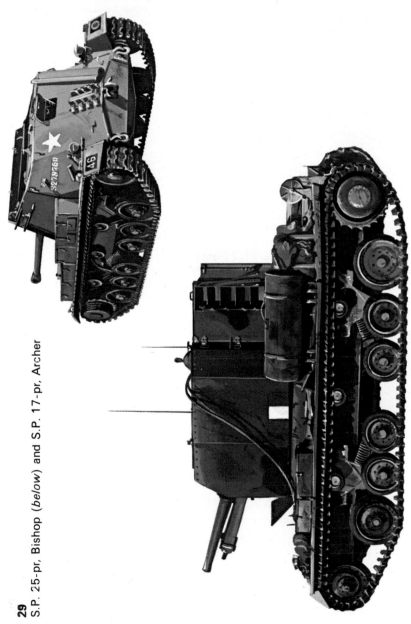

29
S.P. 25-pr, Bishop (*below*) and S.P. 17-pr, Archer

Canada

30
S.P. 25-pr, Sexton

U.K.

31
Sherman D.D.

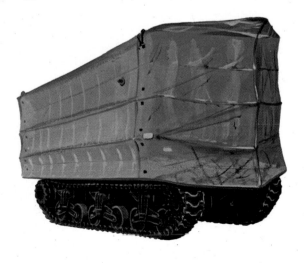

32
Churchill VII Crocodile (*below*) and Grant C.D.L.

33
Matilda Scorpion Mark I (*below*) and Grant Scorpion
Mark IV

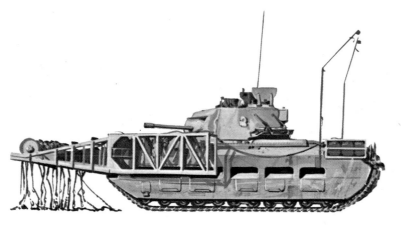

34
Sherman Crab I (*above*) and Crab II

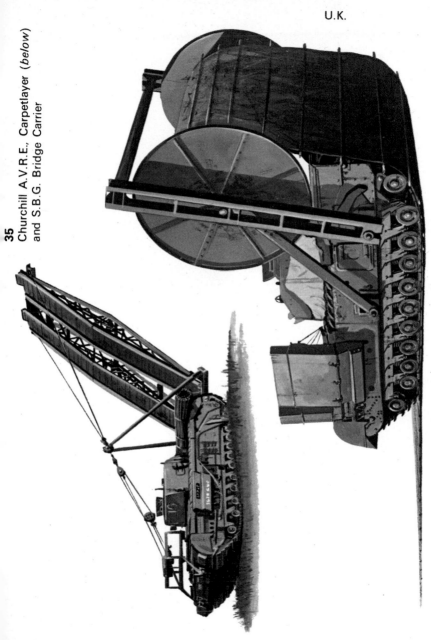

U.K.

35
Churchill A.V.R.E., Carpetlayer (*below*)
and S.B.G. Bridge Carrier

36
Churchill A.R.V., Mark I (*below*) and Sherman B.A.R.V.

37
Carrier, Universal, Mark II (*below*) and Carrier, 2-pr, Tank
Attack (Aust.)

38
South African Armoured Reconnaissance Cars, Mark IV
(*below*) and Mark VI

Armoured Cars, Humber

U.K.

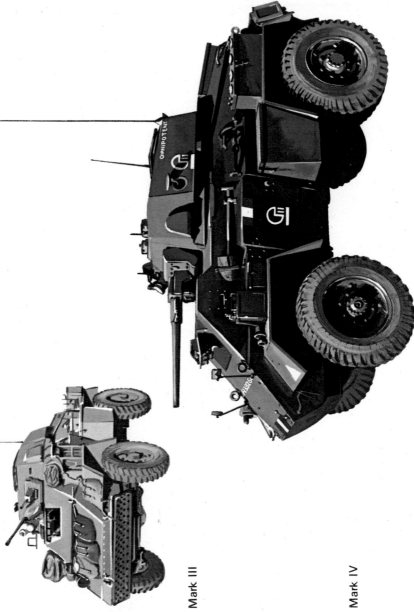

Mark III

Mark IV

U.K.

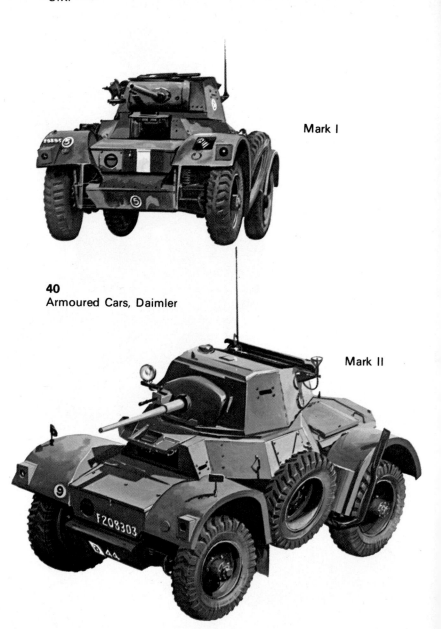

Mark I

40
Armoured Cars, Daimler

Mark II

41
Armoured Cars, A.E.C.,

Mark II

Mark III

42
Car, Scout, Humber, Mark I

43
Car, Scout, Ford, Lynx II (*above*) and Car, Light Reconnaissance, Canadian G.M., Mark I, Otter I

44
Cars, 4 × 4, Light Reconnaissance, Humber, Mark IIIA
(*below*) and Morris, Mark II

45

Armoured Carrier, Wheeled, I.P., A.O.V.

Armoured Carrier, Wheeled, I.P., Mark IIA

46

Armoured Command Vehicle (A.E.C.) 4 × 4, Mark I

U.K.

Armoured Command Vehicle (A.E.C.) 6 × 6, Mark I

47

S.P. 17-pr Gun—Straussler

Carrier, A.E.C., 6-pr Gun, Mark I (Deacon)

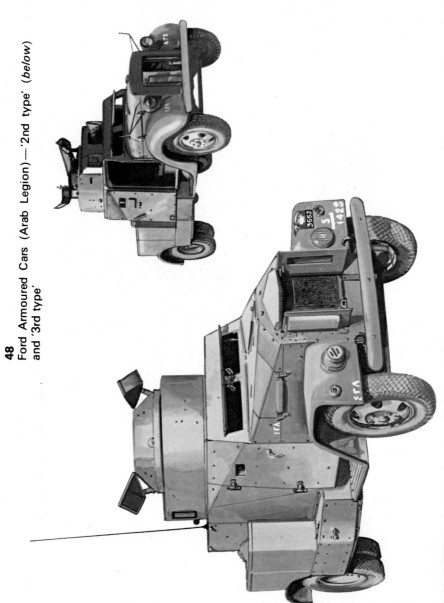

48
Ford Armoured Cars (Arab Legion)—'2nd type' (*below*)
and '3rd type'

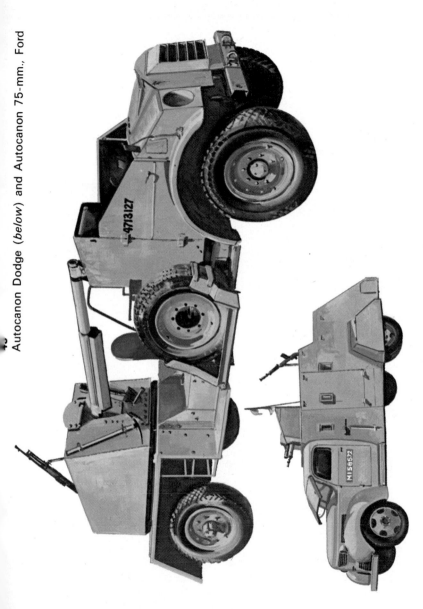

Autocanon Dodge (*below*) and Autocanon 75-mm., Ford

France

Italy

50
Carro Armato M.15/42

51
Carro Armato P.40

Italy

52 Semovente M.42M da 75/34 (*above*) and Semovente
M.42L da 105/23

53
Panzerkampfwagen II, Ausf. L, Luchs

54
Panzerkampfwagen III, Ausf. L (*below*) and Ausf. M

55
Panzerkampfwagen IV, Ausf. H

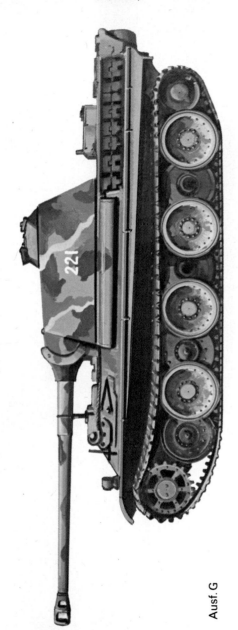

Ausf. G

56
Panzerkampfwagen V, Panther, Ausf. D

57
Panzerkampfwagen VI, Tiger I

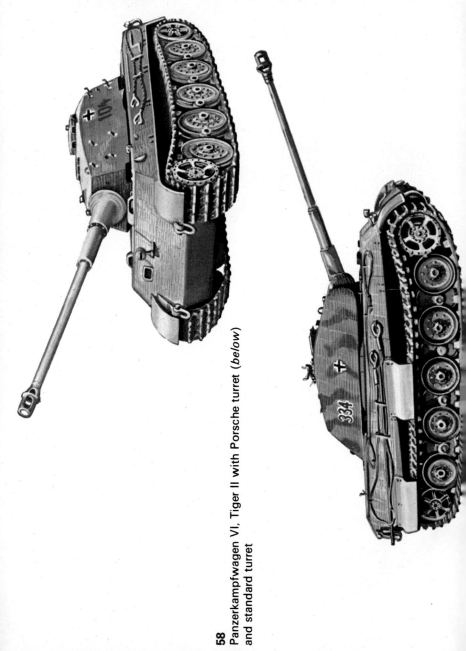

58
Panzerkampfwagen VI, Tiger II with Porsche turret (*below*)
and standard turret

Germany

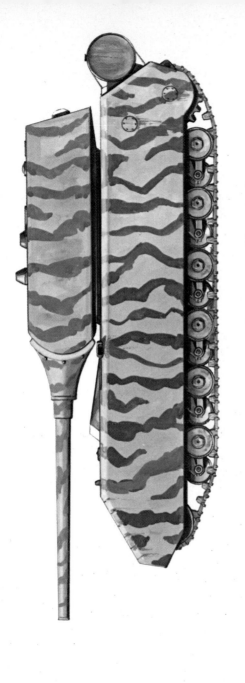

59
Panzerkampfwagen Maus

Panzerkampfwagen E.100

Jagdpanzer 38(t), Hetzer

61
Sturmgeschütz III/10.5-cm. StuH

Germany

62
Sturmpanzer IV, Brummbär (*above*) and Jagdpanzer
IV/70

63
8.8-cm. Panzerjäger Panther-Jagdpanther

Germany

64
Jagdpanzer Tiger (P), Elefant

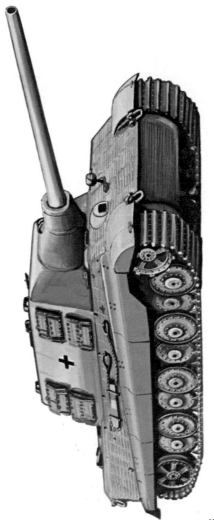
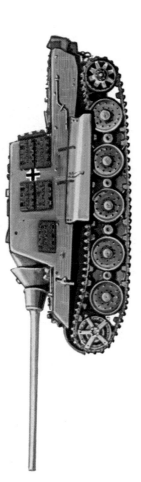

65
Jagdpanzer VI Jagdtiger with Porsche suspension (*above*) and Henschel suspension

66
7.5-cm. Pak auf Gw. 38(t), Marder III, Ausf. M

-cm. sIG33 auf Sf. II (*above*) and 7.62-cm. Pak auf
w. II, Ausf. D

68
15-cm. Pz fH 18 auf Gw. III/IV, Hummel (*below*) a
8.8-cm. Pak 43/1 (L/71) auf Gw. III/IV, Nashorn

69
Flakpanzer IV (3.7-cm.), Möbelwagen (*below*) and
Flakpanzer IV (2-cm.), Wirbelwind

70 Schwerer Ladungsträger (Sdkfz 301) (*above*) and Leichter Ladungsträger (SdKfz 302)

71
Leichter Schützenpanzerwagen SdKfz 250/8 (*below*) and
Leichter Schützenpanzerwagen SdKfz 250/9

Germany

72
Panzerspähwagen SdKfz 234/2 (Puma) (*above*) and
Panzerspähwagen SdKfz 234/3

T-34/85 (Medium Tanks)

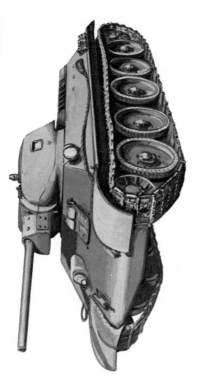

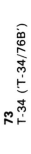

73
T-34 ('T-34/76B')

74
KV-85 (Heavy Tank) (*above*) and SU-85

75
JS-II (Heavy Tank)

76
JSU-122 (*above*) and JSU-152

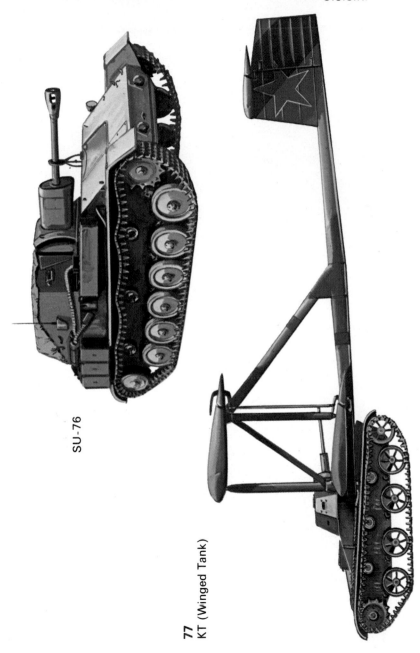

U.S.S.R.

SU-76

77
KT (Winged Tank)

78
BA-64 (Light Armoured Car)

79
Tanque 'Narhuel', Modelo DL 43

Sweden

80
Stridsvagn M/42 (*below*) and Stormartillerivagn M/43

TANKS AND OTHER
ARMOURED FIGHTING VEHICLES

1 Tankette, Type 97 (Te-Ke) and Light Tank, Type 95 (Ha-Go), Japan.

The ultra-light tank was evolved in Japan for a dual purpose—as an infantry supply vehicle (towing a trailer) and as a command and liaison vehicle for tank units. Derived originally from Carden-Loyd designs (examples of which were purchased from Britain) and developed through the Type 95 Tankette series, more emphasis was placed on the second function with the Type 97, as the Tankette was found to be quite a useful fighting vehicle, except against heavier enemy tanks. A two-man 4·25-ton vehicle, built by Tokyo Motor Industry, the Type 97 had a 60-b.h.p. Ikegai air-cooled diesel engine at the rear to the right, a centrally mounted turret with a 37-mm. gun and the driver was located at the front left-hand side. The track-driving sprockets were at the front and the suspension consisted, each side, of a large trailing idler wheel and two two-wheel bogie units on bell-crank arms restrained by a long horizontal coil spring.

The light tank was produced to meet. a demand for a lighter and more mobile tank than the Type 89 Medium for use in mechanized formations. Designed by Mitsubishi Heavy Industries Ltd in 1933, the Type 95 was the first Japanese light tank classified as such and, due to delays in the introduction of later models into production, remained the principal light tank in service throughout World War II.

The official name for this tank was Ha-Go, but it was often known colloquially as 'Kyo-Go' ('ninety-five'). One of its principal features was the air-cooled diesel engine, able to function satisfactorily in the extreme cold of north Manchuria or in tropical climates. This six-cylinder unit of 110-b.h.p. was located at the rear at the right. Another feature was the use of welding in the construction of the armoured hull, which was protected on a 12-mm. basis. The armament of the Type 95 Light Tank consisted of a 37-mm. gun in the turret (manned by the commander) with, additionally, a ball-mounted 7·7-mm. machine-gun at the right side near the back and another 7·7-mm. machine-gun in a ball mounting at the front left-hand side of the hull. The third member of the crew, the driver, sat to the right of the hull machine-gunner. The transmission layout and bell-crank suspension of the Type 95 were similar to those of the Type 97 Tankette. An interesting point with the Type 95 is that tanks used in north Manchuria were modified while they were there so that the bell crank suspension arms were inverted and an extra small road wheel introduced at the centre of each arm. This was to counteract pitching encountered in the furrows of the kaolin fields of the country.

Both the Type 97 Tankette and the Type 95 Light Tank were used widely in World War II. The former was quite effective when used in comparable functions to those of the British Universal Carrier series. The latter, although obviously no match for Allied medium tanks, was a good vehicle in its class and one of the best Japanese tanks of its era.

2 Medium Tank, Type 97 (improved) (Shinhoto Chi-Ha) and Medium Tank, Type 3 (Chi-Nu), Japan.

The first tank built in Japan was a prototype completed in 1927 which was developed into a heavy tank. A second and lighter prototype was classified as a medium, which was standardized as Type 89. The design of the latter was directly influenced to some extent by a Vickers Mark C medium tank purchased from Britain. An indirect effect was a fire in the petrol engine of the British tank, which led to the important decision by the Japanese to develop a tank diesel engine, for economy as well as its low fire risk. Air cooling of the diesel was decided on for its advantages in cold climates and in avoiding problems of water supply.

The Type 89 gave good service but by 1935 developments in other countries made it desirable to introduce a faster medium tank, better-protected without undue increase in weight.

The more successful of two competing designs was adopted in 1937 as the Type 97 medium tank or Chi-Ha. With a new suspension system of medium-sized road wheels carried on internal bell cranks controlled by horizontal coil springs, and a cleaned-up hull design, the Type 97 foreshadowed the general appearance of most modern tanks. The main armament still consisted of the short-barrelled 57-mm. gun, however, and an improved model of Type 97 was designed in which the

original turret was replaced by a new turret mounting a 47-mm. gun with a much higher velocity than the old 57-mm. gun. Type 97s were reworked with the new turret and the Type 97 modified and known as Shinhoto ('new turret') Chi-Ha became from 1942 onwards the most important Japanese medium tank of World War II. The secondary armament consisted of a machine-gun in the rear face of the turret at the left-hand side and another in the hull front, to the left of the driver.

With a 170-b.h.p. twelve-cylinder diesel engine and weighing just under 16 tons, the Type 97 (improved) had a maximum speed of 23 m.p.h.

Prior to the modifications to Type 97 described above, an improved medium tank, known as Type 1 (Chi-He) was designed. This differed little in layout and external appearance from the Type 97 (improved) except that it had a flat driver's plate, without the curved protruberance of the earlier tank. The Type 1, however, had the maximum armour protection increased from the inadequate 25-mm. of the Type 97 to 50-mm. and the engine was the new standardized air-cooled diesel of 240-b.h.p. giving an increase in speed to 25 m.p.h.

All the features of the Type 1 were included in the Type 3 medium tank of 1943, in which a more powerful gun (by then essential) was also incorporated. This new gun requiring a larger turret, made possible fortunately without major changes because of forethought in the design of the Type 97, which allowed for a larger turret ring than was immediately necessary, was a 75 mm. weapon. Early medium tanks

Type 3 had a gun based on the Type 95 field gun; later tanks a gun developed from the Type 90 field gun. The latter had a higher muzzle velocity with a consequently shorter barrel life. Welded construction introduced in the Type 97 was used largely in the Type 3 medium.

Lack of industrial capacity in Japan in 1943–45 meant that relatively few of the later types of medium tanks could be produced and so the 'new turret' Type 97 remained the chief type in use to the end of the war.

3 Medium Tank, Type 4 (Chi-To) and Medium Tank, Type 5 (Chi-Ri), Japan.

To meet the requirement for a medium tank with a more powerful gun and greater protection, the Type 4 was developed. Armour thickness was increased to a maximum of 75-mm. and the powerful Type 88 75-mm. anti-aircraft gun was adapted for tank use. These features meant increased weight up to about 30 tons, so that the chassis of the Type 97 could no longer be used and a lengthened chassis with the same type of suspension but with seven road wheels each side was designed. To ensure that performance was maintained, the 400-b.h.p. supercharged twelve-cylinder V-form air-cooled diesel engine was used. The top speed of 28 m.p.h. was, in fact, better than that of the Type 3.

Development began in 1944 of what proved to be the ultimate Japanese medium tank of World War II. This, the Medium Type 5, was an outgrowth of the Type 4 but as it was even heavier, weighing 37 tons, an extra road wheel each side was added to the suspension, which still employed the system employed in the Type 97 medium.

The turret of the Type 5 medium had the same 75-mm. main armament as that of the Type 4 but the Type 5 had, in addition, a 37-mm. gun mounted in the front of the hull at the left-hand side. Two machine-guns completed the armament.

In order to get Type 5 mediums into the field as soon as possible, when the invasion of Japan was imminent, a German-designed BMW aircraft air-cooled petrol engine was adapted and used, pending the development of the Japanese diesel engine of the requisite horse power. The BMW engine was of 550-b.h.p. and gave a top speed of 28 m.p.h.

Only the prototype of the Type 5 medium had been completed when World War II ended. A small number of Type 4 mediums had been built and these were not sent overseas but allocated for the defence of Japan.

The illustration of the Medium, Type 5, shows the prototype as it existed without the front track guards and the turret (facing to the rear) minus the 75-mm. gun.

4 Gun Tank, Type I (Ho-Ni I) and 15-cm. S.P. Howitzer, Type 4 (Ho-Ro), Japan.

These two self-propelled weapons were both built on the ubiquitous chassis of the Type 97 medium tank, powered with a 170-b.h.p. air-cooled diesel engine. Both were armed with field weapons mounted behind three-sided shields, open at the rear and with only partial overhead protection.

The Ho-Ni I was equipped with a 75-mm. gun Type 90 with a muzzle velocity of 2,260 feet per second and was the only really effective anti-tank weapon available in the field in any quantity. The fixed shield permitted a total traverse of 20 degrees, elevation of 25 degrees and depression of 5 degrees.

A Type 38 15-cm. howitzer equipped the Ho-Ro. This short calibre weapon (12 calibres long) fired a 79-lb high explosive projectile to a maximum range of 6,500 yards. This vehicle formed part of the field artillery element of Japanese armoured formations.

5 Amphibious Tank, Type 2 (Ka-Mi) and Amphibious Tank, Type 3 (Ka-Chi), Japan.

Japan, an island country with widespread interests in the Pacific area in World War II, developed, as might be expected, a number of types of amphibious tanks and support vehicles. One of the most widely used amphibious tanks was the Ka-Mi, which was based on the Light Tank Type 95. The general layout of the Type 95 was retained and the suspension system was identical except that in the amphibious tank the idler was in contact with the ground. The hull, however, was made more box-like, with straight sides, thus increasing the volumetric capacity and hence, inherent buoyancy although the main amphibious capability was provided by two pontoons, one at the front and one at the rear. Propulsion in water was by means of two propellers driven by a power take-off from the engine, a six-cylinder 110-h.p. diesel. Steering in water was by means

of twin rudders attached to the rear pontoon. The freeboard in smooth water was only about 6 inches or so and a tall trunk was fitted over the engine grill as well, occasionally, as a cylindrical extension to the turret cupola. The pontoons could quickly be jettisoned once the tank came ashore.

The armament of the Ka-Mi was one 37-mm. gun and a coaxial machine-gun and the armour was to a maximum of 12-mm. A large crew (for a light tank) of five men was carried, including a mechanic to oversee the land and water power and transmission system. The tank had a speed of 23 m.p.h. on land and 6 m.p.h. on smooth water.

The Amphibious Tank, Type 3, Ka-Chi was a medium equivalent of the Ka-Mi and shared many of its characteristics. From the point of view of the armament it was equivalent to the Medium Type 97 (improved) with its 47-mm. gun and two machine-guns, although mechanically, with a lengthened suspension system with eight road wheels each side and a 240-h.p. Type 100 diesel engine, it had more in common with some of the later Japanese medium tanks. Weighing nearly 29 tons, the Ka-Chi had a water speed of 6 m.p.h. and a road speed of 20 m.p.h. Unlike the light amphibious tank, it is not known to have been employed in action.

The illustrations show both types complete with fore and aft pontoons and with engine air trunks fitted.

6 Flail Tank and Engineer Vehicle —Jungle Cutter (Ho-K), Japan.

These two interesting examples of Japanese specialized armour were both based on the widely used Type 97 medium tank.

The flail tank was intended to clear anti-tank mines by detonation through the beating action of the flail attached to the revolving drum. The type of drive used for the flails is not known, except that it was presumably by means of a power take-off from the tank's own engine, since an auxiliary engine was apparently not carried. The tank was normal in most other respects and retained its turret. This vehicle is not known to have been used in action and may not have progressed beyond the prototype stage.

The jungle cutter was a device developed only by the Japanese. It consisted of a wedge-shaped pointed attachment, rather like the bow of a speed boat in appearance, which was carried at the front of the turretless engineer vehicle. Slightly wider than the vehicle to which it was attached, the device was used for forcing a way through heavy undergrowth. The point of attachment of the jungle cutter was at two lugs on the glacis plate of the engineer vehicle. It could be raised from the normal horizontal position if necessary and is shown raised in the illustration.

An alternative attachment for the engineer vehicle was a conventional bulldozer blade.

7 Tank Recovery Vehicle, Type E and Tank Bridgelayer (Medium Type 97 chassis), Japan.

The Japanese developed several types of engineer tanks in World War II, some of which were equipped to carry out apparently on the same mission, a bewildering variety of tasks.

One of the earlier of these vehicles was the Type E, intended for tank recovery but, as adjuncts to this function, equipped as a bridgelayer, flame-thrower and mine-clearer. The bridge, about 23 feet long and capable of being folded in two, was normally carried opened above the hull of the vehicle on rollers, by means of which it was launched and then finally pushed into position. Some vehicles of this type were equipped with two hinged forks, with four tines each, one fork in front of each track. These were for mine clearance and also possibly for use as earth anchors. The Type E vehicle also had provision for five flamethrowers, with one mounting at the front and two each side. There was also a machine-gun in a ball mounting in the top centre of the glacis plate. No turret was fitted: armour was to a maximum of 25-mm. It must be assumed that the Type E was intended for special tank recovery tasks in which its particular array of equipment was needed. No jib, or even a winch, seems to have been carried and it seems likely that on some occasions vehicles of this type would have been used in conjunction with other types of engineer vehicles having the necessary pulling or lifting ability.

The suspension of the Tank Recovery vehicle was, surprisingly, quite different from that of any Japanese tank and consisted of eight small road wheels each side, carried in two sets of four (each of two two-wheel bogie units), each set mounted on a semi-elliptic leaf spring. The vehicle was powered by a six-cylinder diesel engine of 140-h.p., giving a maximum speed of 18 m.p.h.

The standard Type 97 medium tank chassis was used for the second engineer vehicle shown here, which was a specialist bridgelayer. The bridge, about 30 feet long, was carried above the hull (the vehicle was turretless) on rollers. It was launched by means of rockets attached to the front end of each trackway.

The illustrations show (top) a bridgelayer facing right and a tank recovery vehicle, Type E, complete with bridge, facing left.

8 Armoured Personnel Carrier, Half-tracked, Type 1 (Ho-Ha) and Armoured Personnel Carrier, Tracked, Type 1 (Ho-Ki), Japan.

Several types of armoured personnel carriers were developed by Japan in World War II, both full-tracked and half-tracked. One of each variety is shown here and they have an affinity in that virtually the same track assembly was used in both.

The half-tracked vehicle Ho-Ha was on the general lines of the German SdKfz 251 series but somewhat larger and of far less sophisticated design. It weighed about 7 tons, was protected by armour up to 8-mm. only and could carry fifteen men. It was powered by a six-cylinder 134-h.p. diesel engine. The suspension consisted of four road wheels each side, with the drive sprockets at the front and the idler wheel at the rear.

The full-tracked armoured personnel carrier Ho-Ki used the same track assembly as the half-track vehicle

except that it had two return rollers instead of one and a rear drive sprocket, the transmission being led back from the six-cylinder 134-h.p. diesel engine mounted at the front. Weighing 6½ tons, the tracked personnel carrier could also carry fifteen men, who were protected by 6-mm. armour all round, although the rear compartment had no overhead protection. A similar vehicle was used as a field artillery tractor.

9 Light Tank, M.5A1 and 75-mm. Howitzer Motor Carriage, M.8, U.S.A.

The Cadillac Division of the General Motors Corporation entered into tank production early in 1942 with a new version of the M.3 Light Tank, known as the M.5. This tank, at the suggestion of Cadillac's, was powered by two eight-cylinder V-form Cadillac automobile engines, with Cadillac Hydramatic automatic transmission. A prototype was constructed in October 1941 by conversion of a standard M.3 and after a highly successful five-hundred mile demonstration drive, the design, subject to modifications in detail, was accepted. A total of 2,074 was built by the end of 1942, when the M.5 was succeeded by an improved model M.5A1. This tank was distinguished from the M.5 chiefly by a turret with an extension at the rear for radio. Other improvements included an escape hatch in the floor of the hull, a gun mount including a direct sight telescope, extra turret periscopes and an anti-aircraft machine-gun mount on the right-hand side of the turret protected by a curved armoured shield. The latter, however, was invariably removed on M.5A1s supplied to the British Army (by whom they were known as Stuart VIs) and sometimes, also, on U.S. Army vehicles. Production of the M.5A1 was ended in mid-1944 when 6,810 had been built.

The M.5A1 (and the M.5) was similar in most respects to the earlier M.3. It had a similar overall performance, in spite of being some 2 tons heavier, with thicker armour, but was much easier to drive than the M.3. The armament consisted of a 37-mm. gun with a coaxial 0·30-in. Browning machine-gun and another in the hull front, together with the anti-aircraft machine-gun already mentioned. An M.5A1 of the U.S. Marine Corps in the Pacific theatre of war is shown in the illustration.

A variant of the M.5 light tank was the Howitzer Motor Carriage M.8. This used the same chassis with the upper hull modified to take an open-topped turret with full traverse, mounting a 75-mm. howitzer. Few changes were found to be necessary beyond removing the ball-mounted hull machine-gun and transferring the driver's and co-driver's hatches to the glacis plate, where they would not interfere with the traverse of the turret.

Known as General Scott, 1,778 M.8s were built between 1942 and 1944 and issued mainly as close support vehicles in Headquarters companies of U.S. armoured battalions in Europe. They were also used by Fighting French troops and one belonging to the French in the Italian campaign, is shown in the illustration.

10 Light Tank, M.22 (Locust) and Light Tank, M.24 (Chaffee), U.S.A.

The M.22 was specially designed by the Marmon Herrington Company Inc. as an airborne light tank. The first pilot model was given the experimental designation T.9, and this was followed by two more modified pilot vehicles (T.9E1) late in 1942. After a number of design changes production began in April 1943 and a total of 830 was built by February 1944, by which time the tank was classified 'limited standard' as M.22.

With a layout conventional for medium tanks of the period, the M.22 had a 162-b.h.p. Lycoming engine at the rear, with a 4-speed gearbox and drive to front track sprockets. The driver sat at the front left-hand side. The turret, carrying the other two crew members, was centrally mounted and had a 37-mm. gun coaxial with a 0·30-in. Browning machine-gun. Armour protection was at a maximum of 1 in. and the top speed was 40 m.p.h.

No M.22's were used by the U.S. Army in action and by December 1944 it was decided that there was no need for an airborne light tank. Some M.22's had, however, been supplied to the United Kingdom (where they were named Locusts) and a very small number was used by the British 6th Airborne Division at the Rhine crossing operation in March 1945. Like its British counterpart, the Tetrarch light tank, the Locust's gun was fitted with a Littlejohn Adaptor, converting it to a 'squeeze gun' and greatly increasing the velocity of the projectile. It is not known if Locusts so equipped were used in action, although Tetrarchs with

Littlejohn Adaptors certainly were. A British Locust with the Littlejohn Adaptor is shown in the illustration.

The Light Tank M.24 was the replacement for the M.3–M.5 series which, by 1943, were already considered inadequate, not only in fire power but in other qualities, such as lack of crew space and poor cooling. The layout of the new tank was worked out by the Cadillac Division of the General Motors Corporation in 1943 and Cadillac later became the main producers, together with Massey-Harris —4,070 being built between April 1944 and June 1945.

The most important feature of the M.24, compared with its light tank predecessors, was the adoption of a 75-mm. gun. This was a light weight high velocity (2,050 feet per second) weapon, adapted from aircraft use. It shared a mounting in the turret with a 0·30-in. Browning machine-gun. The twin V-8 Cadillac engine power unit of 220 b.h.p. used successfully in the M.5A1, was adapted for the M.24 and the torsion bar suspension system (with five medium-sized road wheels) was that used on the M.18 gun motor carriage. A crew of five was carried, of which the driver sat at the front left-hand side, with the co-driver-cum-radio operator at the right, where he controlled a ball-mounted 0·30-in. Browning machine-gun in the glacis plate. Separate emergency driving controls were provided for the co-driver. The commander, gunner and loader occupied the turret.

Although only lightly armoured (maximum 1 inch), the Chaffee was a fast, efficient reconnaissance vehicle. During World War II they saw service only at the end of the North West European and Pacific campaigns in 1945, although they were supplied to many different countries in the post-war years. An M.24 of the U.S. Army as it appeared in snow camouflage in North West Europe in the winter of 1944–45 is illustrated.

11 Medium Tank, M.3 (Lee and Grant), U.S.A.

By 1940, the United States had developed a medium tank that was mechanically satisfactory and carried a liberal supply of machine-guns for infantry support. After study of the reports of the German campaign of that year, however, it was felt that the tank's main armament of a 37-mm. gun was inadequate and it was decided to introduce the 75-mm. gun. The existing medium tank M2A1 was taken as the basis and the design modified to carry a 75-mm. gun in the right-hand side of the hull but retaining a turret mounting a 37-mm. gun.

This tank, which in its production form became known as Medium, M.3, had the disadvantage that the 75-mm. gun in the hull had only a limited traverse, but it was accepted that this was only an interim design that would be put into production as quickly as possible in order to get appreciable numbers of new medium tanks into the hands of the troops. For the first time, the enormous resources of the American automotive industry were to be used for tank production and an initial order for 1,000 M.3s to be built at a new tank arsenal at Detroit was awarded even before the factory was built. However, the first M.3 prototype from the Detroit Tank Arsenal was completed in April 1941, only a short time after prototypes from the more traditional heavy industry tank suppliers, the American Locomotive Co. and Baldwin Locomotive works. Nearly 5,000 M.3s of the original type were built by these and other manufacturers, the last being delivered in August 1942.

In the meantime, a British purchasing mission in the United States had ordered M.3 mediums in quantity, as well as light tanks. The tanks made to British orders, and subsequently named Grants, had some special modifications, the principal of which were incorporated in the turret. This did not have the cupola, incorporating a machine-gun, on top and there was an overhang at the rear to incorporate the wireless equipment, in accordance with British practice. Lack of a command cupola and turret overhang were both considered to be deficiencies in design later in the war but the lowering of the M.3's considerable height was, no doubt, on balance an advantage, particularly in the open North African terrain where most of the tanks were to go.

The M.3 in its original (and, numerically, by far the most important) version was powered by a Continental nine-cylinder radial air-cooled engine of 340-b.h.p. and the hull was of all-riveted construction to a maximum armour thickness of 50-mm. The engine was at the rear, the transmission being led forward to a gear-box alongside the driver and the track drive was via front sprockets. The hull-mounted 75-mm. gun at the right had a total

traverse of 30 degrees and 46 rounds were carried. The turret had a full 360 degree traverse and besides the 37-mm. gun (for which 178 rounds were carried) it had a 0·30-in. Browning machine-gun, coaxially mounted. Standard M.3s also had a further Browning in the cupola on the main turret and two more in the glacis plate at the left, operated by the driver. These hull machine-guns were normally removed in all British-used vehicles and, of course, the Grant did not have the machine-gun cupola, although an anti-aircraft machine-gun was sometimes mounted on the turret roof.

The M.3s suspension used the horizontal volute system, already well tried in earlier medium and light tanks. It consisted of three twin-wheel bogie units each side.

The Medium M.3 first saw action (as the Grant) with the British forces in the Western Desert in the spring of 1942. In spite of its design shortcomings, its effective 75-mm. gun mounted in a reliable vehicle with a good degree of mobility (maximum speed 26 m.p.h.) helped considerably to redress the balance against the German armour. A Grant of the 3rd Royal Tank Regiment, one of the first units to receive them, is shown in one of the illustrations.

The U.S. Army also used the M.3 in action in North Africa—in Tunisia. This was in the standard form in which a quantity was also supplied to Britain (where they were known as the Lee) and by which name were, likewise, used in North Africa. M.3s were also employed by British Commonwealth forces in the Burma campaign of 1944; often in hybrid form, where they were commonly referred to as 'Lee/Grants', and were used also by the Australians for home defence. The other illustration shows a later production M.3 (with the longer 40 calibre 75-mm. gun) on issue to the U.S. Army training in Britain in 1942.

12 Medium Tank, M.4 (Sherman), U.S.A.

The Sherman is arguably one of the greatest tanks of World War II, even on numbers alone, because over 58,000 were built. The Sherman was a good straightforward design which proved adaptable, so that armament and armour modification could be introduced to enable it to keep level with its opponents to the end of the war.

Design work on the M.4 as the definitive 75-mm. gun-armed medium tank to replace the medium M.3 model was commenced in March 1941. Many of the elements of the M.3, such as the power unit, transmission and suspension were quite satisfactory and were adopted, but the main feature of the M.4 was the incorporation of the 75-mm. gun in a fully rotating turret. The prototype, known as T.6, was ready by September 1941 and after trials and minor design changes was approved for production commencing in early 1942.

Production of the M.4 in the numbers envisaged would have overrun the supply of Continental engines (as used in the M.3 and original M.4 designs) and so the use of alternative engines, already used in later models of the M.3, and others, was provided for. The most important of these were the General Motors 6046 twelve-cylinder diesel

(two six-cylinder truck engines geared together) used in the M.4A2, the Ford GAA V-8 petrol engine, used in the M.4A3 and the Chrysler A.57 thirty-cylinder petrol engine used in the M.4A4. The latter engine consisted of no less than five six-cylinder truck engines all driving a common crank shaft.

The basic hull shape of all Shermans included a well-sloped glacis plate but the form of construction varied, that of the M.4A1 with a cast, rounded hull being closest to the original design. The M.4 (first in designation sequence but actually the third type to enter production) had an all-welded hull with sharp edges, as did the M.4A2, M4A3 and M.4A4. Some late M.4s, however, had a cast front portion married to the welded rear part of the hull.

Armament of the Sherman consisted originally of a 75-mm. M.3 gun (although short M.2 guns with counterweights were provisionally fitted on some of the very first tanks built) with a coaxial 0·30-in. Browning machine-gun. In the front of the hull was a Browning machine-gun in a ball mounting and, beside it, two more Brownings, fixed to fire forwards only. The latter were eliminated after the early production vehicles. Most tanks in American use had a 0·50-in. Browning machine-gun mounted on a pintle on the turret for anti-aircraft use, although this weapon was not accurate and was commonly discarded in British-used tanks. Changes in the main armament of Shermans during the course of production included the 105-mm. howitzer in place of the 75-mm. gun, and the 76-mm. gun, a long high velocity cannon. These weapons were incorporated in a proportion of tanks during the course of production and some tanks supplied to Britain were modified to take the British 17-pr gun. These were M.4A1s, M.4A3s and M.4A4s but mostly the latter, which were known as the Sherman Vc in Britain. The 105-mm. howitzer tanks were used for close support and the 76-mm. and 17-pr gun versions used to stiffen up the anti-tank fire power of the 75-mm. Shermans.

The Sherman was used by American and British forces on nearly all battle fronts from 1942 onwards and several thousand were supplied to the Russians.

One illustration shows a side view of a typical Sherman armed with the 75-mm. gun and the other a 17-pr-equipped Sherman Vc of a British armoured regiment in Normandy in 1944, where this model was first used in action.

13 Medium Tank, M.26 (Pershing), U.S.A.

Following the abandonment of heavy tanks in the U.S.A., attention was turned to the problem of mounting a 90-mm. gun in a medium tank. A series of experimental tanks was built between 1942 and 1944, trying out various suspension systems, transmissions and other components as well as various guns, including the 90-mm. This series culminated in the T.26E1 completed in January 1944. This tank with some modifications, including a muzzle brake on the 90-mm. gun and increased ammunition stowage, became the T.26E3. By this time the need for a better gun than the 76-mm., the best weapon fitted to M.4 Medium tanks,

was recognized following combat experience in Normandy. There was, therefore, a demand for a 90-mm. gun tank but the T.26E3, now reclassified as a heavy tank was not yet considered battleworthy as it had been insufficiently tested. Twenty tanks out of the first batch to be built were, however, shipped to Europe for field trials and in January 1945 were now declared battleworthy. Allotted to the 3rd and 9th Armoured Divisions of the U.S. First Army, the tanks were named the General Pershing and standardized as M.26. Production was by now well under way and 200 had been issued by the end of the war in Europe, although most arrived at the front too late to see action. Some that did—at Remagen on the Rhine—were some of the original Pershings issued to the 9th Armoured Division.

The M.26 weighed 46 (U.S.) tons. Besides the 90-mm. gun (53 calibres long) it had a coaxial 0·30-in. Browning machine-gun and another Browning in a ball-mounting in the hull glacis plate and a 0·50-in. anti-aircraft machine-gun on the turret top. The crew of five were protected by armour at a maximum of 102-mm.

The M.26's engine was a Ford Model GAF eight-cylinder V-form type of 500-b.h.p. and the transmission was Torquematic with three forward speeds, with the track drive from rear sprockets. Suspension was of the torsion bar type and a maximum speed of 30 m.p.h. could be attained.

Although arriving too late to see much action in World War II, the Pershing was the direct ancestor of a long line of post-war U.S. medium tanks.

14 Heavy Tank, M.6, U.S.A.

A tank which received much publicity in the Allied press in 1941–42 was the American M.6 heavy tank. Sometimes shown crushing motor cars, the 50-ton M.6 was of spectacular appearance and, for its time, was a powerful tank.

Called for in 1940 as a heavy tank to complement the M.3 Medium, the first pilot model, out of several designed to test alternative forms of hull construction, transmission and power unit, was completed at the end of 1941. This model, T.1E2, had a cast hull and a torque converter transmission and was later standardized as Heavy Tank M.6. The T.1E3, which appeared slightly later, had a welded hull but was otherwise similar, and was standardized as M.6A1. The third to appear, T.1E1, was ready in 1943—this model had electric transmission and a cast hull. It was usually known later as M.6A2.

All models of this heavy tank were powered by a Wright G-200 radial nine-cylinder air-cooled engine of 800-b.h.p. which gave a maximum speed of about 22 m.p.h. The main armament consisted of a 3-in. gun (a modified anti-aircraft gun) with a coaxial 37-mm. gun in the turret. (The T.1E2 had also a 0·30-in. Browning machine-gun in a separate cupola on top and a 0·50-in. machine-gun on a high-angle mounting at the right rear of the turret.) Two 0·50-in. machine-guns were mounted in the front hull plate under the control of the co-driver and the driver was responsible for two (later one) fixed machine-guns. Armour was at a maximum of 100-mm. and a crew of six was carried.

Because of disagreement over the need for a heavy tank, the large orders originally envisaged were reduced drastically to one hundred and fifteen in September 1942 and then cancelled altogether at the end of the year, although there were subsequent experiments with 90-mm. and 105-mm. guns. Consequently, no more than forty of all variants of the M.6 series, including prototypes, were built. Apart from propaganda purposes, however, the programme had involved useful work, which was not wasted, on armour design, gun stabilizers and power traverse, horizontal volute spring suspension and transmissions, as all these features of the M.6 were used in various later light and medium tanks.

The illustrations show the M.6 (T.1E2) and (below) the M.6A1.

15 105-mm. Howitzer Motor Carriage, M.7 (S.P. 105-mm., Priest), U.S.A.

In action for the first time with British forces in North Africa, where it formed an important element in the self-propelled artillery available at the Alamein battle in October 1942, the Howitzer Motor Carriage M.7 became the main field artillery component in U.S. armoured divisions during World War II.

The decision to mount a 105-mm. field howitzer on the same chassis as the M.3 Medium Tank was taken in June 1941. Production began in April 1942, so that the first ninety vehicles for British use were delivered in Egypt in September. A Priest (as they were named by the British) belonging to 11th

Regiment, Royal Horse Artillery (of 1st Armoured Division), which received its first Priests on 10 September 1942, is shown in one of the illustrations. This vehicle has the earlier type of 3-piece noseplate.

The M.7 had the 105-mm. howitzer mounted to the right of the hull centre line to fire forwards, with a total traverse of 45 degrees. The driver sat at the left, and a characteristic dustbin-shaped 'pulpit' mounting for a 0·5-in. Browning machine-gun was at the right. The Continental nine-cylinder radial engine, drive train and suspension were all similar to those of the M.3 medium. Maximum speed was about 25 m.p.h. Armour was at a maximum thickness of 62 mm. although there was no overhead protection for the crew of seven, except for the driver.

A later, but generally similar, version of the M.7, the M.7B1, using M.4 Medium Tank components replaced the former in production from March 1944 onwards until the type was gradually replaced by the M.37 in the last months of the war.

The M.7 was used widely by field artillery units in U.S. armoured divisions from 1942 to 1945 in most theatres of war, including North West Europe. An M.7 in this area as it appeared in late 1944 is shown in one of the coloured views. After the North African campaign Priests continued in American and British use in the Sicilian and Italian campaigns which followed (and during which, incidentally, a 10-in. mortar was experimentally fitted in one). They were also employed by British troops in the Burma campaign and in the opening stages of the Normandy operations.

16 3-in. Gun Motor Carriage, M.10 and 76-mm. Gun Motor Carriage, M.18, U.S.A.

It was American philosophy in 1942 that enemy tanks should be engaged wherever possible by specialized 'tank destroyers', rather than by their own tanks. The characteristics required of a tank destroyer were a powerful gun and a good speed, even if these were attained at the expense of reduced protection for the crew. The Gun Motor Carriage M.10 was an adaptation of the M.4 Medium Tank chassis based on these principles. The powerful 3-in. gun was mounted in an open-top fully rotating turret on a modified M.4 tank hull with engines, transmission and suspension, equivalent to corresponding vehicles in the M.4 series. The maximum armour thickness was only 37 mm., although the side plates of the hull were, unlike those of the M.4, sloped to give better protection. The M.10 had twin General Motors diesel engines like the Medium Tank M.4A2, and the M.10A1 (externally similar to the M.10) had the Ford GAA eight-cylinder petrol engine, like the M.4A3. In either case, the maximum speed was 30 m.p.h. A development of the M.10 series was the M.36, a similar vehicle but equipped with a 90-mm. gun—the only U.S. armoured vehicle in the field with this weapon and the only one able to tackle the German Tiger II before the advent of the M.26 heavy tank.

Some M.10's and M.10A1's were supplied to the United Kingdom, and they were used by British and Commonwealth forces in Italy and North West Europe. A British modification to a proportion of the vehicles received was the substitution of the 17-pr for the 3-in. gun.

The Gun Motor Carriage M.18 continued the idea behind the M.10 but on a more modern chassis which, because of its weight of around 19 tons with a high power/weight ratio, turned out to be the fastest tracked fighting vehicle of World War II. Up to 55 m.p.h. could be achieved.

After undergoing several changes in both armament and suspension, the M.18, later nicknamed Hellcat, in its final form consisted of a 76-mm. gun, 55 calibres long, mounted in a partly open top turret on a new chassis with torsion bar suspension, powered by a Continental nine-cylinder radial engine of 340 b.h.p. (400 b.h.p. engines in some). The driver sat at the left front of the hull and the co-driver at the right, with the three other crew members in the turret. The commander sat at the left side of the turret, where he was able to operate the 0·50-in. Browning machine-gun carried on a ring mounting on the turret top.

Between July and October 1944, 2,507 M.18's were built, and all went to the U.S. Army where they were employed, with great success, mainly in the Italian and North West European theatres of war. The M.18 chassis was also used for the development of other vehicles, including the M.24 light tank.

17 Landing Vehicle, Tracked (Unarmored) Mark IV (L.V.T.4) and Landing Vehicle, Tracked (Armored) Mark IV (L.V.T.[A]4), U.S.A.

The great majority of amphibious cargo carriers used in World War II were built by the United States; neither her Allies nor her enemies, apart from Japan, paying very much attention to this class of vehicle.

The type was derived from an amphibian designed by Donald Roebling, intended for rescue work in hurricanes and the swampy Everglades region of Florida. A militarized version of Roebling's 1940 model was ordered as a Landing Vehicle Tracked for the U.S. Marine Corps and known as L.V.T.1. A greatly improved model, L.V.T.2, appeared in 1943. The next development, which finally became the L.V.T.3, had twin Cadillac engines in the pontoons at either side, so enabling a rear-loading ramp to be incorporated. The L.V.T.2, which had a single seven-cylinder Continental radial engine, was also modified to provide an unobstructed hold with a rear-loading ramp by having the engine moved forward, the result being known as L.V.T4.

Armoured cargo and support versions of the L.V.T.'s were also developed, the L.V.T.(A)1 and L.V.T.(A)2, both having a similar chassis to the LVT2, the former being enclosed, with an M.3 light tank turret (37-mm. gun and 0·30-in. Browning machine-gun) mounted on the roof, the latter a cargo carrier only. The L.V.T.(A)4 was similar to the L.V.T.(A)1, except that a 75-mm. howitzer turret from the M.8 gun motor carriage was used.

All the L.V.T. series were propelled in water by means of their tracks, which on all except the original L.V.T.1 had W-shaped grousers added. The water speed for all models was between 6 and 7½ m.p.h. The L.V.T.1 had an unsprung suspension system, but all the later L.V.T.s used an interesting rubber torsion suspension. Each road wheel was mounted independently on an arm, the pivot of which was a hollow tube, fitted over a smaller tube attached to the hull. The space between the two tubes was filled with vulcanized rubber which, in resisting the movement of the tube-carrying road wheel, acted like a spring.

The production of L.V.T.s in the United States amounted to 1,225 L.V.T.1s, 3,413 L.V.T.2s and L.V.T.(A)2s, 509 L.V.T.(A)1s, 1,890 L.V.T.(A)4s and 8,438 L.V.T.4s. The L.V.T.3 appeared late in World War II and was first used in action in April 1945—2,962 were built, many of which saw service after the war. There was also an improved version of the L.V.T.(A)4, the L.V.T.(A)5 with powered turret traverse, of which 269 were built too late to see action.

All the L.V.T.s (except as mentioned above) saw extensive service with the U.S. Army and Marine Corps in the Pacific, taking part in the assaults on the Japanese-held islands. L.V.T.s were also supplied to the British Army (where they were classified as 'Amphibians, Tracked' 2 ton (L.V.T1 and L.V.T.(A)1) or 2½ ton) by whom they were used in the marshy areas of North Italy, and (in company with American-manned L.V.T.s) in the Rhine and other river crossings in North West Europe. Most of the vehicles used by the British were L.V.T.2s and L.V.T.(A)2s—known usually as Buffalo II—and L.V.T.4 (Buffalo IV). One of the latter, carrying a Universal Carrier, is shown in one illustration. The other picture shows a L.V.T.(A)4 as used by U.S. Forces in the Pacific war theatre in late 1944.

18 **Car, Half-Track, M.2A1 and 75-mm. Gun Motor Carriage, M3, U.S.A.**

Half-tracks were produced extensively by the United States, as well as Germany, in World War II and used for a variety of purposes. The American vehicles were generally somewhat less sophisticated, both mechanically and in the hull design, than their German counterparts, although they did have driven front axles.

Nearly all the U.S. half-tracks of World War II were armoured and the design originated, in essence, through the addition of rear tracks (of the type developed in France by Citröen from designs by Adolphe Kégresse) to a four-wheel-drive Scout Car, M.3A1. The first standardized model was a personnel carrier for ten men known as Car, Half-Track, M.2.

The layout of the M.2 was typical of the great majority of U.S. half tracks built during World War II. The engine was in the conventional normal-control truck position and the transmission was led, via a transfer box, forward to the front wheels and back to the track drive wheels at the front of the track assembly. The track suspension consisted of four road wheels each side, carried on a single bogie unit. The tracks consisted of continuous bands, made up of steel cables covered with metal cross pieces (to avoid slip) and metal track guides. A roller was carried in front of the radiator to help prevent the vehicle 'ditching'. The armoured hull, bolted on to the chassis frame, was made up of flat plates of 6·35-mm. thickness, except for the driver's plate and the upper, hinged, parts of the side doors, which were 12·72-mm.

The engine in the M.2 was the White six-cylinder in-line type of 147 b.h.p. The armament consisted of one 0·30-in. and one 0·50-in. Browning machine-guns. These weapons could be mounted on a continuous rail which ran round the perimeter of the inside of the hull.

The M.2 was followed by a similar vehicle with a slightly longer hull, capable of carrying thirteen men, designated Personnel Carrier, Half-Track, M.3. Other differences included a rear door and the omission of the machine-gun 'skate rail', a pedestal mount being provided instead. Newer versions of both M.2 and M.3, standardized in 1943, were the M.2A1 and M.3A1, both of which had an armoured ring mount at the front left-hand side of the hull for the 0·50-in. machine-gun for use against aerial or ground targets.

To meet the demand for half-tracks, the International Harvester Company joined the production programme, and the International six-cylinder engine of 143 b.h.p. was used in the M.5 and M.9 series which were externally much like the M.2 and M.3 series.

One of the earliest of many self-propelled gun mountings on half-track chassis, and the first to be standardized, was the Gun Motor Carriage M.3. This was basically a M.3 Personnel Carrier with a 75-mm. gun, model M.1897A4 (originally a French design) mounted with a shield in the crew compartment, where it had a traverse of 19 degrees left and 21 degrees to the right. The gun was intended as an anti-tank weapon, and the projectile had a muzzle velocity of 2,000 feet per second.

U.S. half-tracked 75-mm. gun motor carriages were used in action in Tunisia and Italy before being declared obsolete in September 1944. They were also used by the U.S. Marine Corps in the Pacific theatre and one of these is shown in the illustration. Some vehicles of this type supplied to Britain were used in armoured car regiments for fire support purposes.

Half-tracked personnel carriers were used widely by U.S. forces and their allies. An M.2A1 belonging to the Fighting French is illustrated.

19 **Armored Car, Staghound I (T.17E1) and Armored Car, Boarhound (T.18E2), U.S.A.**

Relatively few armoured cars were produced in the United States during World War II, because the American preference was for tracked vehicles for most combat tasks, including reconnaissance. However, British experience in the North African desert had shown that good use could be made of armoured cars in this kind of terrain and several American armoured car designs were started in 1941–42, prompted by British needs. The first of these were the T.17 and T.17E1 commenced in June 1941. Both rear-engined armoured cars, equipped with a 37-mm. gun turret (somewhat like that of the Grant medium tank) and generally alike in layout and appearance, the T.17 was a six-wheeled vehicle (6 × 6) by Ford and the T.17E1 was four-wheeled and designed by General Motors (Chevrolet Motor Car Division). Some 3,760 T.17s and 3,500 T.17E1s were on order by June 1942, but in reviewing the overall production of armoured cars, the Special Armored Vehicle Board decided to eliminate the T.17 on the grounds that it was too heavy. Only 250 had been made and these were allocated for internal security duties in the U.S.A. The T.17E1 order was also in danger of being cancelled after 250 were built, but production was continued at the specific request of the United Kingdom, and a final total of 2,844 T.17E1s was built by December 1943, all of which were supplied to Britain or Commonwealth countries, where they were known as Staghound I.

The Staghound was without a chassis as such, the automotive components being attached direct to the armoured hull. The power unit consisted of two six-cylinder G.M.C. Model 270 engines, each of 97 b.h.p., mounted at the rear and driving all four wheels through a Hydramatic (automatic) transmission. The turret carried a 37-mm. gun and a 0·30-in. Browning machine-gun, mounted coaxially, and there was another Browning machine-gun in a ball mount in the glacis plate, controlled by the co-driver at the right. The driver, who enjoyed power steering, sat at the left. Hull armour was at a maximum of ⅞ inches (22 mm.), although the turret was mainly 1¼–1¾ inches thick.

Deliveries of Staghounds to the British forces were too late for them to be used in the Desert fighting, where they would have been ideal. Although easy to drive, they were not popular with armoured car regiments for reconnaissance duties in European terrain, where they were regarded as being too large and lacked the manœuvrability of the smaller British Daimler armoured cars. None the less, Staghounds found useful employment as command vehicles at squadron and regimental headquarters, where their roominess and provision for a crew of five were advantages. (A Staghound belonging to the regimental headquarters of a British armoured car regiment is shown in the illustration.)

A Staghound A.A. armoured car (T.17E2) was also built for Britain and 1,000 of them were produced. This had an open top turret, designed by Frazer-Nash in England and built by the Norge Division of Borg-Warner in Detroit, mounting twin 0·50-in. anti-aircraft machine-guns. British modifications of the Staghound I included the Staghound II, in which the 37-mm. gun was replaced by a 3-in. howitzer for close support use, and the Staghound III, in which a British Crusader cruiser tank 75-mm. gun turret was mounted in place of the original turret.

The heavy armoured car T.18E2 had all the characteristics required for open desert warfare to an even greater degree than the Staghound and, like it, unfortunately was ready only when the campaign in North Africa was over. It weighed over 26 (short) tons and was over 20 feet long, but the armament was only a 6-pr gun and two 0·30-in. Browning machine-guns (one in the glacis plate). This was much inferior to that of many tanks better armoured and weighing less, although with two G.M.C. engines totalling 250 b.h.p. the T.18E2, named Boarhound by Britain, was capable of a speed of 50 m.p.h. Only 30 T.18E2s out of the original order for 2,500 were completed by the Yellow Truck and Coach Company division of General Motors. All of these were delivered to Britain where they were stored in ordnance depots, none being used in action.

20 Light Armored Car, M.8 and Armored Utility Car, M.20, U.S.A.

The best American armoured car of World War II was designed in response to a requirement by the Tank Destroyer Force for a 37-mm. Gun Motor Carriage. Intended to replace the 37-mm. Gun Motor Carriage M.6—an anti-tank gun on an unarmoured ¾-ton truck—the T.22, prototype of the M.8, was later re-classified as a light armoured car.

The T.22 was designed by the Ford Motor Co. in competition with other 6 × 4 and 4 × 4 projects by Studebaker and Fargo. Out of these and many other armoured car designs at this time (some of which had even received large production orders) only the T.17E1 and the T.22, which was completed in early 1942, modified as T.22E2 and standardized as M.8, remained to be produced in quantity after a critical survey had been carried out by the Special Armored Vehicle Board.

A six-wheeled, six-wheel-drive vehicle with a rear-mounted engine—the 110-b.h.p. six-cylinder Hercules JXD—the M.8 had a welded hull (armoured to a maximum of ¾ in.) and a circular cast turret with an open top. The armament consisted of a 37-mm. gun and a 0·30-in. Browning machine-gun in the turret with provision for a 0·50-in. heavy machine-gun to be mounted on the turret top. With a four-speed gear-box, the maximum speed of the M.8 was 55 m.p.h. The car had a four-man crew.

The Armoured Utility Car M.20 was a companion vehicle to the M.8, to which it was mechanically identical. Intended as a command vehicle or armoured personnel or cargo carrier, it differed from the M.8 in having no turret and a square, raised centre section of the hull. This was open-topped and was surmounted by a ring-mounting for a 0·50-in. machine-gun. The M.20 could carry up to six men, according to function.

A total of 8,523 M.8s was built in World War II and 3,791 M.20s. They were used in numbers by the U.S. Army—the M.8 was, in fact, the only armoured car to be employed in action by the Americans. The M.8 (but not the M.20) was also supplied to the United Kingdom for use by the British and Commonwealth armies, by whom they were employed in action chiefly in the Italian campaign towards the end of the war. Named Greyhound in British service, the M.8's characteristics were summarized by one armoured car regiment as having a magnificent cross-country performance; being hard to reverse; difficult to protect against mines (the thin hull floor armour—⅛ inch to ¼ inch—was often reinforced by sandbags) and the useful advantage in a reconnaissance vehicle of being able to cross Class 9 bridges.

The illustrations show an M.8 of the U.S. Army in North West Europe (the fifteenth vehicle in C Troop of a reconnaissance unit) with impedimenta as carried in a campaign, and an M.20 in 'parade ground' condition.

21 Tank, Light, Mark VII, Tetrarch and Tank, Light, Mark VIII, Harry Hopkins, U.K.

The Light Tank, Mark VII, was a drastic departure from earlier light tanks (culminating in the Mark VIc) designed by Vickers-Armstrongs Limited. Although owing something to the track-warping steering device of the Vickers Carriers, the Light Mark VII had an entirely new form of steering in that all four road wheels on both sides could be turned into a curve for steering in a wide radius. This warped the tracks in the direction desired, although for sharper turns steering brakes on either track were brought into action.

Developed from a prototype completed at the end of 1937, the Light Mark VII, later known as Tetrarch, although armoured only up to a maximum of 16 mm., had the main armament of a contemporary British cruiser tank—a 2-pr gun with coaxial 7·92-mm. Besa machine-gun. The Littlejohn Adaptor, to greatly increase the muzzle velocity of the 2-pr was fitted to some Tetrarchs and this device is shown on the vehicle (belonging to 6th Airborne Division) illustrated. Although the first Tetrarchs were delivered in 1940, production (by the Metropolitan-Cammell Carriage and Wagon Company Limited—a Vickers-Armstrongs subsidiary) was seriously interrupted by damage caused by an air raid on the factory and the last of the 171 vehicles built was not delivered until 1942. The first use in action of the Tetrarch was during 1942—some with the Russians, who received a small quantity, and some

forming a half squadron in the British attack on Madagascar. The remaining stock of Tetrarchs was then reserved for airborne operations.

The Tetrarch created history on the eve of D-Day 1944 by being glider-landed in Normandy. Only about half a dozen tanks were used, and mainly in a defensive role, but their fire power gave useful support to the parachute troops.

Developed from the Tetrarch and weighing a ton heavier, the Light Tank, Mark VIII, named after President Roosevelt's Lend-Lease administrator, had armour protection up to 38 mm. and the design of the hull and turret was ballistically improved. The Harry Hopkins's armament was the same as the Tetrarch's but the maximum speed was reduced from 40 m.p.h. to 30 m.p.h. Following the Tetrarch in the Metropolitan-Cammell production line, 102 Light Mark VIII's were built. They were never used in action and were the last British light tank before the advent of the Alvis Scorpion in the 1960s

22 Tanks, Cruiser, Mark VI, Crusader I and Crusader III, U.K.

The Crusader arose from a proposal by the Nuffield organization for a 'heavy cruiser' development of their earlier model, Cruiser Mark IV. This the War Office accepted: the pilot model was running in July 1939 and full scale production was under way in 1940.

Although the armour protection was increased to a maximum of 40 mm., an extra pair of road wheels added, the main turret redesigned and an auxiliary turret added, the Cruiser Mark VI had many features of the Cruiser Mark IV. These included the same form of Christie suspension, the 340 b.h.p. Nuffield Liberty engine and the same turret armament. Nevertheless, it proved to be far less reliable than its predecessor, particularly when subjected to desert conditions in North Africa. Mechanically, the engine fan drive and the air cleaner were particular sources of weakness, and the cramped auxiliary turret mounting a single 7·92-mm. Besa machine-gun was unsatisfactory. The Crusader's good speed of nearly 30 m.p.h. was an asset in the desert, though, and was a feature liked by its crews and admired by the Germans and Italians—the latter to the point of building an experimental tank of their own modelled on the Crusader.

The demand for heavier armour led to the introduction of the Crusader II, in which the frontal protection was increased to 49 mm. The auxiliary turret was usually omitted in this model, the aperture plated over and the space created used for extra stowage. (Some Crusader I's were also retrospectively modified in this way.)

The 6-pr gun having by then become available, the Crusader III was designed to use it, and the first tanks of this model came off the production lines in May 1942. Basically the same turret was used, with the mantlet redesigned, but the bigger gun meant a reduction in the crew to three (Crusader I had five men, Crusader II without the auxiliary turret had four.)

A total of 5,300 Crusaders was built by a group of firms under the parentage of Nuffield Mechanizations and Aero Limited. This total includes tanks which were later in the war converted to anti-aircraft tanks and 17-pr gun tractors and chiefly employed in action in the North West Europe campaign. The Crusader I's action was in the North African desert in 1941 and the illustration shows one in the markings used at the end of that year. Crusader III's were used by both the Eighth and First Armies in North Africa, and one belonging to a regiment of 6th Armoured Division of First Army in Tunisia in 1942 is shown.

23 Tanks, Cruiser, Centaur and Cromwell, U.K.

As a successor to the Crusader, a new cruiser tank was planned in 1940 to have much heavier armour, a 6-pr gun, and to greatly improve the power/weight ratio by using a de-rated version of the Rolls-Royce Merlin aero engine. The design was completed but as the new engine could not be ready for some time, the Nuffield organization produced an interim model, known as Cruiser Mark VII (and later as Cavalier), which employed the Nuffield Liberty engine, gearbox, transmission and radiators of the Crusader, for which they were also responsible. The Cavalier (of which the prototype appeared early in 1942) was mechanically rather unreliable and only a few hundred were built. It was, however, redesigned by Leyland Motors Limited, retaining the same engine modified and linked to a Merrit-Brown gearbox. The suspension was also improved, although the armour (a basic 76-mm. frontal protection) and the 6-pr gun, coaxial and hull 7·92-mm.

Besa machine-gun armaments were unchanged. This tank was known as Centaur I. The British 75-mm. replaced the 6-pr gun in Centaur III, and Centaur IV was a close support version armed with the 95-mm. howitzer.

Cavaliers and Centaurs were used mainly in secondary roles in the North West Europe campaign, the former only as an artillery observation post vehicle and the latter mainly as O.P., bulldozer and anti-aircraft tanks. Some eighty Centaur IV's of the Royal Marines Armoured Support Group did, however, see action as gun tanks, both in support of the landings, firing from landing craft offshore, and subsequently in continuing to give fire support inland. A Centaur IV of this formation is shown in the illustration.

The Cromwell appeared as the natural development of the Centaur, which had been designed so that the Nuffield Liberty engine could easily be replaced by the new engine, when the Meteor engine was ready for it. The first batch of Meteors (adapted from the Merlin aero engine) were built by Rolls-Royce (although other manufacturers then assumed production) and the Cromwell was produced in series from January 1943 onwards. After some changes, Leyland Motors Limited some months later became production 'parents' for the Cromwell as well as the Centaur—which was, of course, replaced on the assembly lines by the newer tank as soon as possible. Some Centaurs were later re-engined with Meteors and re-designated as Cromwells.

Running through eight basic Marks, the Cromwells I–III had the 6-pr gun, the IV, V and VII had the 75-mm., and the VI and VIII had the 95-mm. howitzer. The early Cromwells were exceedingly fast, with a maximum speed of 40 m.p.h., but this was governed down to 32 m.p.h. on later models to lengthen the life of the Christie suspension. Welded hull construction was first used in British tanks on the Cromwell V w and VII w, and in these tanks the maximum thickness was increased from 76 mm. to 101 mm. British armoured reconnaissance regiments in North West Europe in 1944–45 were equipped with the Cromwell which, additionally, equipped the armoured brigade of 7th Armoured Division in the earlier stages of the campaign. The illustration shows a Cromwell (with 6-pr gun) of 5 Troop, A Squadron, 15th/19th Hussars in 1943, when it formed part of 9th Armoured Division. This regiment, still equipped with Cromwells, became, in 1944, the Armoured Reconnaissance Regiment of 11th Armoured Division in North West Europe.

24 **Tank, Cruiser, Challenger,** U.K.

The Challenger was designed in 1942 as a cruiser tank to mount the new 17-pr gun. Prototypes were produced in the same year by the design firm, Birmingham Railway Carriage and Wagon Company, the use of many components of the Cromwell series easing many problems. Development of the turret was undertaken by Stothert and Pitt Ltd who were specialists in A.F.V. turret design. Problems were encountered during trials with the suspension and the turret and mounting, and then it was suggested that the 17-pr gun should be mounted in the Sherman, which was becoming available in increasing numbers to Britain.

The latter proved ultimately to be the best answer to the question of getting a powerful tank gun into the field where it could tackle the latest German tanks. Nevertheless, 200 Challengers were ordered and, the design snags eliminated, delivered during 1944. They were used chiefly by British regiments equipped with Cromwells in North West Europe, from Normandy onwards.

The illustrations show a tank of 8th King's Royal Irish Hussars, the armoured reconnaissance regiment of 7th Armoured Division.

25 Tank, Cruiser, Comet, U.K.

The Comet was the last of the line of British cruiser tanks and by far the best. It had a good gun and was fast and reliable.

Leyland Motors Limited undertook the design of the Comet: work was commenced during 1943 and the first prototype was completed in February 1944. Designed around the new 77-mm. gun—a shorter version of the 17-pr— some of the best features of the Cromwell were used, including the same Meteor engine. All-welded construction was used for the hull and turret, a system also employed with some of the later versions of the Cromwell. The Christie suspension system was again used but in a heavier form, since the Comet's weight was about 4½–5 tons heavier than that of the Cromwell.

After trials with the prototype, wider tracks were used and track return rollers (four each side) were added. A hull Besa machine-gun position like the Cromwell's was retained in the new design, and this was one point of subsequent criticism, because of the vertical plate it needed—far more vulnerable than the sloping glacis plate of the German Panther, one of the Comet's adversaries. The hull floor protection against mines was also felt to be not fully satisfactory.

The first production Comets arrived in September 1944 and, when delivered to armoured regiments towards the end of the year, met with general approval. The 77-mm. gun did not have quite the penetrative ability of the 17-pr but was very accurate and also had good high explosive ammunition. As a result of the German offensive in the Ardennes, which interrupted training, the Comet was not used in action until after the Rhine crossing in 1945. The first formation to be re-equipped with the Comet was the 29th Armoured Brigade of 11th Armoured Division, and tanks of Regimental Headquarters, 2nd Fife and Forfar Yeomanry of this brigade are shown in the illustrations.

26 Tank, Cruiser, Ram and Armoured Personnel Carrier, Ram Kangaroo, Canada.

A cruiser tank designed and produced in Canada, the Ram foreshadowed some of the features of the U.S. Sherman Medium Tank, M.4.

Using the running gear of the U.S. M.3 Medium, the hull was completely redesigned in the light of British experience and the clumsy sponson of the M.3 was eliminated so that the main armament was concentrated in the turret. As only the 2-pr gun was available to start with, this was used in the prototype, which was running in June 1941. This gun (in an adapted Valentine mounting) also equipped the first fifty production vehicles to be built, and these were named Ram I. The turret design incorporated a removable front adapter plate, however, so that when the much more powerful 6-pr gun came along later, the turret was readily changed to accept this weapon. All the subsequent vehicles (of which 1,899 were built, production ending in 1943) had the 6-pr and were known as Ram II. The Ram (in both Marks) also carried two mounted 0·30-in. Browning machine-guns—one coaxial with the main armament and the second in the hull at the front left-hand side. On all the earlier vehicles this hull machine-gun was in a small auxiliary turret, although on the final vehicles to be built a ball and socket mounting was used instead. A further Browning machine-gun was carried for anti-aircraft use.

The engine used in the Ram tanks was the nine-cylinder radial Continental, developing 400 b.h.p.; the gearbox had five speeds and the steering was of the controlled differential type. With a top speed of 25 m.p.h., the Ram had maximum armour protection of 3 inches (76 mm.).

The Ram was used widely for training Canadian armoured units, but was never used in action as a battle tank, as the American Sherman became available in large quantities and was adopted

more or less as the standard medium tank of the Allied Forces. However, when there was a call in 1944 for armoured personnel carriers to carry infantry into battle in the North West Europe campaign, the Ram chassis was used. Following earlier armoured personnel carriers, improvised for use in Normandy by the removal of the guns from Priest S.P.s (Priests and Shermans were also converted in Italy) the Ram Kangaroo became the standard British armoured personnel carrier. With the turret removed, the Ram could carry an infantry section of eight men, well protected by the hull armour, although lacking overhead cover. A British and a Canadian regiment were each equipped with Ram Kangaroos by December 1944 and, with a combined strength of 300 Kangaroos, operated under 79th Armoured Division until the end of the War.

The illustrations show a Ram II as used for training about 1942, and a Ram Kangaroo based on one of the later production vehicles with the hull ball m.g. mounting and no side doors.

27 Australian Cruiser Tanks, Mark I and Mark III, Australia.

The first pilot model of the first tank ever to be built in Australia was completed in January 1942. As World War II progressed, it became an increasing possibility that supplies of fighting vehicles from Britain or other Commonwealth countries for the Australian Army could not be counted on. Several hundreds of tracked carriers, based on designs adapted from drawings received from the United Kingdom were built in 1940-41, but when it was decided to undertake the production of cruiser tanks in Australia, it was felt preferable to develop an entirely new design consistent with Australian resources. The resulting design by Colonel W. D. Watson, a tank designer on loan to Australia from the United Kingdom, was entirely original.

The hull of the A.C.I. was cast in one piece—an unusual practice, but made necessary by the lack of capacity of Australian heavy industry to undertake the manufacture of the rolled plate, which it was originally intended to use in conjunction with smaller castings. A power unit of adequate performance was the next problem and, as no engine was available in Australia, or could be imported at that time, this was made up by combining three Cadillac V-8 cylinder petrol engines to form a 330 b.h.p. unit. These were at the rear of the hull in an arrangement of two beside each other, and the third centrally placed behind them. The power from all three engines was collected in a transfer box and thence forwards by one Carden shaft to the clutch and 5-speed crash gearbox. The track drive sprockets were at the front.

It had originally been the intention to adopt a suspension system, and tracks like those of the U.S. M.3 medium tanks but, although U.S. type tracks were used, the suspension finally chosen was the American type re-designed as a horizontal-volute spring type, resulting in a similar arrangement to that of the French Hotchkiss H-35 tank. The armament for the A.C.1 had to be based on weapons of British design available in Australia, and this resulted in a turret-mounted 2-pr gun with coaxial 0·303-in. Vickers water-cooled machine-gun and another Vickers machine-gun centrally mounted in the front of the hull.

The armour was between 65 mm. and 25 mm. and, with an all-up weight of 28 tons, the A.C.I. had a top speed of 35 m.p.h. It was found to be not entirely reliable in service and, as by 1943 British and American tanks were available for Australia, no more than sixty-six A.C.I.s were built. In the meantime, however, improved Australian cruiser tanks were under development. As no heavier anti-tank gun than the 2-pr was to be had, the A.C.3 (the A.C.2 was a light cruiser design both started and abandoned in 1941) used the 25-pr field gun. A Vickers 0·303-in. machine-gun was mounted co-axially with the 25-pr. The hull machine-gun mounting of the A.C.1 was omitted, the extra space being used for stowage of the larger 25-pr ammunition.

The Cadillac engine arrangement in the A.C.3 was improved and made more compact by their being mounted in a semi-radial pattern, so that all three engines were linked to a common crankcase.

The ultimate development of the A.C.1 was the mounting of the 17-pr gun, this version to be known as A.C.4. After recoil tests with twin 25-pr guns in a special turret on an A.C.1, the 17-pr gun then produced in Australia was mounted successfully. Around 700 tanks of the A.C.3 and A.C.4 types were needed by the Australian Army, but apart from the experimental models none of these were built, because of the change in priorities in

Australian war production brought about by supplies of A.F.V.s from overseas. The A.C.1s built were, however, used by the Australian Army for many years for defence, and then training, the last of them being declared obsolete in 1956.

28 Tanks, Infantry, Mark IV, Churchill III and Churchill VII, U.K.

The first versions of the Infantry Tank Mark IV, to appear in 1941—the Churchills I and II—were equipped, of necessity, with 2-pr gun turrets. However, as a supply of 6-pr guns became available the Churchill III entered the production line, using a welded turret designed by Babcock and Wilcox Limited. Mechanically the same as its predecessors, having the 350-h.p. Bedford twelve-cylinder with a Merritt-Brown 4-speed gearbox, the Churchill III differed from the Churchill I–III mainly in the different turret and ammunition stowage. A little later, the Churchill III was joined on the production lines by a further version, Churchill IV, with the same armament but having a cast instead of a welded turret.

At the earliest opportunity, earlier marks of Churchill were reworked and had their 2-pr turrets replaced by new turrets with the 6-pr gun.

The Dieppe Raid in August 1942 was used to try out the Churchill in action for the first time. Some thirty Churchill tanks, mostly Churchill IIIs, but with a handful of Churchill Is and IIs (the latter equipped with flamethrowers), were used in support but had little

chance of proving themselves, as few were able to surmount the sea wall and penetrate inland.

Some Churchill IIIs and other Marks were among the tanks supplied to the U.S.S.R. in 1942, but it was not until the Tunisian campaign of 1942–43 that the Churchill, represented mainly by Mark IIIs and IVs, really proved its worth, particularly in mountainous country.

Development in the meantime resulted in the Churchill V, a close support version equipped with a 95-mm. howitzer and the Churchill VI, similar to the Churchill IV but with a British-built 75-mm. gun in place of the 6-pr.

An entirely new version of the Churchill was designed by Vauxhall Motors Limited, the original 'parent' company for the group of Churchill tank manufacturers, to meet a new War Office specification A.22F (later renumbered A.42) for an infantry tank with 6-in. frontal armour. The new model, known as Churchill VII, although superficially similar to earlier Churchills, used a completely different form of hull construction in that a hull frame was dispensed with, the armour plate itself forming the hull. Many detailed improvements were incorporated, the most obvious being circular side doors and driver's vision port instead of the rectangular variety. A commander's turret vision cupola was introduced after the first few Churchill VIIs were built. The Churchill VII had main armament of a 75-mm. gun with a coaxial 7·92-mm. Besa machine-gun and another Besa in the hull front. A close support tank, Churchill VIII, was identical except for the 95-mm. howitzer which replaced the 75-mm. gun.

A ton heavier than earlier models, Churchills VII and VIII had a heavier suspension system and slightly lower ratios in the gearbox, and the governed top speed was reduced from about 16 m.p.h. to about 13 m.p.h.

Reliable, with heavy armour and a reasonably satisfactory gun, the Churchill VII (together with earlier models brought up to roughly the same standard) was one of the most important British tanks in both the Italian and North West Europe campaigns until the end of the war, during which 5,640 of all Marks were built.

The illustrations show a Churchill III of 142nd (Suffolk) Regiment, Royal Armoured Corps, at the time of the Tunisian campaign, and a Churchill VII in the colours of 6th (Guards) Tank Brigade.

29 S.P. 25-pr, Bishop and S.P. 17-pr, Archer, U.K.

The war in the North African desert emphasized the need for both increased mobility and protection for field and anti-tank artillery. The Bishop was designed hurriedly in 1941 in response to an urgent request from the Middle East for a self-propelled mounting for the 25-pr field gun—a weapon that had often been found to be the only effective answer to the German medium tanks. Designed by the Birmingham Railway Carriage and Wagon Company Limited, the sturdy and reliable Valentine tank chassis was used as the carrier for the 25-pr gun, which was mounted in a fixed shield with a total

traverse of 8 degrees, elevation of 15 degrees and depression of 5 degrees.

One hundred Bishops were built by July 1942, and nearly all of them were used in the North African campaigns.

As a design to meet an emergency, the Bishop served its purpose but was never entirely satisfactory and, although some continued in action in Sicily and Italy in 1943, it was replaced as soon as possible by the U.S.-built Priest S.P. 105-mm. or the Canadian Sexton S.P. 25-pr.

The Bishop design was proposed as the basis of a self-propelled mounting for the new 17-pr anti-tank gun in 1942, but this was found to be impracticable. Nevertheless, the Valentine chassis was again used but this time with a rearward-facing layout for the gun. Two prototypes were completed in the first part of 1943 by Vickers-Armstrongs. After some modifications to the gun traverse system, frontal armour and other features, production began: the first vehicles were delivered in 1944, and a total of 665 of them were finished by the end of the war.

The rear-facing arrangement of the 17-pr gun in the Archer permitted a compact design—particularly useful in an anti-tank gun—and a total traverse of 45 degrees allowed reasonable flexibility in use. The welded upper hull had armour protection up to 20 mm.—effective against small arms. A 0·30-in. Browning machine-gun was carried for protection against local ground attack and aircraft.

The Bishop used the Valentine II chassis with an A.E.C. 131 b.h.p. diesel engine, but the Archer chassis was equivalent to that of the later models of Valentine tank with the

General Motors diesel of 192 b.h.p., giving a top speed of 20 m.p.h.—compared with the slightly heavier Bishop's 15 m.p.h.

Although the merits (rapid withdrawal in emergency, for one) and demerits of the rearward-facing gun were often debated, the Archer was generally acknowledged as reliable and the effectiveness of the 17-pr gun was never in doubt. The Archer was used by anti-tank regiments in North West Europe and Italy from 1944 onwards, and continued to be employed by the British Army for several years after the war. An Archer of the anti-tank regiment of 15th (Scottish) Division in Germany in 1945 is shown in the illustration. The Bishop shown is as it appeared in the Sicily campaign in 1943.

30 S.P.25-pr Sexton, Canada.

The Sexton was probably the most important Canadian-built tracked vehicle to be used in action—it was the principal self-propelled field artillery piece employed by British and Canadian armoured formations in 1944–45.

Based on the chassis of the Canadian Ram cruiser tank (which never saw combat as a battle tank) the Sexton was designed by the Canadian Army Engineering Design Branch. Intended as a replacement in the Commonwealth Armies for the U.S. M.7 Priest S.P. 105-mm., the Sexton was not unlike the M.7 in appearance, and the suspension of both vehicles shared a common ancestry with the U.S. M.3 Medium tank.

The British 25-pr field gun was mounted slightly to the left of centre in an open-top welded armoured superstructure, where it had a traverse of 25 degrees left and 15 degrees right, and an elevation of 40 degrees. Eighty-seven high explosive and smoke shells were carried together with eighteen armour-piercing shells for anti-tank use. Two 0·303-in. Bren machine-guns were carried (but not normally mounted) for local protection, although in some vehicles a 0·50-in. Browning heavy machine-gun was mounted at the front of the hull at the left.

The nine-cylinder Continental engine of 400 b.h.p. (484 b.h.p. in later models), used in the Ram and in some models of the U.S. M.3 and M.4 medium tanks, in the Sexton gave a top speed of 25 m.p.h.

Production of the Sexton took place at the Montreal Locomotive Works Tank Arsenal, and a total of 2,150 of them was completed by the end of World War II.

The illustrations show (top) a Sexton belonging to the 5th Royal Horse Artillery (7th Armoured Division) and (below) to the 147th (Essex Yeomanry) Field Regiment, Royal Artillery (8th Armoured Brigade), both operating in the North West Europe campaign.

31 Sherman D.D., U.K.

One of the most ingenious, yet basically simple, devices of World War II was Nicholas Straussler's D.D. amphibious tank. By water-proofing the hull and raising the freeboard, it was found that an ordinary tank could be made to float without the necessity for the clumsy buoyancy chambers or pontoons, or a boat type of hull as used in earlier amphibious tanks. The means used by Straussler to increase the free-board was to add a canvas screen around the edge of the hull. Tried out first on a 7½-ton Light Tank Mark VII in 1941, the screen was raised by means of inflatable rubber tubes and held erect by metal struts. Production of 625 D.D. tanks based on the 17-ton Valentine tank then took place and deliveries were made in 1943–44. It was, however, desired to extend the use of the D.D. device to the Sherman, virtually the standard medium tank used by the British Army, and Sherman D.D. prototypes were built and proved as successful as the earlier models, although the 30-ton tank needed higher screens to produce the buoyancy required to make it float.

As in earlier D.D. tanks, the Sherman had Duplex Drive (hence the initials)—normal propulsion on tracks on land and propellers for movement on water. The tracks of the Sherman were also run in water because the power take off to drive the twin 3-bladed propellers was implemented through stub axles on the rear idler wheels. The propellers were movable for steering, which was operated by the tank commander through either mechanical linkage to the propellers or a hydraulic system.

The water speed of the Sherman D.D. was up to 6 m.p.h. and, as the tracks were running all the time the tank was afloat, it could climb ashore the moment it touched ground. The screens could be lowered quickly, and the Sherman's armament, a 75-mm. gun and 0·30-in. Browning in the turret (the hull machine-gun had had to be eliminated in the D.D.) could then be used.

A tactical surprise was achieved with the first use of Sherman D.D. tanks in action on some Normandy beaches in 1944, because in the water they were not immediately recognized as tanks. They were also used later on in the Italian campaign (together with a small number of Valentine D.D.s) and at the Rhine crossing in March 1945.

The illustrations show a Sherman D.D. (with screens folded) of 4th Armoured Brigade in Germany in 1945, a Sherman D.D. afloat, and one on land with the screens raised.

32 Churchill VII Crocodile and Grant C.D.L., U.K.

The first British tank-borne flame-thrower to be sent into action was the Churchill Oke. Three Churchill IIs with this hastily produced flame-thrower equipment were among the tanks used in the raid on Dieppe in August 1942 but, as it happened, the landing craft carrying all three never reached the beach, being sunk offshore.

A more satisfactory design of tank flamethrower was already in hand and twelve pilot models were ordered by the War Office at the end of July 1942. Mounted in the Churchill IV, the flamethrowers were of the Wasp type already used successfully in Carriers. The fuel for the flame projector, which replaced the hull machine-gun, was carried in an armoured trailer and was pumped through under pressure obtained from compressed gas cylinders. A range of between 100 and 200 yards was attainable. One thousand Crocodile equipments were ordered and some 800 were completed by the end of the war. The Churchill VII was used as the basis of the production Crocodiles and a rectangular hatch in the hull floor for the mounting of the flame equipment was included as standard in all Churchill VIIs and VIIIs, so that they could readily be adapted for this role. Apart from the hull machine-gun, all the rest of the normal Churchill VIIs armament was carried in the Crocodile.

Crocodiles equipped a tank brigade in the North West Europe campaign and were also used in smaller numbers in Italy. A Churchill VII Crocodile of C Squadron, 51st Royal Tank Regiment in the latter theatre of war is shown in the illustration.

Another form of special armour used in the North West Europe campaign, the development of which began several years earlier, was the C.D.L. tank. The initials stood for Canal Defence Light—a deliberately misleading code name, since by dazzling enemy gunners the tank was intended to support attacks. The device consisted of a high intensity arc lamp, the beam of which was, by reflectors, projected through a vertical slit in the armoured face of the special turret. The dazzle effect could be enhanced by operating a shutter, causing the beam to flicker.

Originally fitted to Matilda infantry tanks, and used on training in the United Kingdom and the Middle East, the C.D.L. was later standardized on the U.S.-built Grant. The advantage in using this tank was that the main armament of a 75-mm. gun in the hull sponson could be retained, only the small 37-mm. gun turret having to be removed to fit the C.D.L. turret.

Because of the wish to keep this weapon secret for an important action in which it could be used to the best effect—and perhaps because of ignorance of its potential (or existence) by senior commanders—the C.D.L. was not used in action until nearly the end of the war, at the Rhine and Elbe river crossings. Even so they seem to have been used as little more than ordinary static searchlights, rather than in a true assault function.

The Grant C.D.L. tanks, like the Crocodiles, in North West Europe came under the aegis of 79th Armoured Division, and one belonging to that formation is shown here.

33 Matilda Scorpion and Grant Scorpion, U.K.

The most effective device for clearing minefields devised in World War II, the flail tank, was the idea of Major A. S. J. du Toit, a motor engineer serving with the South African Union Defence Force. A working model to demonstrate the idea was built, and details were given to the Middle East Mechanical Experimental Establishment, before Major du Toit was despatched to the United Kingdom where better resources for development of the device were available.

The anti-mine flail was a power-driven revolving drum to which rows of heavy chains were attached which, beating the ground in front of the vehicle to which the device was fitted, exploded mines on contact.

The Mechanical Experimental Establishment in the Middle East first fitted the device to a lorry and then, after trials, to a Matilda tank. This equipment was then called Matilda Scorpion Mark I.

The flails of the Matilda Scorpion I were made up of wire cable to the ends of which short lengths of chain were attached. The rotating drum was driven by a Ford V-8 engine, mounted in an armoured box on the right-hand side of the tank's hull. A cardan shaft took the transmission along the supporting girder to a bevel box and from it to the rotor. The flail engine was operated by an extra crew member who had the unenviable job of sitting at the rear of the armoured box behind the engine. In this position he was nearly choked by dust and fumes from the flail engine.

An order for twenty-four Matilda Scorpion Mark Is was completed in time for them to be used to help clear minefields for the Battle of Alamein in October 1942. Still beset by mechanical difficulties and with a flailing speed of only ½ m.p.h., nevertheless the Scorpions were considered reasonably satisfactory. A better version in which the flail operator was carried in the tank itself, and the design of the side girder was changed and other improvements effected, was known as the Matilda Scorpion Mark II and was ready by early 1943.

In order to take advantage of the greater mobility of the American Grant, the Scorpion Mark II flail equipment was adapted to this tank, the combination being known as Grant Scorpion Mark III. The hull-mounted 75-mm. gun had to be removed, but the 37-mm. gun turret could be retained although this was also, in fact, removed when it was necessary to reduce the overall dimensions to be carried in landing craft. Grant Scor-

pions were used in the Sicily campaign in the summer of 1943.

The final developments of the flail tank which took place in the Middle East, parallel to work in the same field in the United Kingdom, were the Grant Scorpion IV and the Sherman Scorpion. The former used two Dodge engines, mounted at the rear of the hull, driving the rotating drum by means of cardan shafts each side. This equipment was used in very similar form on the Sherman tank, and Sherman Scorpions in small numbers were used in the Italian campaign.

A Matilda Scorpion Mark I and a Grant Scorpion Mark IV are shown in the illustrations.

34 Sherman Crab I and Crab II, U.K.

From the end of 1941 onwards development of the flail tank, initiated by Major A. S. J. du Toit, took place at the works of A.E.C. Ltd in the United Kingdom. At first undertaken independently of the parallel experiments in the Middle East, later on ideas were exchanged. The best design of flail tank to enter service in World War II, the Sherman Crab incorporated ideas from both centres of development.

The first U.K. flail tank, known as Baron, used the Matilda chassis. Early models had one engine to drive the flail but the final model had two flail engines. Sixty were built in 1943 for training purposes. The next type, the Valentine Scorpion, was based on designs received from the Middle East, although the rotor was like that of the Baron. Again, only a small order

(150 vehicles) for training only was given.

Next, flail development was transferred to the Sherman tank—this had the advantage of using the same basic vehicle that was to equip many British armoured regiments.

Prototypes of three models were built in 1943, the Sherman Marquis, turretless and based on the Baron and Scorpion; the Sherman Pram Scorpion, retaining its turret and taking its flail drive from the tank's main engines; and the Sherman Crab. The latter was considered to be the best design and was the one adopted for production in quantity for employment in the forthcoming campaign in North West Europe.

Fitted to the Sherman V, powered by a Chrysler thirty-cylinder 350 b.h.p. engine, the flail was operated through a power take off on the right-hand side of the hull, leading through a universal-jointed cardan shaft to a bevel gear at the rotor. The rotor arms could be lifted by hydraulic rams to make transport in landing craft etc. easier. A lane 9 ft 9 in. wide could be cleared of mines at a maximum speed of 1¼ m.p.h. Six hundred and eighty-nine Crabs were ordered and were widely used throughout the North West Europe campaign in 1944–45, where they operated under the command of 79th Armoured Division.

A later model, Sherman Crab II (which did not become available until nearly the end of the war) was developed to overcome the fault of Crab I and all other earlier flail tanks, in that mines buried in hollows in the ground could be passed over without being detonated because the flails operated at a constant height above a level surface. The left hand hydraulic lifting ram was replaced by a counter weight attached to the rear end of the rotor arm. This enabled the rotor arm and bearing chains to maintain a constant height over the contours of the ground.

The illustrations show a Sherman Crab I with the rotor arm at beating height (attachments on the rear of the hull are station-keeping-lights—for the benefit of following vehicles—mounted above the box containing markers to indicate the swept lane) and a Sherman Crab II flailing in a depression in the ground.

35 Churchill A.V.R.E. Carpetlayer and S.B.G. Bridge Carrier, U.K.

The Dieppe Raid of 1942, in which heavy losses were sustained by both armour and infantry, chiefly because the tanks were unable to penetrate inland, indicated the need for protection for engineers working to surmount or destroy obstacles. A suggestion by Lieutenant J. J. Denovan, of the Royal Canadian Engineers, that a tank should be adapted for this purpose was followed up by the R.C.E. using a Churchill tank. The Churchill was chosen because it had a well-armoured, roomy hull. It also had a relatively large door on each side of the hull, suitable for use by sappers under fire and for loading stores and equipment. The prototype with rearranged stowage was ready by December 1942 and a spigot motor, developed separately, was ready by February 1943 and mounted in the modified turret. The spigot motor, known as Petard, could throw a 40-lb projectile (containing a 26-lb charge) up to an extreme range of 230 yards, and was capable of destroying concrete obstacles.

The Assault Vehicle, Royal Engineers, or A.V.R.E. as it was usually called, was adjudged successful after trials and modifications to the original design which took place in 1943, and production was ordered. The Churchill III or IV was used as the basis, and a total of about 700 A.V.R.E.s was built by 1945.

Most production A.V.R.E.s were fitted with brackets on the hull for the attachment of fittings for special tasks. One of these fitments was the carpet-layer device for crossing soft patches on beaches, for example. The carpet—the most common form was hessian matting reinforced by steel tubes—was carried on a large bobbin at the front of the A.V.R.E. and was unwound by the vehicle itself running over it. A number of these were employed on the D-Day landing beaches. There were several versions, and the Carpetlayer Type D (waterproofed for landing from a landing craft) is shown in the illustration.

Another important use of the A.V.R.E. was as a carrier for the Small Box Girder (S.B.G.) bridge, which could carry a 40-ton load (the weight of a Churchill tank) over a 30-ft span. This could be laid mechanically under fire.

The A.V.R.E. was used in action in Italy and in North West Europe. Three Assault Regiments, Royal Engineers, under the command of 79th Armoured Division, with A.V.R.E.s and a variety of fitments, took part in many actions from D-Day onwards. An A.V.R.E. with S.B.G. bridge as it appeared in the attack on the Le Havre fortifications is illustrated.

36 Churchill A.R.V., Mark I and Sherman B.A.R.V., U.K.

The weakness of the British organization for the recovery of disabled tanks was brought out particularly in the early campaigns in the North African desert, where the Germans proved to be well in advance in this respect.

Early in 1942, a Royal Electrical and Mechanical Engineers experimental section undertook the design of armoured recovery vehicles on tank chassis. The idea was to use adaptations as A.R.V.s of the same kinds of tanks used by the armoured regiments, in so far as the basic chassis was suitable for use also as a recovery vehicle. The three most important A.R.V. types which emerged were based on the Cromwell, Sherman and Churchill, corresponding with the principal tanks in use from 1943 onwards.

The Churchill A.R.V., Mark I, was a turretless vehicle carrying a 3-ton jib. This was stowed on the hull for travelling but was mounted between the front 'horns' when in use and was capable of lifting out tank engines or other major assemblies for maintenance and repair. A 100-ft length of heavy steel cable was carried for hauling out bogged-down A.F.V.s and a pulley block and ground anchors were available for indirect or difficult recovery jobs. The A.R.V. also carried a 4½-in. vice and oxy-acetylene and welding plant among its equipment. Sherman and Cromwell A.R.V.s, Mark I, were also built and had similar equipment to the Churchill A.R.V.

Mark II versions of the Churchill and Sherman A.R.V.s were also produced and began to become available in 1944. These had fixed turrets with dummy guns: a fixed jib (with a 9½-ton lift) was carried at the rear and a demountable 3½-ton jib at the front. Other improved equipment included a 60-ton-pull-winch, the operator of which sat in the turret.

Development of an A.R.V. to recover disabled tanks or vehicles, both in the water and on the beaches, was commenced in 1943 specially for the forthcoming invasion of Europe. Churchill and Sherman tanks were tested in this role, but the former was abandoned because of the far greater amount of waterproofing it needed. The diesel-engined Sherman III was finally selected as the standard chassis for the Beach Armoured Recovery Vehicle (B.A.R.V.). Fully waterproofed and able to operate in up to 10 feet of water, the Sherman B.A.R.V. was intended only for simple recovery operations, such as towing vehicles 'drowned' in landing from landing craft or pushing off stranded landing craft, for which wooden railway sleepers mounted on the front were provided.

The Sherman B.A.R.V.s well served their purpose in 1944 by helping to keep the D-Day beaches clear. One B.A.R.V. was inadvertently the cause of more direct alarm to the enemy because, landed in error at a very early stage of the invasion, it was taken to be a new 'secret weapon'.

The illustrations show a Churchill A.R.V., Mark I, belonging to the 3rd (Tank) Battalion Scots Guards, and a standard Sherman B.A.R.V.

37 Carrier, Universal, Mark II, and Carrier, 2-pr, Tank Attack (Aust.), U.K. and Australia.

The British Army's demand for tracked carriers of the Bren and Scout types, and for a variety of functions, remained high throughout World War II, but even by 1940 the need was felt to standardize the design as far as possible. This resulted in the introduction of the Carrier, Universal. Mechanically the same as the earlier carriers, the Universal was powered by a Ford V-8 engine which drove the tracks via rear sprockets. Steering was by lateral displacement of the front bogie unit for gentle turns, with track braking for more abrupt turns. Although the driver's and gunner's compartments were very much the same in all carriers, the position of the armoured rear compartment varied. In the Universal Carrier, the whole of the rear was armoured, providing an open-top compartment on either side of the engine.

As before, both British and imported Ford V-8 engines were used in the Universal Carrier, and the final list of these was as follows:

No. 1   British-built engine.
No. 2 and 2a American-built engines—
             models   G.A.E.   and
             G.A.E.A. respectively.
No. 3   Canadian-built engine.

The British-built engines were originally rated at 65 b.h.p., the American engines at 85 b.h.p. and the Canadian ones at 95 b.h.p., although at the end of the war the War Office rated them all at 85 b.h.p. In any event, engines from all three sources were inter-changeable.

The Mark II version of the Universal Carrier included some improvements, such as a spare road wheel as a standard fitting, a larger kit box on the rear of the hull, and either one or two foot-step brackets each side of the hull. Some further improvements were incorporated in the Mark III Carrier. There were also other carriers such as Carriers M.M.G., Mortar, and Armoured Observation Post, but these had basically the same hull form as the Universal Carrier, with only relatively minor adaptations to fit their specialized roles.

Some 40,000 or more Carriers of the Universal and later associated types were built in the United Kingdom alone during World War II but, even so, it was felt necessary that Common-wealth countries should also undertake the production of tracked carriers. In Canada 29,000 of the Universal-type were built to a similar specification to the U.K. version (about 5,000 of the larger Windsor carriers were also built in Canada and the U.S.A. produced 14,000 T.16 series Carriers). A Carrier, Universal, Mark II, belonging to an infantry battalion of 43rd (Wessex) Division is illustrated.

In Australia and New Zealand carriers were also built. The earliest N.Z. carriers were built from plans sent from the United Kingdom, although later models were more like the Austra-lian ones. Australian production was much greater, to meet the heavier demand in that country, and the basic U.K. carrier design was simplified mechanically in that the track displace-ment device for steering was omitted. Although in other respects broadly the same as the U.K. carriers, the later Australian carriers had a modified hull with a sloping glacis plate. Also, welded construction was used—a feature em-ployed only in some models of the U.K.-built carriers.

In 1942 an experimental version of the Australian carrier with a stronger, lengthened chassis was built as a mounting for the 2-pr anti-tank gun. The Ford V-8 engine was brought forward alongside the driver and the gun, on a field mounting with shield, was on a turntable at the rear. Trials of the 2-pr carrier showed various faults; among others it rode badly, was slow and underpowered; was insufficiently strong and mechanical components failed; the driver was too cramped and the crew and gun were inadequately protected. It did not, therefore, go into series production, although the 5,600 standard Universal-type Carriers built in Australia gave useful service.

38 South African Armoured Re-connaissance Cars, Mark IV and Mark VI, South Africa.

Experience with the South African Reconnaissance Car, Mark II, on active service in East Africa and Libya in 1940–41, showed the need for further improvements and some of these were incorporated in the next model, Mark III, also using a Ford Marmon-Herring-ton chassis. However, neither model was armed with an anti-tank gun, and as a temporary expedient armoured car regiments often fitted heavier weapons of calibres of 20 mm. upwards, taken from captured enemy A.F.V.s or derelict British tanks.

Consequently, it was decided to build the next model to take a 2-pr gun. This vehicle, the South African Armoured Reconnaissance Car, Mark IV, once again used Marmon-Herrington automotive components but it was a complete redesign, in which the welded armoured hull acted as the chassis to which the engine, suspension, etc., were attached directly. A rear-engine layout was adopted, with the driver at the front and a central fighting compartment. Of fairly light construction, it was felt that the turret could not absorb the recoil of a tank-pattern 2-pr gun and so a 2-pr field mounting was used, with the prominent recuperator under the barrel. A coaxial 0·30-in. Browning machine-gun was added in the final standard form of the Mark IV, together with a 0·50-in. or (more usually) a 0·30-in. Browning on an anti-aircraft mount on the turret roof.

There was a strong demand for South African-built armoured cars from the War Office, as well as the Union Defence Force and, as the supply of components from Marmon-Herrington in the U.S.A. seemed unlikely to meet requirements, the design of the Mark IV was modified to employ instead automotive components from Canadian Ford F 60L 3-ton, 4-wheel drive lorries. These lorries were diverted to South Africa from War Office orders for the Middle East Forces. The Canadian F 60Ls already incorporated driven front axles of Marmon-Herrington design, so they could readily be used. The resulting vehicle was known as South African Armoured Reconnaissance Car,

Mark IV F (the 'F' probably denoting the Ford connection). In British War Office nomenclature, the two types were known as 'Armoured Car, Marmon-Herrington'—Mark IV and Mark IV F.

A total of 2,116 Mark IV and Mark IV F cars was built and, although they were used for defence in South Africa and were issued to the Arab Legion and some Allied Forces, none were received in time to be used in combat in North Africa. The same fate applied to the much larger South African Armoured Reconnaissance Car, Mark VI.

The Mark VI resulted from the strong impression created by the German eight-wheeled armoured cars, which proved to be well suited to desert conditions. Again, the well-proven Ford Marmon-Herrington components were used, this time two sets with two engines, each of 95 b.h.p. Armament and, to a degree, armour was to be of cruiser tank standard, and consisted of a 2-pr gun and a coaxial 0·30-in. Browning machine-gun, with 30-mm. maximum protection. There was also a turret ring mounting with two 0·30-in. Browning machine-guns for anti-aircraft use. The second prototype was armed with a 6-pr gun and coaxial 7·92-mm. Besa machine-gun, with a 0·50-in. Browning anti-aircraft machine-gun.

By the time that production of the Mark VI could commence—delayed as it was by a shortage of components in South Africa—the North African campaign was well-nigh over. Armoured cars from other sources were becoming available in better quantities and, as the Mark VI was considered less well suited to the European terrain, the production orders were cancelled.

The illustrations show a standard S.A. Armoured Reconnaissance Car, Mark IV, and the first prototype S.A. Armoured Reconnaissance Car, Mark VI—operating during trials before the anti-aircraft ring mounting was fitted.

39 Armoured Cars, Humber, Mark III and Mark IV, U.K.

Humber Armoured Cars were numerically the most important British-built armoured cars of World War II, well over 5,000 being produced by the Rootes Group between 1940 and 1945.

The earliest Humber Armoured Car, the Mark I, was almost identical externally to the Guy Mark IA Armoured Car, and its mechanical layout although based, of course, on Rootes components was on similar lines to that of the Guy. Service experience suggested improvements and a cleaned-up front end, incorporating the driver's visor in the glacis plate, and radiator intake improvements were introduced in the Mark II.

The Armoured Car, Humber Mark III, which entered production in 1942 had a more roomy turret than the Marks I–II, which allowed the crew to be increased to four. The first three Marks of Humber Armoured Car all had an armament of two Besa machine-guns, one of 7·92-mm. calibre and the other 15-mm. The latter was never an entirely satisfactory weapon, being prone to stoppages, and in the Humber Mark IV Armoured Car the American 37-mm. gun was introduced in its place. Because this reduced the turret

space available, the crew was reduced to three men.

All the Humber Armoured Cars weighed about 7 tons and their 90-b.h.p. six-cylinder engines gave them a top speed of 45 m.p.h. They were used by both armoured car regiments (where they tended to be used at regimental and squadron headquarters if Daimlers were also available) and Reconnaissance Regiments (of infantry divisions) in most theatres of war in which British and Commonwealth troops were engaged up to the end of the war. The illustrations show a Mark III as it appeared in the North African desert about 1942, and a Mark IV of 1st Reconnaissance Regiment in Italy in 1944.

40 Armoured Cars, Daimler, Mark I and Mark II, U.K.

Inspired to a large extent by the design of the Car, Scout Mark I, the Daimler Armoured Car was built to the 'Tank, Light, Wheeled' formula of a wheeled vehicle having performance, armour and armament comparable to that of contemporary light tanks. After some initial difficulties it turned out to be one of the best armoured cars of World War II.

The mechanical layout of the Daimler Armoured Car consisted of a rear-mounted, 95 b.h.p. six-cylinder engine from which the transmission was taken via a 'Fluid Flywheel' and pre-selector gearbox to a centrally mounted transfer box with a single differential. From this the power was transmitted via four parallel driving shafts and Tracta universal joints to each wheel, with final reduction gears in each hub. This arrangement helped to keep the height down, as there were no central transmission shafts, and a further point making for compact design was that all the automotive components were attached direct to the hull, there being no chassis as such. Although regarded as being somewhat underpowered, the Daimler Armoured Car had a good cross-country performance and a top road speed of 50 m.p.h. Two other interesting features were the early use of disc brakes, and the inclusion of a second steering wheel facing the rear, together with basic driving controls, to enable the car to be driven rapidly in reverse in emergency.

The armament of the Daimler Armoured Car was identical to that of the Tetrarch Light Tank (with which it shared the turret design), a 2-pr gun and coaxially mounted 7·92-mm. Besa machine-gun.

Some improvements suggested by experience in service of the Daimler Mark I were incorporated in the Mark II, which followed the Mark I into production towards the latter end of the war. The most important changes were a 2-speed dynamo, a driver's escape hatch in the hull roof, an improved gun mantlet, and a different radiator and grill. Both Marks of Daimler (a total of 2,694 of which was built) sometimes had Littlejohn Adaptors added to the 2-pr guns, which greatly increased their penetrative ability.

The Daimler Mark I Armoured Car was first used in action in North Africa in 1942, and subsequently with the Mark II in Europe and the Far East. Many British and Commonwealth armoured car regiments used these cars and the illustrations show a Mark I of the 1st Derbyshire Yeomanry (6th Armoured Division) in Tunisia, and a Mark II of 11th Hussars (7th Armoured Division) in Germany in 1945.

41   Armoured Cars, A.E.C., Mark II and Mark III, U.K.

The original A.E.C. Armoured Car (Mark I) was conceived by the Associated Equipment Company Limited in 1941 as a heavy armoured car with both armour and armament equivalent to that of a cruiser tank and, in fact, used the 2-pr turret of a Valentine tank. This private venture was successful and 122 of them were built, many being sent to North Africa in 1942. When British tank armament increased, the A.E.C. Mark II Armoured Car was designed to use the 6-pr gun (with a coaxial 7·92-mm. Besa machine-gun) and, at the same time, the opportunity was taken to redesign the shape of the front hull and introduce other improvements. The Mark II had a more powerful A.E.C. diesel engine of 158 b.h.p. (which gave a top speed of 41 m.p.h.) and a crew of four. It weighed 12·7 tons and the armour protection was at a maximum of 30 mm.

The next step, in the Mark III, was to substitute the British 75-mm. gun for the 6-pr. The Mark III was very similar to its predecessor in most other respects, except that it had two (rather than one) electric fans installed in the turret roof. A total of 507 Armoured Cars, A.E.C. Marks II and III was built.

Some A.E.C. Mark IIs were supplied to the Yugoslav partisans in 1944 and one of these is shown in the smaller illustration. A.E.C. Mark IIIs were used principally in the Heavy Troops of British Armoured Car Regiments in the North West Europe campaign, and a car of 2nd Household Cavalry Regiment (then in VIII Corps) is illustrated.

42 Car, Scout, Humber, Mark I, U.K.

Production of the Daimler Scout Car (introduced into service at the beginning of World War II) was continued throughout the war. Only relatively minor changes were made in the design because it was a highly successful vehicle. However, as the number built could not meet the demand, the Rootes Group was asked to design and manufacture a scout car to supplement the Daimler Scout Cars.

To avoid unnecessary production complications the Rootes Group design which became known as Car, Scout, Humber, Mark I, employed a high proportion of components used in existing Humber 4-wheel drive military vehicles, such as the Light Reconnaissance Car, but adapted for a rear engine layout. The ubiquitous Rootes 87 b.h.p. six-cylinder engine was linked to a 4-speed gearbox and gave a top speed of 60 m.p.h. Rather larger than the Daimler Scout Car and with room for three men, the Humber Scout Car was of a mechanically less sophisticated design, and the maximum frontal protection was only 14 mm. compared with the Daimler's 30 mm. For some or all of these reasons, given a choice, armoured regiments tended to use

Humbers for liaison purposes rather than scouting.

The Mark II version of the Humber Scout Car was externally similar to the Mark I but had synchromesh added to 2nd gear as well as in 3rd and 4th. A total of 4,300 Humber Scout Cars was built between about late 1942 and the end of the war.

The illustrations show vehicles belonging to 11th Armoured Division.

43 Car, Scout, Ford, Lynx I–II, and Car, Light Reconnaissance, Canadian G.M., Mark I, Otter I, Canada.

As well as manufacturing large numbers of tanks, Canadian industry made a significant contribution to the production of wheeled armoured vehicles for the Commonwealth during World War II. Many chassis were supplied for armoured vehicles built in India and South Africa, but among the most important produced complete in Canada itself were the Lynx Scout Car and the Otter Light Reconnaissance Car—products of Ford and General Motors respectively.

The drawings of the Daimler Scout Car were sent from the United Kingdom to Canada so that an equivalent vehicle could be built to supplement British production, which lagged behind demand. It would have been impracticable to undertake the extensive re-tooling and conversion of standard measurements that would have been needed to produce a replica of the Daimler Scout Car in Canada, so the Daimler's hull design was adapted to accept a Ford V-8 engine and Ford 4-

wheel drive automative components. As the Ford transmission was of the conventional pattern for 4-wheel drive vehicles, with centrally placed transmission shafts to front and rear axles, the Canadian Scout Car was of necessity nearly a foot taller than the Daimler.

Known originally in British nomenclature simply as Car, Scout, Mark III (and later as Lynx I) the early versions of this car were found to be unreliable and some components needed strengthening. Later vehicles were modified in various ways, including a revision of the radiator protection at the rear. A second model, known as Car, Scout, Ford Mark II, Lynx II, incorporated the results of both production experience with Lynx I and British operating experience with Scout cars generally, which led to the omission of the armoured roof, which was rarely used. The Lynx II was considered to be reliable and had a better performance than its predecessor. The chief external difference (apart from the roof) was the sand channels carried at the rear in the Lynx II, instead of across the front locker.

A Lynx II is shown in the illustration. The Ford V-8 95 b.h.p. engine in the Lynx Scout cars gave a top speed of between 55 and 60 m.p.h. and the armour protection, like that of the Daimler Scout cars, was at a maximum of 30 mm. on the sloping glacis plate.

A total of 3,255 Lynx I and II Scout cars was built. They were used by the Canadian Army in Italy and North West Europe, and by British and Indian troops in the Far East.

The Canadian-built Car, Light Reconnaissance, Canadian G.M. Mark I,

Otter I was built to the same general specification as the British Humber Mark III Light Reconnaissance Car. The use of Canadian components, however, resulted in a shorter bonnet and a higher, more humped hull, although provision was made for the same armament—a Bren 0·303-in. machine-gun in the turret and a 0·55-in. Boys anti-tank rifle in the hull front beside the driver. Alternatively, a No. 19 wireless set was carried in the latter position. The six-cylinder General Motors engine developed 104 b.h.p., and gave a maximum speed of 45 m.p.h. The crew of three were protected by armour varying between 12 mm. and 6 mm.

Although of less good performance than the Humber Light Reconnaissance Car (mainly because it was over a ton heavier and lacked an auxiliary gearbox) the 1761 Otters built gave useful service in all the main theatres of war with the Canadian and British Armies (and, in addition, the Royal Air Force Regiment, which equipped some with 20-mm. cannon in the hull front and twin Browning machine-guns in the turret).

44 Car, 4 × 4, Light Reconnaissance, Humber, Mark IIIA and Car, 4 × 4, Light Reconnaissance, Morris, Mark II, U.K.

The Rootes Group were responsible for the major part of the production of Light Reconnaissance cars in the United Kingdom in World War II (3,600 in total), commencing with the Mark I (known as Ironside I) of 1940. This was followed by the Mark II which had an enclosed roof mounting a small turret, and in turn by the externally similar Mark III. This model, however, introduced 4-wheel drive. It was succeeded in 1942 by the Mark IIIA, shown here, which had various minor improvements, the most noticeable of which were extra observation ports at the front corner angles of the hull. A 3½-ton vehicle powered by an 87-b.h.p. Humber six-cylinder engine, which gave it a top speed of 50 m.p.h., the armament of the Humber Mark IIIA Light Reconnaissance Car consisted normally of a 0·303-in. Bren light machine-gun mounted in the turret, to which was sometimes added a 0·55-in. Boys anti-tank rifle usually mounted in the hull front. Often a smoke discharger was also carried. The car had a crew of three, and light armour of up to 10 mm.

The Car, 4 × 2, Light Reconnaissance, Morris, Mark I was put into production by the Nuffield Group to supplement the Humbers and the later versions of the Beaverette being built by the Standard Motor Company. A rear-engined vehicle, the Morris Mark I's cross country performance was enhanced by the smooth enclosed design of its underbelly. Nevertheless, a 4-wheel drive version, the Mark II, was introduced to take the place of the Mark I. With a 71·8 b.h.p. Morris engine and weighing slightly more at 3·7 tons and with 14-mm. armour, the specification and performance of the Morris Mark II was similar to that of the Humber Mark IIIA. The layout of the armament differed, however, in that the Boys anti-tank rifle, when carried, was operated from a hatch, to the left of the turret mounting the Bren

gun, and the gunner was protected by the raised armoured hatch cover. About 2,290 Morris Marks I and II Light Reconnaissance Cars were built.

Intended originally as equipment for the Reconnaissance Corps, both the Morris and Humber Light Reconnaissance Cars were also used extensively by armoured car units of the Royal Air Force Regiment, and the Humber Mark IIIA in the illustration is one belonging to the R.A.F. Regiment in the North West Europe campaign. Both makes of car were used also for reconnoitring and liaison purposes by Royal Engineers field companies and the Morris Mark II shown is in the markings of a field company, R.E., of the 43rd (Wessex) Infantry Division.

45 **Armoured Carrier, Wheeled, I.P., Mark IIA and Armoured Carrier, Wheeled, I.P., A.O.V.,** India.

The wheeled Armoured Carrier, Mark I, built in India in 1940–41, was followed throughout World War II by a series of armoured carriers of successive Marks—a total of 4,655 of them were built by the War's end.

A rear-engine layout was adopted for the Indian wheeled carriers after the Mark I. The Marks II, IIa and IIb were very similar to each other, the two latter having slightly larger tyres and the Mark IIb a slight modification to the roof plate. All employed chassis supplied direct from Canada by the Ford Motor Company of Canada. These were 4-wheel drive chassis with 95 b.h.p. Ford V-8 engines. The armour plate was designed and manufactured in India and assembly took place mainly at factories of the Tata Iron and Steel Co. and the East Indian Railway Workshops.

The Carrier, Wheeled, Mark IIC was very much like its predecessors in appearance but had a number of further improvements, including heavier springs and front axles, wider track, larger tyres and a 12-gallon auxiliary petrol tank. An Armoured Observation Vehicle version of the Mark IIC, with a small turret mounting a light machine-gun was built. This tended to be used as a light reconnaissance car, although there was also a Carrier, Mark III, which had a turret with a Boys 0·55-in. anti-tank rifle and a Bren 0·303-in. machine gun and was, in fact, specifically intended for this purpose.

The final version, Mark IV, differed from all earlier vehicles in that the driver sat separately from the rest of the crew in an armoured cab.

The Mark II series carriers were used in the North African campaigns, in Italy and in the South East Asia campaign, whereas the A.O.V. and the Marks III and IV are not known to have been employed outside Asia. The standard carriers, wheeled, were employed for a variety of purposes, in much the same way as the British tracked Universal-series carriers, by both infantry, artillery and reconnaissance units.

An Armoured Carrier, Wheeled, I.P., Mark IIA (with a Boys anti-tank rifle mounted, although a Bren light machine-gun was more often used), belonging to the Reconnaissance Unit (Indian Cavalry) of the 8th Indian Division in Italy in 1943 is shown,

together with a Carrier, Wheeled, A.O.V. in Burma in 1945.

46 Armoured Command Vehicle (A.E.C.) 4 × 4, Mark I and Armoured Command Vehicle (A.E.C.) 6 × 6, Mark I, U.K.

The limited number of Guy Lizard and smaller Morris armoured command vehicles built at the beginning of World War II, was almost entirely replaced for the greater part of the war by vehicles on A.E.C. chassis.

The A.E.C. Matador chassis was used as the basis of the 4-wheeled A.C.V.—known at first officially as 'Lorry, 3 ton, 4 × 4, Armoured Command, A.E.C.' This consisted basically of an armoured body (12-mm. armour) fitted out internally for command purposes and carrying two wireless sets. These were a No. 19 H.P. and a No. 19 in the Low Power version, and an R.C.A. receiver and a No. 19 set in the High Power version. The A.C.V. Mark II (in a Low Power version only) differed in having an internal partition, dividing it into staff and wireless compartments.

Weighing nearly 12 tons, the A.E.C. 4 × 4 Armoured Command Vehicle was powered by an A.E.C. diesel engine of 95 b.h.p. which gave it a top speed of 35 m.p.h. No armament was fitted but a Bren light machine-gun was carried for defence.

A total of 416 4 × 4 A.C.V.s was built, and these were supplemented in 1944-45 by 151 vehicles of a new model—on an A.E.C. 6-wheel-drive chassis. This was very much more roomy than its predecessor, being 6 feet longer, but slightly lower. It was also very much heavier at 19 tons loaded, and was powered by a more powerful A.E.C. diesel engine of 135 b.h.p. Two versions were again produced, L.P. and H.P., the former having one No. 19 H.P. wireless set and one No. 19, and the latter one No. 53 and one No. 19. Both versions were divided internally, the front compartment being for staff and the rear for the wireless equipment. As in all the earlier vehicles, eight men were carried.

The A.E.C. 4 × 4 armoured command vehicles were first used in action in the North African campaign, where, incidentally, three were captured and used by German generals, two of them by Rommel himself and his staff. These two vehicles were nicknamed 'Max' and 'Moritz', although the type was given the generic name of Mammut (Mammoth) by the Germans.

The armoured command vehicles were large and conspicuous and, of course, as they carried senior officers, valuable targets, so Major Jasper Maskelyne (a well-known stage magician in civilian life) commanding a camouflage unit of the Royal Engineers, was asked to design special camouflage for them. What he did was to disguise them as ordinary lorries, similar to the standard A.E.C. Matador gun tractors which were widely used by the British Army. This involved black shadow painting on various parts of the hull, the addition of a canvas cover to the top surfaces and an extension to the armoured noseplate. This disguise is shown in the illustration of an A.E.C. 4 × 4 A.C.V. in North Africa.

47 Carrier, A.E.C., 6-pr Gun, Mark I (Deacon) and, S.P. 17-pr Gun—Straussler, U.K.

The 6-pr gun was the best British weapon available for tackling German tanks in early 1942, and the Deacon was designed as a means of increasing its mobility, chiefly for use in the North African theatre of war. The 6-pr (on a field-type, not a tank mounting) was mounted on a turntable, with a light shield open only at the rear, and carried on an armoured A.E.C. Matador chassis. The Deacon weighed 12 tons and powered by an A.E.C. six-cylinder 95-b.h.p. diesel engine had a top speed of only 19 m.p.h. Despite their bulk and slowness, the Deacons did good work in the North African campaign, after which they were handed over to the Turkish Government. A total of 150 was built in 1942 and they were supplied ex-works already painted in a bright sand yellow. A further twenty-five vehicles without the gun and a platform body were built as armoured ammunition carriers.

In 1943, an experimental wheeled self-propelled mounting for the new and very much more powerful 17-pr anti-tank gun was designed by Nicholas Straussler. Entirely original in concept, the 17-pr gun with split trail was, in effect, added to a rectangular skeleton chassis. A motive unit, consisting of Bedford type QL lorry components, was added, the engine (at the right-hand side of the chassis) driving the two front wheels for transport. When the gun was in position, the two rear wheels could be swivelled until they were at right angles to the front wheels. The right hand rear wheel could then be driven through a power take-off from the engine, so enabling the whole carriage to be rotated through 360 degrees. Sometimes known as Monitor, the Straussler S.P. 17-pr was not adopted for service because it was felt that the mounting offered insufficient protection for the gun and its crew. The illustration shows the vehicle in its travelling position.

48 Ford Armoured Cars (Arab Legion), Transjordan.

The Arab Legion of Transjordan (now the Kingdom of Jordan) originally had the tasks of patrolling the frontier and of internal security but after the outbreak of war the Arab Legion, now including a mobile unit known as the Desert Mechanized Force, served alongside the British Army in the Middle East, and was in action in Iraq and Syria in 1941. Following the success of the Arab Legion in these operations, it was decided to expand the Desert Mechanized Force, which included only six armoured cars, into a mechanized regiment (and subsequently into a mechanized brigade of three regiments).

The original six armoured cars of the Arab Legion were purchased in Palestine and were very similar to some used by the Palestine Police. No further supplies from this source, or from Britain, were available to equip the new mechanized regiments, and it was decided that the Arab Legion should build its own armoured cars in Transjordan. Four hundred Ford commercial truck chassis were ordered from the United States, although only 250 were delivered, the ships carrying the balance being torpedoed *en route*.

The Arab Legion armoured cars were designed by their commander, Glubb Pasha (John B. Glubb), and were modelled broadly on the original six vehicles (the first type of Arab Legion armoured car), which also used Ford chassis. Glubb's original model (called here for convenience the Arab Legion 2nd type) had built-up front mudguards and bevelled edges on the bonnet and front corners of the hull, but his second model (Arab Legion 3rd type) used the original truck mudguards and had a simpler bonnet design. In both models, the turret had provision for a mounted machine-gun (usually a Vickers 0·303-in.) and a Boys 0·55-in. anti-tank rifle, and an anti-aircraft machine-gun (often a Lewis 0·303-in.). Some cars were fitted with wireless, carried in the hull behind the turret. As supplies of armour plate were not available, the armour was made up of a double skin of mild steel with a sheet of plywood sandwiched between the plates.

A total of 100 armoured cars of these two types was built, and they equipped the Arab Legion mechanized regiments until being replaced by Marmon-Herrington Mark IV F armoured cars in 1945.

49 Autocanon Dodge and Autocanon 75-mm., Ford, France.

The Fighting French contingent which fought alongside British forces in the North African campaign in 1942–43, included an armoured car unit which was equipped partly with South African built Marmon-Herrington armoured cars and partly with vehicles of French design, although based on

American or Canadian chassis. This unit was formed from what was originally an infantry regiment of soldiers from French Morocco—the 1er Regiment de marche de Spahis Marocains (R.M.S.M.).

The Marmon-Herrington armoured cars (Mark III) supplied to the Fighting French were armed with machine-guns only, but these were supported by a number of vehicles (captured from the Vichy French in Syria) that were equipped with a French short 37-mm. gun and a 7·5-mm. machine-gun coaxially mounted in a small turret, open at the rear. A further 7·5-mm. machine-gun could be mounted on a pillar mount in the body of the vehicle. The chassis used for these armoured cars was a 4 × 2 U.S.-built Dodge 1940 model. The lorry cab was retained (with the addition of light windscreen armour) and only the rear part was fully armoured, although, even so, the back portion had an open top.

Later in 1943, the R.M.S.M. received a number of vehicles with very much greater fire power, designed by one of their officers, Lieutenant Conus. This type was based on the Ford F 60L 3-ton lorry supplied by Canada for the British Army. A French 75-mm. field gun was mounted at the rear (using the turntable from a captured Italian tank) where it had a full 360 degrees traverse. The crew were protected by a three-sided shield, and the rear of the chassis and the driver's cab were also armoured, although the latter appears to have been mainly to protect the driver from the blast of the gun. An anti-aircraft pillar mounting for a machine-gun was provided on the front of the gun shield. A lorry canvas hood was carried to disguise the gun when not in action. These 'autocanons' were used in action from about October 1942 until the end of the North African campaign.

These two types of Fighting French equipment are shown in the illustrations in typical Middle East colours, the Dodge bearing a French registration number and the Ford F 60L still carrying its original British W.D. number.

50   **Carro Armato M.15/42, Italy.**

The Italian medium tank M.15/42 was a logical development of the M.13/40 of 1940 and its derivative the M.14/41. Very much like its predecessors in appearance, the M.15/42's 47-mm. gun was, however, of 40 calibres length (compared with 32 calibres of the earlier tanks) which gave it a far higher muzzle velocity and greater penetrative power.

The other most important change compared with the M.13/40 and M.14/41 was a more powerful engine, the S.P.A. 15TB which produced 192 b.h.p. and gave a better maximum (road) speed of 25 m.p.h., despite the increase of a ton in weight. Although the new engine provided the extra power needed, it was a petrol engine and it seems to have been something of a backward step to abandon the diesel type previously used.

Other features of the M.15/42 were a crew of four, an armament of three 8-mm. Breda machine-guns (one coaxial, two in a dual mount in the front of the hull) besides the 47-mm. gun; and maximum armour protection of 45-mm. (50-mm. on the gun mantlet).

About 2,000 M.13/40s and M.14/41s were completed (of which about the last 800 were the latter) but production of the Carro Armato M.15/42 ceased after only 82 of them were built by early 1943. Following this, Italian armoured fighting vehicle production was concentrated on self-propelled guns.

One illustration shows the fifth tank of the 1st Company, 2nd Platoon, of an Italian armoured battalion in Italy in 1943; the other an M.15/42 in desert colours.

51 Carro Armato P.40, Italy.

The only Italian heavy tank of World War II, the P.40, which entered production in 1943, had its origin in design studies commenced in 1938. One of two Ansaldo designs (in competition with two drawn up by the official Direzione della Motorizzazione) was chosen in 1940, although the first prototype to be built did not appear until early 1942.

A 26-ton vehicle, protected up to a maximum of 50 mm., a high velocity 75-mm. gun was chosen as the main armament. As the gun being developed for it was not ready when the prototype was completed, however, the 75/18 howitzer was mounted instead. This was replaced in the second prototype by the interim gun 75/32 until, with the third prototype, the 75/34, with a muzzle velocity of 610 metres per second, could be used.

The suspension of the P.40 followed the common Italian practice of two groups of four road wheels each side carried on a semi-elliptic leaf spring for each group—a somewhat crude but well-tried system. The hull and turret layout were conventional, the armament of the 75-mm. gun and coaxial 8-mm. machine-gun being concentrated in the turret—the front hull machine-gun which existed in the first two prototypes was eliminated in the final version.

The engine was at the rear, the transmission being led forward via the gearbox and clutch to track drive sprockets at the front. The prototypes used a 330-h.p. diesel but a new twelve-cylinder-V petrol engine of 420 h.p. was ready for use in the production models, to which it gave a maximum speed of 25 m.p.h.

Only twenty-one P.40s had been completed by the time of the Armistice in 1943. Two Italian tank battalions to be equipped with P.40s were in the process of formation at this time, but in the end only the Germans employed in service the few P.40s available.

52 Semovente M. 42M da 75/34 and Semovente M.42L da 105/23, Italy.

Some of the most effective Italian armoured fighting vehicles were the series of assault guns based on medium tank chassis which appeared from 1941 onwards.

These vehicles were fully armoured and enclosed, and mounted weapons ranging in power from the 75/18 (75-mm.; 18 calibres long) howitzer originally used on the M.13/40 chassis, to the 105/23 on the M.15/42 chassis.

The 75/18 Semovente was in production between 1941 and 1943: later vehicles used the M.14/41 and M.15/42 chassis. In all, 780 vehicles were built. They gave good service with the Ariete and Littorio Divisions in North Africa and later on Italian soil.

A new weapon for the P.40 tank and assault guns, the 75/34, was in the process of development in 1942. In the meantime as an interim measure the 75/32 was introduced, although only a few dozen assault guns of this type were built, by the Ansaldo concern.

The prototype for the Semovente 75/34 was completed by the end of 1942, by which time a total of 500 had been ordered. Due to problems over the design of the mounting for the 75/34, however, 75/18s or 75/32s were fitted in M.15/42 chassis intended for the new gun. In the end, only just over ninety 75/34 assault guns were built. They were intended to replace the artillery in the armoured units, the 75/18s then to be transferred to support the infantry of armoured formations. Their main use was, however, by the Germans, who acquired all those available in Italy in 1943.

The Semovente M.42M da 75/34 was considered to be a good 'tank hunter', its gun having a muzzle velocity of 610 metres per second and a range of 12½ kilometres. Apart from the longer gun, it was similar in most external respects to the early 75/18 and 75/32 assault guns on the chassis of M.13/40, M.14/41 and M.15/42 tanks, all of which had similar running gear. Weighing 15 tons, the Semovente M.42M da 75/34 was powered by a S.P.A. eight-cylinder petrol engine of 192 b.h.p. which gave it a top speed of about 25 m.p.h. The vehicle had a crew of three men and an 8-mm. machine-gun was carried for anti-aircraft defence.

The Semovente M.42L da 105/23 was in general appearance like the 75-mm. assault gun but had a much larger 105-mm., 23-calibre length, howitzer, specially developed as an assault gun. The final prototype was ready in January 1943, and firing trials took place later in that month. Deliveries began in May 1943 but, although 454 of them were finally ordered, only a relatively small number was completed. Part of the artillery group of the Ariete Division was equipped with Semovente 105/23s in the summer of 1943. Some of these assault guns were used by Italian units in the defence of Rome in September 1943. Later the Germans requisitioned all those available and employed them in Italy.

With the same 192-b.h.p. petrol engine, the Semovente 105/23 weighed somewhat more at 15·6 tons than earlier models and had a top speed of 22 m.p.h. The 105-mm. gun was a good anti-tank weapon, notably with the special ammunition developed for it and, mounted in a compact chassis, this combination represented one of the best Italian armoured fighting vehicles of World War II.

53 **Panzerkampfwagen II, Ausf.L, Luchs, Germany.**

The PzKpfw II as a battle tank was, as early as 1940, recognized as being outdated. Its development, as a reconnaissance vehicle was, however, continued and the final model, Ausf.L, known as Luchs (Lynx) was produced in 1942–43.

Although retaining the same general layout of the earlier vehicles of the

PzKpfw II series, the Ausf.L's design was derived mainly from Daimler-Benz prototypes (based on their earlier Ausf.D and E) rather than the M.A.N. design used for the great majority of PzKfw IIs built. The main external difference of the Ausf.L from all earlier production PzKpfw IIs was the overlapping road wheels, with torsion bar suspension, and wide tracks. With a maximum armour thickness of 30-mm. (excluding spaced armour added later to some vehicles), the armament of the Luchs consisted of a 2-cm. gun and one machine-gun, mounted coaxially in the turret. A few vehicles were fitted instead with a 5-cm. gun—a fairly heavy weapon for a vehicle of under 12 tons. The engine of the Luchs was a 178-b.h.p. six-cylinder Maybach which gave it a maximum speed of about 40 m.p.h.

54 Panzerkampfwagen III, Ausf.L and Ausf.M, Germany.

Production of the PzKpfw III, the first models of which were built in 1937, was not finally ceased until the summer of 1943, when it was still an important element in the German armoured forces. Successive increases in armament, from the 3·7-cm. gun of the early models, through the 5-cm. L/42 of 1940 to the long 5-cm. L/60 of the late models, Ausf.L and M, associated with increased armour protection, justified the retention of the PzKpfw III. Even when superseded as a tank, the Panzer III chassis remained in production as the basis of assault guns.

Among the features shared by the Ausf.L and M with earlier models of the PzKpfw III were the transverse torsion-bar suspension system and the twelve-cylinder Maybach engine of 300-h.p. and the secondary armament of one machine-gun coaxial with the gun in the turret and one machine-gun in the right side of the hull, beside the driver. The maximum armour protection of the Ausf.L and M was 70-mm. in spaced armour at the front and the combination of the increased armour and heavier gun made it necessary to reinforce the suspension. Skirt armour on hull sides and turret was also carried on some tanks. The Ausf.L and M were almost identical in appearance but in the latter, to simplify production, some vision ports and the hull escape doors were eliminated—with the introduction of skirt armour, these were, in any case, of little use.

The final version of PzKpfw III, the Ausf.N was the same as Ausf.L or M but with the short-barrelled 7·5-cm. KwK L/24. In all, 5,644 PzKpfw IIIs were produced between 1937 and 1943.

The upper illustration shows a PzKpfw III, Ausf.M, and the lower one a PzKpfw III, Ausf.L, in winter camouflage in Russia, with the guns sheathed as protection from the cold.

55 Panzerkampfwagen IV, Ausf.H, Germany.

The Panzerkampfwagen IV, which originally entered production on a limited scale in 1937, was steadily improved in armament and armour during World War II so that it remained in production right to the end of the war, by which time about 9,000 of them had been completed. The fact that, latterly, production was continued mainly because of the urgent need for serviceable tanks in large numbers, rather than changing completely to a more modern design, is no reflection on the excellent basic design of the PzKpfw IV.

A medium tank originally specified in the 20-ton class, although in its final form at around 25 tons, the Panzer IV was powered by a 300-b.h.p. twelve-cylinder Maybach at the rear with the gearbox and final drive sprockets at the front. The suspension consisted of eight road wheels each side, suspended in pairs on leaf springs.

When the Ausf.H appeared in 1943, the main armament was the long-barrelled 7·5-cm. L/48, increasingly powerful guns having been introduced in successive models, starting with the low-velocity 7·5-cm. L/24 of the early Panzer IVs. The secondary armament remained as two machine-guns—one in the hull front and one in the turret, coaxial with the 7·5-cm. gun. The maximum armour protection was 80-mm., having been increased fourfold over that of the original version, Ausf.A. Skirting plates (or wire mesh, in some cases) were often added to the turret and hull sides to give protection against hollow charge projectiles.

The Ausf.J, which followed, the final version of PzKpfw IV, was very similar externally to the preceding model but incorporated detail changes. One of the most important (and a retrograde step) was the deletion of the turret power traverse, leaving only a 2-speed hand traverse system, in order to make room for increased fuel capacity (680 litres, compared with 470 for AusfH) to give the extra range called for by 1944.

One of the illustrations shows a tank partly painted with 'Zimmerit', an anti-magnetic paste to repel sticky bombs; both tanks shown have both hull and turret skirting plates.

56 **Panzerkampfwagen V, Panther,** Germany.

The Panther, together with the Russian T-34 which was the direct cause of its inception, was one of the best tanks of World War II and one which has had much influence on post-war tank design.

Once the full effect of the T-34 was appreciated, it was at first proposed that a close copy should be built in Germany to counter it, but this was soon proved to be impracticable because of the fresh tooling that would have been required and the absence of suitable raw materials. The main features of the T.34 were, however, reproduced in the two designs submitted, ranging from the Daimler-Benz VK 3002, which was closely similar to the T.34, to the M.A.N. version, which had more traditional German features. In spite of Hitler's preference for the Daimler-Benz design, the M.A.N. model was chosen for production, which commenced in November 1942.

The Panther, as the Pzkpfw V was named, had the long sloping glacis plate of the T.34, inward sloping hull sides above track level, a turret mounting a long 7·5-cm. gun (L/70—70 calibres long) and interleaved road wheels, sprung on transverse torsion bars. Armour protection was at a maximum of 120-mm. on the turret and 80-mm. on the hull. A Maybach twelve-cylinder engine developing 642-b.h.p. (increased to 690-b.h.p. in the later models, Ausf.A and G) gave a top speed of about 28 m.p.h.

The Ausf.D was followed in production by the illogically designated Ausf.A which incorporated various improvements, one of the most obvious of which was the replacement of the unusual vertical-letter box type of mounting for the hull machine-gun by a more conventional ball-mounting. The turret was equipped with a new type of cupola and the pistol ports and loading door, present in the Ausf.D, were eliminated.

The final model of Panther, Ausf.G, had further changes, partly to compensate for shortages of raw materials and to simplify production. The driver's vision port was replaced by a rotating periscope, leaving the glacis plate clear except for the machine-gun ball mount; the hull sides were more sloped and stowage boxes at the rear were included inside the armour. This latter change was not always apparent, however, as side skirting plates were always likely to be fitted on all models of Panther. Finally, later production vehicles had all-steel road wheels with resilient hubs instead of the rubber-tyred wheels used earlier.

The illustrations show a Panther Ausf.D (bottom view) and an Ausf.G.

57 Panzerkampfwagen VI, Tiger I, Germany.

Perhaps the tank which created the greatest impression on British troops in World War II, from the time it was first encountered by them in Tunisia in 1943, was the Tiger. First used in action in September 1942 in Russia, the Tiger's design was completed before features exemplified by the Russian T.34 could be incorporated. Nevertheless, the heavy armour (at a maximum of 110-mm. on the turret and 100-mm. on the hull) and the powerful 8·8-cm. gun (KwK 36 L/55) made the Tiger a very formidable tank right to the end of the war.

Work on various heavy tank projects was started as early as 1937. These were modified with changing requirements and with the incorporation of an 8·8-cm. gun resulted in 1942 in the specification V.K. 4501, for which the design competition was won by the Henschel firm.

In spite of its size, the Tiger was fairly conventional in layout and design except that interleaved road wheels in the suspension system were used for the first time in a production tank although they were, of course, already a familiar feature in German half-tracks.

The engine—at the rear, the transmission being led forward via an 8-speed gearbox to front drive sprockets —was a V-form twelve-cylinder Maybach of 650-b.h.p., increased to 700-b.h.p. in the later vehicles to be built. This produced a top speed of 24 m.p.h., quite satisfactory for a 54-ton tank.

A total of 1,350 Tiger Is was manufactured and they were used in action in North Africa, Sicily, Italy, North West Europe and Russia.

58 Panzerkampfwagen VI, Tiger II, Germany.

Known to the Western Allies as King Tiger or Royal Tiger, the Tiger II or

Tiger Ausf. B was even more feared by its opponents than Tiger I. With an even more powerful gun (8·8-cm., 71 calibres long, compared with Tiger I's 56 calibres) thicker armour and a sloping hull glacis plate, the Tiger II had all the best features of its predecessor, together with improvements suggested by experience in Russia. Development of the type was called for in the autumn of 1942 and when the Tiger IIs were delivered to the troops in 1944 they were the most powerful tanks in service in the world, as well as the heaviest, and the position remained unchanged until nearly the end of the War.

Fortunately for its opponents, the Tiger II was mechanically unreliable, a fault perhaps due to insufficient time being allowed for development. Fourteen tons heavier than Tiger I, the King Tiger had a similar mechanical layout but the road wheels, sprung on independent torsion bars, were not interleaved, as in Tiger I, although they were overlapped. Four hundred and eighty-five Tiger IIs were built, of which the first fifty had different, more rounded, turrets than had been built for a Porsche-designed Tiger II, although the Porsche tank itself was rejected.

The relatively few Tiger IIs built were used in 1944–45 with considerable effect on both Germany's East and West fronts.

59 **Panzerkampfwagen Maus and Panzerkampfwagen E.100,** Germany.

These two colossal tanks, Maus and E.100, weighing around 150 tons, were produced in prototype form in Germany in 1944–45.

Maus, the earlier of the two, was the result of an instruction by Hitler to Dr Porsche in 1942 to design in conjunction with Krupp's a super-heavy tank in the 100-ton class. The first prototype (without turret and armament) was running by December 1944. The turret, mounted at the rear, with an armament consisting of a 15-cm. L/38 gun with a coaxial 7·5-m. KwK was only fitted at a late stage in development of the prototype, most test runs being carried out with a simulated turret.

The final all-up weight of Maus was no less than 185 tons, which few bridges could have withstood, so provision was made for the tank to ford rivers up to a depth of 14 feet, with air supply through a submarine-type snorkel tube. A 1200-b.h.p. Daimler-Benz petrol engine (a diesel was the ultimate type) with electric transmission was used and this produced a top speed of 12 m.p.h.

Panzerkampfwagen E.100 was the 'official' design by the Army Weapons Department for a tank in the 100-ton class and the heaviest in a proposed family of tracked fighting vehicles of between 5 and 100 tons, in which it was hoped to standardize as many components as possible. A somewhat more conventional design than Maus, being developed by Adler from the basis of the Tiger series, the E.100 was rather like a scaled-up Tiger II in appearance, with a 15-cm. gun and a coaxial 7·5-cm. gun in the turret, which was mounted centrally. The engine was a 700-b.h.p. twelve-cylinder Maybach for trials, although a 1,200-b.h.p.

version was proposed and was needed to produce the required performance.

The suspension system, like that of Maus, abandoned the torsion bars used for the later German medium and heavy tanks. It used a form of coil springing—Belleville washers. The weight of E.100 was about 138 tons and the maximum armour protection for both Maus and E.100 was 240-mm.

Two prototypes of the Maus were completed and tested in 1944-45; the E.100 prototype was never finished. Although overcoming engineering problems in the design of such heavy vehicles, the tactical value of tanks of this size was questionable as was, to an even greater degree, the diversion of A.F.V. design and production effort. There was certainly little excuse at all for two separate and competing designs at a critical stage of the war for Germany.

60 Jagdpanzer 38(t), Hetzer, Germany.

The Jagdpanzer 38(t) Hetzer ('Baiter') was one of the best self-propelled mountings for its size of World War II, being compact, well-armoured and mobile, with a top speed of about 25 m.p.h. The gun—the 7·5-cm. Pak 39 (L/48) was mounted in the right-hand side of the sloping glacis plate, which was armoured to a maximum of 60-mm. The driver sat at the left, the 150-b.h.p. six-cylinder Praga engine being at the rear. The suspension was of the leaf spring variety, the large road wheels being sprung in pairs.

An interesting feature of the Jagdpanzer 38(t) was the type of machine-gun mounted on the roof in some vehicles. This was fitted with a deflection device which enabled it to 'fire round corners', thus making it more effective in close-up defence.

The last type on the Czech LT-38 chassis to go into production, 1,577 Hetzers were built in 1944 and the design was considered good enough to be adopted by the Swiss Army in the post-war years.

61 Sturmgeheschütz III/10·5-cm. StuH, Germany.

The Sturmgeschütz III was one of Germany's most enduring armoured fighting vehicles, production of which commenced in 1940 and continued right through to the end of the war, when over 10,500 vehicles had been built.

In its standard form the StuG III was originally equipped with the low-velocity 7·5-cm. L/24 gun, suitable for close support of infantry. This was replaced in 1942 by the much more powerful L/43 and L/48 weapons which were also capable of tackling tanks. Also developed in 1943 was a new version for the close support role, but with a much heavier gun—the 10·5-cm. howitzer. The first vehicles had the 1eFH18 (light field howitzer) but the StuH.42 (assault howitzer) was soon standardized for the majority of 10·5-cm. StuG. III that were produced.

The chassis of the StuG III remained throughout production that of the contemporary model of Pzkpfw III, although the tank itself was eventually withdrawn from production in favour of the assault gun. The armour protection in the later StuG III was at a maximum of 80-mm. and side skirting plates were usually fitted. The total weight was nearly 24 tons, although the maximum speed of 24 m.p.h. remained the same as in earlier models.

The upper illustration shows a vehicle with 'Zimmerit' finish and skirting plates.

62 Sturmpanzer IV, Brummbär and Jagdpanzer IV/70, Germany.

Two self-propelled mountings developed from the Stu.G III concept, but taking advantage of the greater scope offered by the larger Pz IV chassis, the Brummbär (Grizzly Bear) appeared in 1943 and the Jagdpanzer IV/70 in 1944.

Armed with the short (12 calibres) heavy 15-cm. StuH.43, the Brummbär was armoured to a maximum of 100-mm. on the front plate. Weighing over 28 tons the chassis was overloaded, although a top speed of 25 m.p.h. was attainable. Only 315 of them were built and to compensate for a shortcoming discovered in service, the last ones produced had a machine-gun added in a ball-mounting at the left-hand side of the sloping front plate.

The Jagdpanzer IV/70 was the outcome of the policy to produce heavily armoured turretless self-propelled anti-tank guns at the expense of tank production—a token of the realization of Germany's need for vehicles suited more for defence than attack. In addition, production of turretless vehicles rather than tanks helped to increase the total number available. Earlier vehicles on the PzKpfw IV chassis used the 7·5-cm. L/48 in a superstructure like that of the Stu.G III until the redesigned Jagdpanzer IV appeared. At first also

armed with the 7·5-cm. L/48, the final version had the powerful 7·5-cm. L/70—the same gun as the Panther's. This exceptionally long weapon caused nose heaviness, resulting in heavy wear on the rubber tyres of the front two road wheels each side. Accordingly, steel-tyred resilient road wheels were substituted in these positions. Also, to simplify the suspension, only three, instead of four, return rollers each side were used in the later vehicles built. Output of Jagdpanzer IV with both the L/48 and L/70 guns (mostly the former) amounted to over 1,500 vehicles.

63 8.8-cm. Panzerjäger Panther-Jagdpanther, Germany.

Like the tank on which it was based, the Jagdpanther was a formidable vehicle. Following the standard German practice of using a tank chassis to mount a heavier gun in a limited traverse mounting, thus keeping the weight within reasonable bounds, the Panther chassis was used to create a highly mobile heavily armed 'tank hunter'.

The running gear and lower chassis of the Panther (Ausf.G) was retained but the hull was increased in height and the gun—the 8·8-cm. L/71 (71 calibres long)—was mounted in the centre of the sloping glacis plate. A ball-mounted machine-gun was retained but higher up the glacis than in the tank.

Produced in 1944 the Jagdpanther was considered by some at the time to be an undesirable dilution of Panther production, but in the defensive operations of 1944–45, the Jagdpanther was probably an even more effective weapon than the tank.

64 Jagdpanzer Tiger (P), Elefant, Germany.

Dr Ferdinand Porsche's design to the V.K. 4501 specification—the Tiger tank—had interesting and unusual features, such as petrol-electric drive and longitudinal torsion-bar suspension, but the more conventional Henschel design was chosen for the production order for the Tiger. Nevertheless, a limited order for ninety Porsche Tiger chassis was awarded. Five were completed at the Nibelungenwerke in Austria as tanks (and used for trials only) and the rest were modified at the Alkett concern in Berlin as 'tank hunters'. This involved the addition of a fixed superstructure (armoured to a maximum of 200-mm.) in which an 8·8-cm. Pak L/71 was mounted, with a limited traverse. The original engine intended by Porsche was replaced by two twelve-cylinder Maybach engines, totalling 640-b.h.p. but the electric transmission was retained. Weighing 67 tons, the top speed was only 12½ m.p.h.

Named at first Ferdinand (after Dr Porsche) and later Elefant, these Jagdpanzers were employed at first in Russia and later, in reduced numbers, in Italy. Experience in Russia showed that the lack of a hull machine-gun was a serious fault, and one was incorporated later.

65 Jagdpanzer VI—Jagdtiger, Germany.

In accordance with the usual German practice, a companion 'tank hunter' version of Tiger II was produced, in which the rotating turret was replaced by a fixed superstructure mounting a heavier gun than that carried in the tank. This was the Jagdtiger, armed with a 12·8-cm. Pak 44 L/55—the most powerfully armed fighting vehicle to go into production in World War II, although Germany's circumstances in 1944 made it possible for a total of only forty-eight to be built. With a similar power train and suspension (although lengthened) to that of Tiger II, the Jagdtiger was protected to a maximum thickness of no less than 250-mm., weighed 70 tons and had a top speed of 23 m.p.h. It was the heaviest and one of the most formidable fighting vehicles of its era to enter service.

During the course of its short production life, the suspension of the Jagdtiger was changed from the Henschel system of transverse torsion bars used in Tiger II to a longitudinal torsion bar system, designed by Ferdinand Porsche, in which the wheels were mounted in four pairs each side. In the illustrations a vehicle with the Porsche suspension is shown at the top, and a Jagdtiger with the Henschel system, which had nine overlapped wheels each side instead of eight, at the bottom.

66 7·5-cm. Pak auf Gw. 38(t), Marder III, Ausf.M, Germany.

The Czech LT-38 tank was continued in production after the German take-over of Czechoslovakia. By 1942, the Pzkpfw 38(t), as it was then called, was outclassed as a battle tank, but it was thought well worth while to continue output of the reliable, sturdy and easily maintained chassis as a mounting for self-propelled weapons.

The earlier self-propelled mountings (Geschützwagen—Gw.) used the chassis with the original layout in which the engine was located at the rear. The later versions, built in 1943–44, had the engine (a six-cylinder 150-b.h.p. Praga) moved forward to a position alongside the driver, and were designated Ausf.M (M = mitte [middle]), the earlier version being Ausf.H = heckmotor [rear engine]). Apart from better weight distribution, a lower silhouette was possible with the engine relocated and there were advantages in the crew having access to the gun from the rear.

The weapon used was the 7·5-cm. Pak 40/3, of a calibre length of 46, and mounted behind a shield open at the rear and with no overhead protection. One machine-gun was usually carried for local defence.

Seven hundred and ninety-nine Marder III, Ausf.M were built in 1943–44, together with four hundred and eighteen of the earlier Ausf.H in 1942–43.

Two views of different vehicles are shown in the illustrations.

67 15-cm. sIG33 auf Sf. II and 7·62-cm. Pak auf Gw. II, Ausf. D, Germany.

These two self-propelled mountings both used the chassis of different models of the PzKpfw II. The heavy infantry gun (sIG) carrier was, however, by far the better vehicle, being low and inconspicuous and the addition of an extra road wheel each side in the later version (which appeared in 1943) gave a better weight distribution and more space for crew and ammunition. With a crew of five and a loaded weight of about 13 tons this self-propelled gun (Selbstfahrlafette—Sfl.), which was powered by the standard six-cylinder 140-b.h.p. Maybach engine, had a top speed of 25 m.p.h. Vehicles of this type on both lengthened and normal PzII chassis were used in North Africa and Russia.

The 7·62-cm. Pak—a captured Russian anti-tank gun, rechambered to take German ammunition—on the Pzkpfw II Ausf. D (also Ausf. E) chassis was, by contrast, one of the crudest of the improvised self-propelled mountings produced by the Germans in World War II. Nevertheless, it served its purpose in helping to get the greatest possible number of anti-tank guns into the field in the shortest possible time. The long-barrelled gun, protected by its own shield, was mounted towards the rear of the vehicle on top of the armoured superstructure with the end of the barrel projecting over the front. The Ausf.D of Pzkpfw II had a 180-b.h.p. six-cylinder Maybach engine and the Gw II for the 7·62-cm. Pak weighing 11·5 tons had a top speed of about 35 m.p.h.

68 15-cm. Pz. fH 18 auf Gw. III/IV, Hummel and 8.8-cm. Pak43/1 (L/71) auf Gw. III/IV, Nashorn, Germany.

A modified Panzer IV chassis, incorporating features of the Panzer III, was used between 1942 and 1944 for the production of two specially designed heavily armed but relatively lightly armoured self-propelled mountings. Known as Geschützwagen III/IV, the chassis had the Panzer IV suspension with the engine (300-b.h.p. twelve-cylinder Maybach) moved forward to allow room for a fighting compartment at the rear.

Hummel (Bumble Bee) was the 15-cm. field Howitzer (Pz.H.18) on this chassis: 666 vehicles were built in 1943-44, together with 150 similar vehicles without guns for use as armoured ammunition carriers.

The 8·8-cm. Pak 43/1 (L/71) on the same chassis with minor variations for the gun mounting, ammunition stowage etc. was known at first as Hornisse (Hornet) and later as Nashorn (Rhinoceros). Four hundred and seventy three were made in 1943–44 and although, like Hummel, armoured only to a maximum of 30-mm., the powerful gun made them a formidable weapon.

69 Flakpanzer IV (3·7-cm.), Möbelwagen and Flakpanzer IV (2-cm.), Wirbelwind, Germany.

The overwhelming Allied air superiority by 1943 made it increasingly necessary for Germany to direct a greater proportion of armoured fighting vehicle production to the output of anti-aircraft tanks.

The Pzkpfw IV chassis was used for some of the more important of the A.A. tank designs which entered service in 1943–44. The commonest of the lighter weapons were the quadruple 20-mm. and the single 3·7-cm. guns. The earlier design for both of these mountings (called Möbelwagen—furniture van—in the case of the 3·7-cm. mounting) consisted of the guns with their normal shield, surrounded by a hinged four-sided square armoured structure, which folded flat, when required, to give unimpeded all-round traverse.

The later design, again generally similar for both 20-mm. and 3·7-cm. guns called Wirbelwind (Whirlwind) for the former and Ostwind (East Wind) for the latter, dispensed with the clumsy folding shields and used instead a multi-sided pot-shaped turret, open at the top. Although only lightly armoured (16-mm.) this turret gave better protection to the gun crew.

In addition to the anti-aircraft weapon, Wirbelwind and Ostwind (unlike the Möbelwagen types) retained the front hull machine-gun of the standard Pzkpfw IV.

70 Schwerer Ladungsträger (Sdkfz 301) and Leichter Ladungsträger (SdKfz 302), Germany.

These two machines, heavy and light demolition vehicles, were more commonly known as B.IV and Goliath, respectively. The B.IV, designed by the Borgward company of Bremen and produced from 1942 onwards, carried a 500 kg. explosive charge in a wedge-shaped bin at the front. With a seat for one man, the B.IV could be driven close to the scene of the action. In the attack, the vehicle was radio controlled. At the target, the bolts holding the demolition charge were destroyed by an electrically detonated charge, allowing the explosive bin to slide to the ground. The vehicle was then reversed away before the demolition charge was detonated. Powered by a petrol engine, the B.IV could be controlled by radio up to distances of about 1¼ miles. The first model, Ausf. A, shown in the illustration, weighed 3·6 tons. A total of 1,193 B.IVs (in three models) was produced between 1942 and 1944. They were used chiefly by heavy tank units to help destroy fixed defences.

The lighter demolition vehicle SdKfz 302 or 'Goliath' was, unlike the B.IV, expendable. About 5 ft 4 in. long, the Goliath (Ausf. A) carried a 60 kg. explosive charge. Driven by one electrical starter motor for each track, the vehicle was guided, and detonated when it reached its target, through a 3-core electric cable, of which about 670 yards was carried on a drum at the rear. In front of the drum was a compartment containing the control gear and the explosive was in a third compartment. Some 2,650 Goliaths of this type were built between 1942 and 1944 together with 5,079 (between 1943 and 1945) of a later and slightly heavier model, Ausf. B or SdKfz 303, powered by a Zündapp petrol engine. The employment of Goliaths was similar to that of the B.IV.

In the illustration of a Goliath (Ausf.A) the cover over the rear compartment is shown raised, revealing the electric control cable reel.

71 Leichter Schützenpanzerwagen SdKfz 250/8 and Leichter Schützenpanzerwagen SdKfz 250/9, Germany

The light armoured semi-tracked armoured personnel carrier SdKfz 250 which first appeared in action as a troop carrier in 1940, had by the end of the war appeared in twelve main variants, many of which were support vehicles for the basic infantry carrier.

The SdKfz 250/8 was a self-propelled mounting for the 7·5-cm. KwK L/24— the gun used in the earliest versions of the Sturmgeschütz III although in a 6-ton vehicle only light protection could be afforded. The gun was mounted just behind the driver together with a machine-gun (MG 42) both for ranging the 7·5-cm. KwK and for general targets.

Virtually a semi-tracked light armoured car (Panzerspähwagen) the SdKfz 250/9 had the same turret as the Leichter Panzerspähwagen SdKfz 222. This turret carried a 2-cm. gun and machine-gun on a mounting also capable of anti-aircraft fire: the only overhead protection was a hinged wire mesh frame to guard against grenades.

With good mobility and a high top speed of nearly 40 m.p.h., the SdKfz 250 series were powered by a Maybach six-cylinder engine of 100-b.h.p., which drove the tracks via front drive sprockets. The front wheels were for steering only and were not driven. An efficient vehicle, although with a somewhat complicated suspension and track design making heavy demands on maintenance time, the SdKfz 250 and its larger counterpart the SdKfz 251 was not replaced in production by semi-tracks of simpler design until 1944.

72 Panzerspähwagen SdKfz 234/2 (Puma) and Panzerspähwagen SdKfz 234/3, Germany.

An improved version of the successful German eight-wheeled armoured car, first issued in 1938, appeared in 1944. Although the chassis was basically unaltered and only minor changes were made to the armoured hull, the use of a diesel engine of greatly increased power (the Czechoslovakian Tatra twelve-cylinder V-form of 220-b.h.p.) led to improved performance. An air-cooled diesel engine was specified in 1940, when the design work began, with the object of facilitating operation in hot countries but this type of engine was also an advantage in subsequent operations in the cold weather in Russia and the fuel economy of the diesel resulted in a much wider range.

The first model of the new eight-wheeled armoured car, SdKfz 234/1, was armed only with a 2-cm. KwK and one machine-gun in an open-topped turret—no more than that of the 5-ton light armoured car SdKfz 222, and very inadequate for a vehicle of this size. The next model, SdKfz 234/2, was equipped with a 5-cm. (L/60) gun and a machine-gun in an enclosed turret, which made it capable of engaging tanks, although it was still intended only as a reconnaissance vehicle.

Two further models of the SdKfz 234 were produced as self-propelled mountings with guns mounted to fire forwards, with only limited traverse. The SdKfz 234/4 was a highly mobile 'tank hunter' with a 7·5-cm. Pak L/48 and the SdKfz 234/3—shown in one of the illustrations, together with SdKfz 234/2—was a close support vehicle with the low velocity 7·5-cm. Stu.K L/24.

73 T-34 ('T-34/76B') and T-34/85 (Medium Tanks), U.S.S.R.

The immense superiority of the T-34 over its opponents when it first appeared in action in 1941 was countered by the Germans with the introduction of the Panther and Tiger, and by up-gunning the PzKpfw IV. Nevertheless, successive improvements in the armament and protection of the T-34 kept it in the forefront of medium tanks throughout the rest of the war.

These improvements were accompanied by various other changes, although the main basic features of the T-34's design were retained throughout its long life. All this was achieved without undue interruption to the production flow although it led to many transitional models. The Russians did not allocate model numbers at all but the main differences between T-34 variants were, however, classified by the Western Allies and the Germans, and the model letters they allotted have been used here.

The original production version of the T-34, the T-34/76A, as it became known outside the Soviet Union, had a turret design which was unsatisfactory in some respects. This was replaced in the T-34/76B by a new turret incorporating a 76·2-mm. gun with a length of 41·2 calibres (compared with the earlier gun's 30·5 calibres) and increased muzzle velocity. Vision arrangements were improved and the 'pig's head' type of mantlet was replaced by a bolted one of more angular shape in which the gun was mounted relatively higher. (This incidentally resulted in the depression of the gun being no more than 4 degrees, one of the weaker points of the T-34's design, but accepted because one solution—raising the height of the turret roof—would have increased vulnerability). The earlier turrets of Model B were of rolled plate, welded, but during 1942 a cast version was introduced and this pattern is shown in the illustration.

Good as it was, it became necessary to increase the hitting power of the T-34 and during the summer of 1943, A. A. Morozov, who had taken over as chief designer from M. I. Koshkin, who died in 1940, redesigned the tank to accept a new turret armed with an 85-mm. gun. The gun was an adaptation of a pre-war anti-aircraft gun and was in a turret designed for the KV-85 heavy tank, so, once more, introducing standardization between the two classes of Russian tank. Later, though, this turret was re-designed and the second model of the T-34/85, using the new turret is shown in the illustration in this book.

The T-34/85's roomier turret enabled a five-man crew to be used and the protection was increased to a maximum of 75-mm. at the front. The main essentials of all T-34s remained, however, including the V-12 cylinder diesel engine of 500 h.p. driving rear sprockets and the Christie suspension of large road wheels on pivot arms controlled by long coil springs. Although many improvements had been introduced since 1940, the T-34 was still basically a simple and rugged but effective design, well suited to mass production. Nearly 40,000 T-34s of all types were built during World War II.

74 KV-85 (Heavy Tank) and SU-85, U.S.S.R.

The need to improve the armament of the KV-1 heavy tank was emphasized during the great battle of Kursk in 1943, in which the Soviet tanks encountered the German Tiger tanks in appreciable numbers. The 85-mm. gun in a new turret was fitted to the KV-1 in that year and the first of the new tanks, designated KV-85, were in action by the Autumn of 1943. The new combination was roughly equivalent to the German Tiger I (although more lightly armoured) and the Russians took the opportunity of reworking existing KV-1s to the new standard in order to make available quickly larger numbers of tanks capable of taking on the Tiger on equal terms. By Russian standards only small numbers of KV-85s were built—but the design was used as the basis of the Stalin tank which succeeded the KV series.

Roughly at the time the KV-85 appeared in service in 1943 and when a heavy tank with a more powerful gun than the 85-mm. was already envisaged, the SU-85 was designed. This SU (the initials stand for Samachodnya Ustanovka—self-propelled [gun] mounting) was intended as a 'tank hunter' and carried the high velocity 85-mm. gun in a mounting with limited traverse in a low (and hence less conspicuous) well-armoured hull on the T-34 chassis. This device, of using a standard (or, sometimes, obsolescent) chassis to to mount a heavier gun and, at the same time, achieve better protection and/or mobility than with the same weapon on a tank, was widely used by the Germans in World War II.

Often used in conjunction with T-34/76s, the SU-85 was in production from about the end of 1943 for about a year, when it gradually began to be replaced by the SU-100, with a more powerful gun, which used the same chassis and which was similar in appearance. Another widely used self-propelled gun on the T-34 chassis was the SU-122, a 122-mm. low velocity howitzer, which was in service from early 1943 onwards.

75 JS-II (Heavy Tank), U.S.S.R.

The Josef Stalin or JS-II heavy tank with its long 122-mm. gun was one of the most powerful tanks to go into service with any army in World War II.

A tank which traced its ancestry directly back to the KV series, the JS-II was another product of the design team headed by General Z. A. Kotin. Taking the KV-85 as a base, the best points were retained but others, including the suspension and transmission, were redesigned. A two-stage planetary transmission, combined with an improved engine led to better manoeuvrability and overall performance. At the same time, the opportunity was taken of rearranging the internal layout in a more compact form, allowing for armour increases while decreasing the total weight compared with KV-85.

The earliest JS tanks had the same 85-mm. gun as the KV. This was then replaced by a 100-mm. weapon and then, finally, by the 122-mm. gun. As this gun needed a wider turret ring, the hull at that point had to be extended out over the tracks each side but to avoid increasing the height, the top run of the track was lowered, although in most other respects the torsion bar suspension of the JS was similar to that of the KV's.

Known as JS-I or JS-122, the first 122-mm. gun-armed Stalin tanks entered service in late 1943. The JS-II which followed was generally similar but had the hull redesigned to give greater protection, notably in the better slope on the glacis plate.

The 122-mm. gun on the JS-II had a 7·62-mm. machine-gun as a coaxial weapon. The tank was served by a crew of four. The combat weight was 45 tons and with a 600-b.h.p. twelve-cylinder-V diesel engine had a top speed of 23 m.p.h. Armour was at a maximum thickness of 120-mm.

Over 2,000 JS-IIs were produced during the war, before being superseded by even the better JS-III, which became one of the most formidable tanks of the post-war years.

76 JSU-122 and JSU-152, U.S.S.R.

Two powerful self-propelled guns based on the Stalin heavy tank chassis, the JSU-122 and JSU-152 both entered service in 1944. Superseding similar weapons mounted on the earlier KV chassis (known as SU-122 and SU-152) to which they bore a strong resemblance, these two self-propelled guns had a better mechanical performance and, among other detail improvements, improved fire control arrangements.

The 122-mm. gun used in the earlier JSU-122s (one of which is shown in the illustration) was 45 calibres long and had a range of over 14,000 yards. Later models had a 43-calibre gun with a muzzle brake. The 152-mm. gun (29 calibres long) of the JSU-152 was a howitzer with a range of well over 9,000 yards. The ammunition (weighing 96 lb for high explosive and 107 lb per round for armour piercing) was so bulky, however, that only twenty rounds could be carried.

Carrying a crew of four (five if the vehicle was fitted with radio) the two JSUs were mechanically the same as their heavy tank counterparts and had much the same performance. This was important, because they were generally employed integrally with heavy tank regiments equipped with JS tanks.

77 KT (Winged Tank) and SU-76 U.S.S.R.

By the end of 1942, the Russians were already beginning to regard light tanks as a class as obsolete and although the type was developed from the T-40 of 1941 through the T-60 and T-70 to the T-80 of 1943, production of light tanks was tailed off in that year and had ceased before the war ended. At one time regarded mainly for their amphibious qualities, the Russians also gave some consideration to the potential of the light tank as an airborne vehicle. One of the most interesting tank experiments by any country in World War II was the Russian design for a Kyrliatyi Tank (KT) or 'winged tank'.

This design, by a team led by O. Antonov, consisted of a T-60 light tank, more or less in standard form, to which biplane wings, twin booms and a tail assembly were attached. These aerodynamic structures were made of wood, mainly, it seems, because of the shortage of aircraft alloys for experi-

ments of this kind. Rudimentary flying controls were led from the wings and tail to the tank, which formed the 'fuselage' of the machine.

The first test flight took place in 1942 and was curtailed only because of a fault in the engines of the towing aircraft. The winged tank apparently performed satisfactorily, but eventually the project had to be cancelled because of a shortage of the four-engined towing aircraft that would have been needed in some quantity to justify production of the tank gliders.

The T-60 light tank, as used in this experiment, was a 6-ton vehicle armed with a 20-mm. gun and a 7·62-mm. machine-gun. Maximum armour protection was 20-mm. and a 70-b.h.p. GAZ—202 six-cylinder petrol engine gave the tank a top speed of about 27 m.p.h.

The successor to the T-60 light tank was the T-70, which weighed 9 tons and had a 45-mm. gun and 7·62-mm. machine-gun. Several thousand were produced in 1942–43. Before production ceased, however, it had already been decided to utilize the T-70 chassis as the basis of a self-propelled mounting for the 76·2-mm. anti-tank gun.

The vehicle which emerged, the SU-76, used automotive and running gear similar to that of the T-70, although an extra road wheel each side was added to accommodate the longer hull needed as a self-propelled mounting. The power unit, mounted at the right-hand side of the hull, consisted of two engines, GAZ-202 of 70-b.h.p. each in earlier vehicles and GAZ-203 of 85-b.h.p. each in late production vehicles. Independent torsion bars for each road wheel were used for the suspension. The 76·2-mm. gun, 41·5 calibres long, was mounted at the rear in an open-topped compartment with a total traverse of 32 degrees. The relatively light armour and absence of overhead protection made the SU-76 less suitable as an anti-tank vehicle once the gun began to be outranged by more powerful German weapons. It was replaced by the SU-85 as an anti-tank vehicle, therefore, and switched to the infantry support role.

The SU-76 shown in the illustration is one of the earlier production vehicles.

78 BA-64 (Light Armoured Car), U.S.S.R.

Armoured car development in the Soviet Union in World War II was very limited indeed because, apart from improvements to the two main pre-war designs, only one new model appeared. This was the BA-64, which went into production in 1942. A light armoured scout car with 4-wheel drive, said to have been inspired by the German SdKfz 222, to which it bore a slight resemblance, the BA-64 had a crew of two—the driver and the commander, who had a small open top multi-sided turret equipped with a machine-gun. This was normally a 7·62-mm. weapon, mounted in the turret face, or on top for anti-aircraft use, but alternatively a heavy 14·5-mm. machine-gun on a pintle mount could be carried.

Weighing about 2½ tons, the BA-64 was powered by a four-cylinder 50-b.h.p. GAZ petrol engine, which gave it a maximum speed of 31 m.p.h.

79 Tanque 'Narhuel', Modelo DL 43, Argentina.

Designed in Argentina in 1943 and produced in that country, the 'Narhuel' was a medium tank weighing 35 tons. The name 'Narhuel' is a South American Indian name for the jaguar. Although owing much in inspiration and configuration to the United States M.4 Medium, the 'Narhuel' was otherwise entirely original in design. The main armament consisted of a 75-mm. gun. A machine-gun was mounted coaxially with the 75-mm. gun on the left side and there were up to three others in the hull glacis plate, with another for anti-aircraft use.

The crew consisted of five men and with a 500-h.p. engine the maximum speed was 25 m.p.h. and the range was about 150 miles. The maximum armour protection was 80-mm.

Only sixteen of these tanks were built, the need for further production of medium tanks in Argentina ceasing to exist after 1944 when supplies of U.S. M.4 mediums and other equipment became available.

80 Stridsvagn M/42 and Storm-artillerivagn M/43, Sweden.

Swedish armoured fighting vehicle development during World War II followed a policy of steady progress in mechanical improvement and up-gunning, as far as was possible with the resources available.

The 22½-ton Strv. M/42, designed by Landsverk, had a family resemblance to that concern's earlier, much lighter, series taken into Swedish Army service as Strv. M/38, M/39 and M/40. The latter were armed only with 37-mm. guns, however, which by 1942 were inadequate, and it was decided to adopt a short calibre 75-mm. gun for the Strv. M/42. With a crew of four and armour protection to an 80-mm. maximum, the Strv. M/42 was powered by an eight-cylinder Volvo water-cooled engine developing 380 b.h.p. which produced a top speed of 29 m.p.h. Two 8-mm. machine-guns were mounted to the right of the 75-mm. gun in the turret and a third machine gun was in the front of the hull.

In 1945 the Strv. M/42 was re-designated Infanterikanonvagn 73 (Ikv 73) to reflect the new role for this tank as an infantry support vehicle.

The Stormartillerivagn M/43 (Sav. M/43), which appeared in 1944, used the chassis of the Czech-designed LT-38 built under licence in Sweden by Scania-Vavis A.B. as Stridsvagn M/41. This assault gun mounted a 10·5-cm. howitzer in a fixed, enclosed armoured superstructure. Weighing 12 tons and with a crew of four, the Sav. M/43 had a six-cylinder Scania-Vabis engine of 140 b.h.p., which gave it a maximum speed of about 27 m.p.h. The Strv. M/41 design, on which the Sav. M/43 was based, had a very long life for a fighting vehicle, incidentally, because in 1962 chassis of this type were rebuilt as armoured personnel carriers.

APPENDIX

Armoured Fighting Vehicle Camouflage and Markings 1942-45

The artist in conjunction with the author has tried to show camouflage colours as they are likely to have appeared, and tactical and other markings for specific vehicles have been included where practicable. However, in some cases, information has been unobtainable or incomplete: black and white photographs, for example, are an unreliable guide as to whether a vehicle is painted a medium brown or medium green colour. Even reproductions of colour photo transparencies are often very misleading—for example, one photograph in colour of a Churchill tank which was reproduced in a journal showed it as something very much like middle bronze green, whereas the original transparency, which the author has examined, proves that the tank in question was actually khaki brown!

Apart from the difficulties of colour reproduction in a book, the colours used on the actual vehicles often varied for many reasons—the exact colours for camouflage were not always considered important and wide discretion was allowed to unit and tank commanders; the quality control on paints issued—always difficult to maintain—sometimes allowed quite wide variations; and colours, once applied, could sometimes be changed out of all recognition by ageing, frequently helped by terrain such as desert sand. References to official colour standard specifications are given below in some cases and these are the surest basis of information available today on exact shades as they were supposed to be applied. Even so, allowance has to be made for variations from causes such as those mentioned above and it must always be borne in mind that, for example, a dark colour, particularly in bright sunlight, will appear much lighter when spread over a wide surface and, of course, the reverse applies to a light colour in deep shadow.

For those wishing to pursue the subject, useful articles discussing the problems involved as well as details of actual colour schemes have appeared in the journals *Tankette* and *A.F.V. News*, details of which are given in the Foreword.

Argentina

The colour for fighting vehicles was either plain olive green or, where necessary, a three-colour disruptive pattern of olive green, brown and dark green.

Australia

Camouflage and markings were on similar lines to those used by the United Kingdom except that for A.F.V.s in Australia itself a two- or three-colour scheme using shades better matching the local terrain was used. For operations in New Guinea and Borneo, tanks were painted 'Jungle green'—a very dark green.

Tactical signs were as for the United Kingdom, except that independent squadrons used an inverted triangle symbol.

Canada

See under United Kingdom.

France (Fighting France)

Vehicles in the Western Desert were usually sand colour, as for contemporary British vehicles. Original French vehicles had French registration numbers, vehicles supplied by the British usually carried the original W.D. numbers. When American equipment was provided in the Italian campaign and for use in France itself in 1944–45, U.S. camouflage colours (usually olive drab) were used.

Germany

In 1942 grey, ranging from medium to dark was in general use, except in North Africa where sand yellow was normally used. A mottled pattern of green or brown was sometimes added in North Africa, more often in Tunisia near the end of the campaign.

An order dated 18 February 1943 instructed that all A.F.V.s leaving the factories should be finished in a standard dark sand (yellow) colour, although in 1944, perhaps due to paint shortages, some vehicles again left the factories in a grey finish. Tank crews in the field were issued with a supply of paint (diluted with water or petrol before use) for each vehicle—usually reddish-brown, olive drab and dark yellow—so that a camouflage pattern appropriate to the terrain could be added to the basic colour.

Thus the degree of dilution of the paint applied in the field and/or the skill and whims of the crews resulted in a very wide range of colours and patterns in German A.F.V. camouflage. A German expert has said that exceptions to the rule were very common. The German black cross, on hull and/or turret sides and rear, outlined in white, was shown on most A.F.V.s.

The basic colours used were allotted RAL numbers by the department responsible for paint standards and although a full list is not available, some of these were as follows (an asterisk following the number denotes that the colour is still a published standard in West Germany in 1975)—RAL 6006★ (dark green), RAL 6007★ (medium-dark green), RAL 7016★ (very dark bluish-grey), RAL 7017 (very dark brownish grey), RAL 7021* (very dark grey), RAL 8002 (khaki-brown), RAL 8020 (dark cream).

A tactical number was usually carried on most German A.F.V.s, although more often omitted on armoured cars and half-tracks. This number was usually in black or red, outlined in white, or sometimes in white or white outline only. The system for allocating these numbers was usually as follows, although there were exceptions to the general rule.

R 01	regimental commander
R 02	regimental adjutant
R 03	ordnance or signals officer
R 04 etc.	regimental staff etc.
I 01	commander of I battalion
I 02	adjutant of I battalion
I 03	ordnance officer of I battalion
I 04	staff of I battalion
II 01 etc.	commander of II battalion etc.
101	officer commanding Ist company, I battalion
102	2nd in command 1st company I battalion
111	Leader, 1st platoon, 1st company, I battalion
112	2nd vehicle, 1st platoon, 1st company, I battalion
133	3rd vehicle, 3rd platoon, I battalion
201 etc.	officer commanding 2nd company
301–801 etc.	Panzer battalions consisted of three or four companies and the above system was continued up to 801 etc. for the 8th company of the II battalion.
901 1001 1101 etc.	Tiger battalion of a special Panzer division, such as the 'Grossdeutschland' in 1944. Also independent Tiger or Sturmgeschütz company (9th) of some divisions or reconnaisance companies (10th and 11th) in others.

The system included even higher serials in some special cases. Only the final digit, denoting the individual vehicle in the platoon, was used in some instances.

A battery letter (in plain or Gothic letters) was sometimes carried on self-propelled guns, denoting the battery to which the vehicle belonged.

Small symbolic signs indicating the type of unit and the sub-unit within that unit were carried on some armoured vehicles, but not often on tanks.

Small divisional signs, usually in yellow, but white or black was also used, were sometimes stencilled on A.F.V. hulls or turrets.

Vehicle registration serial numbers, prefixed by WH for the Army, by the double lightning flash for the SS, and WL for the Luftwaffe (e.g. Hermann Göring Division) were carried on armoured cars and half tracks but not on full tracked A.F.V.s. The letters/numbers were in black on a white background.

India

See under United Kingdom.

Italy

Sand yellow, with or without a darker disruptive pattern, in North Africa; dark greenish-grey in Europe, with sometimes a shadowy or sharp reticulated pattern added.

Tactical markings consisted firstly of the regimental number in white arabic figures and the battalion number in white Roman figures. These were usually carried on rear surfaces of the tank's fighting compartment. Battalion command tanks were denoted on the turret or hull by a rectangle divided vertically into red, blue and yellow strips or, where there were only two companies in the battalion, red and blue only. The company signs, carried on the sides and rear of the turret (or hull, in turretless vehicles) were as follows:

1st company—red rectangle
2nd company—blue rectangle
3rd company—yellow rectangle
4th company—green rectangle

Platoons were indicated by one, two or three vertical white bars on the company sign, indicating 1st, 2nd or 3rd platoon respectively. The position of the individual tank in the platoon was shown by an arabic number in white or the company colour above or below the company sign.

These markings were generally used in Africa, less frequently so in Europe.

A vehicle registration number was usually carried at front and rear. The number was in black on a white background, preceded by RoEto (Regio Esercito = Royal Army) in red.

Japan

A three-colour camouflage scheme was generally used, consisting of a sand (yellow) colour, brown and dark green, although dark green alone also appeared.

Tactical signs were not standardized and were used only in some units. Sometimes these consisted of large Western figures in white on hull or turret, with or without Japanese characters. A red sun symbol, with or without the rays, sometimes was used and appeared on turret, nose plates or front mudguards of tanks. A yellow star was sometimes embossed or painted on the glacis plate of tanks.

Registration plates, when carried on tanks, appeared on the rear plate of the hull only. These showed a white star, Japanese characters and a number in Western figures.

Jordan

Arab Legion armoured cars were a mustard colour to which sometimes a disruptive pattern was added. British-style geometric tactical signs were sometimes carried. The vehicle number usually appeared in both Western and Arabic figures on the mudguards on opposite sides.

South Africa

See under United Kingdom.

Sweden

A camouflage system of grey, brown, green and black, in patches. In winter, vehicles were overpainted in white.

A small reproduction of the Swedish flag was generally carried on A.F.V.s after 1941.

Large tactical numbers in black, outlined, were sometimes carried on A.F.V.s, including armoured cars.

U.S.S.R.

Russian tanks were usually painted in a single colour of green or brown shade. Sometimes, but only infrequently, a disruptive pattern in a dark shade was added. A.F.V.s in winter were frequently painted over in white.

Sometimes (but rarely in combat) a red star was shown on the turret or hull. Slogans—generally of a patriotic nature—were rather more frequently shown on tanks in combat. Call signs, usually painted in white (black on snow-camouflaged vehicles) and enclosed in geometric shapes, often came increasingly to be shown. Large white numbers on turrets or hulls of A.F.Vs were also sometimes shown towards the end of the war.

British A.F.V.s in the United Kingdom at the beginning of 1942 were permitted to be painted in a basic colour of either a shade of dark green, Middle Bronze Green (British Standards Institution specification No. 381—1930, colour No. 23 or B.S.I. 987c Shade No. 7) or a khaki brown colour, known as Standard Camouflage Colour No. 2 (published in B.S.I. No. 987c—1942). Khaki brown predominated, however, and appeared also in various lighter shades, including Shade No. 4 in B.S.I. 987c—1942. Nevertheless, several Regimental histories of British armoured regiments in the Eighth Army refer to the dark green of the First Army vehicles (newly out from the United Kingdom) encountered in Tunisia in 1943 or of repainting their own desert-camouflaged vehicles in green for the forthcoming campaign in Italy.

If a dark disruptive colour was to be added to either the green or the brown basic colour, the War Office instructed that this was to be the very dark brown known as Standard Camouflage Colour No. 1A (also published in B.S.I. 987c—1942).

In 1944, a new instruction laid down that the brown Standard Camouflage Colour No. 2 should be replaced by olive drab, officially known as Shade No. 15, an amendment to B.S.I. 987c—1942. This colour was much like the green used in 1942 but somewhat duller. It was similar to the U.S. Army standard 'olive drab'. Also in 1944, the use of a dark disruptive colour was no longer authorized.

British armoured fighting vehicles in North Africa (except those of the First Army in Tunisia) were painted in various sand colours, ranging from yellow through various stone-coloured shades to pink. To these were added, when required, various darker disruptive shades. In some regiments with cruiser tanks with large road wheels, the inner wheels were painted black to make them 'disappear' and so cause the tank to look more like a lorry—an effect heightened by the use of 'sun shields' (canvas on iron hoops) to conceal the turret and upper surfaces.

Armoured fighting vehicles of British and Indian formations in Burma were painted 'jungle green'. This was, contrary to some belief, a very dark colour, an olive drab darker than that used in Europe. In 1942 it would have been Shade No. 13 in B.S.I. 987c—1942, replaced in 1945 by Shade No. 16, 'Very Dark Drab'. Australian tanks in New Guinea and Borneo were also painted in a dark 'jungle green'.

Formation signs were carried by British A.F.V.s, normally at the front and rear of the hull. All British units were allotted a unit code sign, usually applicable to the type of unit, which was often unique *only* in conjunction with the formation sign. The code sign was a white number on a coloured square. Code numbers were usually allocated to armoured regiments in the brigade in accordance with their seniority in the Army List. The main exception to these rules were signals units which had the code number in red on a square divided horizontally white over blue. The code numbers used were of those of the headquarters of the formation served by the signals unit.

The most important of these unit code numbers for A.F.V.s in Armoured Divisions in 1942–45 were as follows:

	Europe 1942–45	Libya 1942
Armoured Division Headquarters	40	49
Headquarters (I) Armoured Brigade	50	71
Armoured Regiment (Battalion) (1)	51	40
Armoured Regiment (Battalion) (2)	52	86
Armoured Regiment (Battalion) (3)	53	67
Headquarters (II) Armoured Brigade (a)	60	
Armoured Regiment (Battalion) (1)	61	
Armoured Regiment (Battalion) (2)	62	
Armoured Regiment (Battalion) (3)	63	
Armoured Car Regiment (b)	44	76
Armoured Reconnaissance Regiment (c)	45	

Notes
   (a) The second armoured brigade was deleted during the course of 1942 although in North Africa, divisions still often had two or even three armoured brigades on an *ad hoc* basis. These extra brigades sometimes had the same unit code numbers as the (I) brigade, although they were usually distinguished by their brigade signs.
   (b) At first 47 in the United Kingdom. Deleted from armoured divisions to become Corps Troops in 1943, but restored in 1945.
   (c) Added to armoured division in 1943.

The coloured squares for the unit code signs were black for Divisional Headquarters, red for Headquarters and units of (I) Brigade, and green for Headquarters and units of (II) Brigade. The unit code numbers of the latter, incidentally, were taken over by the Lorried Infantry Brigades after the 1942 reorganization. For armoured car regiments the colours varied, although at first black in the U.K. and finally, in 1945, as for Armoured Reconnaissance Regiments, namely blue and green, divided horizontally.

Independent tank brigades and armoured brigades used various code-sign numbers (155, 156, 157 for the three tank units of the 34th Tank Brigade in 1944 for example) although the numbers were standardized as 51, 52, 53 (as in the armoured divisions) by 1945. White bars to denote allocation to a higher formation—above the code sign for Corps Troops, below the sign for Army Troops, and diagonally for Army Group—were added as appropriate.

Tactical signs were standardized by 1942 as the following hollow geometric shapes, painted on turrets and/or hulls, as follows:

Regimental (Battalion) Headquarters—diamond

'A' Squadron (Company)—triangle

'B' Squadron (Company)—square

'C' Squadron (Company)—circle

'D' Squadron (Company)—vertical bar

Canadian units sometimes used an inverted triangle for 'A' Squadron.

These tactical signs were in the following colours:

Senior Regiment in Brigade—red

Second Regiment in Brigade—yellow

Third Regiment in Brigade—blue

Fourth Regiment in Brigade—green

In armoured formations, only armoured car regiments or infantry motor battalions had a fourth squadron or company and the fourth unit in an armoured brigade was usually the motor battalion. From about 1943 onwards some British armoured regiments adopted a numbering system to supplement or replace the tactical signs. Large serial numbers were shown on hull or turret sides and rear. Unlike the German system, this did not denote battalion, company and platoon but ran through the unit, the order differing between regiments, although pains were usually taken to avoid numbering regimental headquarters tanks with the lowest numbers, and thus make them stand out.

British A.F.V.s frequently carried individual names, usually allocated in associated groups for squadrons and/or sub units, and/or bearing the same initial letter as the squadron letter. They were often names associated with regimental tradition or links, such as battle honours, recruiting towns or districts. In the battalions of the Royal Tank Regiment, the World War I tradition of naming all tanks with a letter equivalent to the battalion number (e.g. 4th Battalion tank names—Destroyer, Devil, Duck etc.) was continued in World War II.

The War Department registration number (prefixed by T for tanks, F for armoured cars, and so on) was carried in white (or black for light-painted vehicles) on the front and rear of the hull and/or hull or turret sides, according to the type of vehicle.

Varying A.F.V. recognition signs were used at different times. The white/red/white strips adopted in the Middle East in late 1941 were abandoned about March 1942 to be followed by a white St Andrew's cross on upper surfaces (principally for air recognition) and then in turn by R.A.F.-type roundels (blue, white and red—the latter in the centre). In the United Kingdom, red/white/red strips were painted on A.F.V.s in March 1942 as a recognition sign and this applied also to the First Army vehicles in Tunisia and was later used in Italy until mid-1943. The white five-pointed star (with or without an enclosing ring) first used by American forces in the North African landings in 1942 was adopted by the War Office for general use as an 'Allied Star' by British forces in June 1943. Usually shown on top surfaces as an air recognition sign, it also appeared sometimes on hull or turret sides, particularly on tanks in the Far East.

Finally, a bridge group number was usually carried by British A.F.V.s. This denoted the maximum loaded weight of the vehicle in tons and the figure was in black on a yellow disc or within a yellow ring, shown at the front.

U.S.A.

The most common basic colour finish for U.S. A.F.V.s was green, although the shade varied widely. In 1942, however, the dark green commonly used (U.S. Army Ref. No. 320, similar to the British B.S.I. 987c—1942, shade No. 7) was generally superseded for Army vehicles by olive drab (Ref. No. 319). A range of other basic colours, suited to different terrains, was available, though, and recommended styles of application of darker disruptive patterns (in one or two colours) were published by the U.S. War Department. The U.S. Marine Corps also came to use olive drab as the basic colour, although forest green (a colour not dissimilar to olive drab but less brown) was standard. Landing Vehicles Tracked were sometimes finished in naval grey. Disruptive patterns, sometimes somewhat bizarre, were used, but not consistently.

A system of tactical signs including full details from formation down to company level was introduced in 1943. This consisted of small white numbers, symbols and letters, carried at front and rear, of which 7 △ 31 △ B-13 is an example, denoting 7th Armored Division, 31st Armored Battalion, B company, 13th vehicle (actually a Sherman tank). (In the Cavalry, the signs represented squadron and troop, and in the Artillery battalion and battery.) Prior to this, only the Company and vehicle designator was usually shown (sometimes in conjunction with the divisional sign, though), but even late in the war, where security necessitated it, other symbols were painted out leaving only the company and vehicle sign. The U.S. 1st Armored Division in Tunisia in 1942 used a permutated system of white geometric shapes denoting battalion, company and platoon, with a number added to indicate the individual tank.

United States Marine Corps vehicles sometimes carried geometric shapes (diamond, semi-circle, rectangle etc.) surrounding a number indicating regiment, battalion and company. Tactical letters and numbers or larger numbers alone also were used on A.F.V. hulls and/or turrets.

Vehicle registration letters were shown in white or pale blue prefixed by 'USA' (for Army vehicles) usually, on tanks, on the hull sides near the rear. The first digits were standardized for the type, tanks always having 30 (e.g. USA 3031428—an M.4 Medium tank), half tracks and tracked vehicles except tanks (such as S.P. guns) —40; armoured cars—60; tracked tractors (including L.V.T.s)—9. U.S. Marine Corps vehicles did not conform to this system and carried the prefix 'U.S.M.C.'.

The general recognition sign of a five-pointed star was used by the U.S. forces from 1942 onwards. This was normally white, with or without a white outer ring.

The bridge group sign of a black figure (denoting the maximum laden weight in tons) on a yellow disc was often carried at the front of U.S. armoured vehicles in Europe.

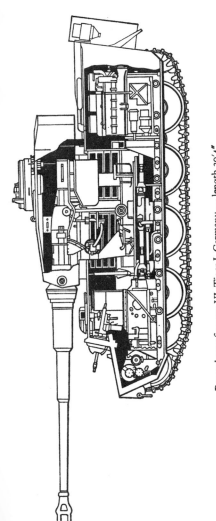

Panzerkampfwagen VI, Tiger I, Germany — length 20'4"

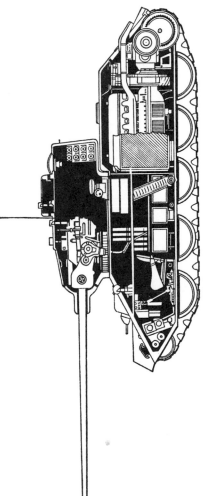

T-34/85 (Medium Tank), U.S.S.R. — length 19'8"

165

The dimensions and weights given here should be taken as a rough guide only: in some cases they a[re?] tions. Most of the specialized armoured vehicles are not included in these tables, because in most cases the[y?] the standard vehicles from which they have been developed and due allowance has to be made for the effe[ct?]
Gun calibre lengths are not shown here but these should always be taken into account (and also th[e?] ment' column, 'm.g.' has been used to denote machine-guns of rifle calibre and 'h.m.g.' for weapons

FULL-TRACKED

Ref. No.	Type	Weight tons	Length ft	in	Width ft	in	Height ft	in	Armour max. mm.	Armament
	Japan									
1	Tankette, Type 97	4·25	12	0	5	11	5	10	12	1 37-mm.
1	Light, Type 95	7·50	14	1	6	11	7	3	12	1 37-mm., 2 m.g.
2	Medium, Type 97 (new turret)	15·80	18	1	7	8	7	11	25	1 47-mm., 2m.g.
2	Medium Type 3	19·00	18	6	7	8	8	7	50	1 75-mm., 2 m.g.
3	Medium Type 4	30·00	20	9	9	5	9	5	75	1 75-mm., 2 m.g.
3	Medium Type 5	37·00	24	0	10	0	10	0	75	1 75-mm., 1 37-mm, 2 m.g.
5	Amphibious, Type 2	12·50	24	7	9	2	7	6	12	1 37-mm., 2 m.g.
5	Amphibious, Type 3	28·80	33	9	9	10	12	6	50	1 47-mm., 2 m.g.
8	Armoured Personnel Carrier, Type 1	6·5	15	1	6	11	8	3	6	—
	U.S.A.									
9	Light M.5A1	15·13	15	10	7	6	7	10	67	1 37-mm., 3 m.g.
10	Light M.22	7·32	12	11	7	4	5	8	25	1 37-mm., 1 m.g.
10	Light M.24	18·08	18	0	9	4	8	1	63	1 75-mm., 3 m.g.
11	Medium M.3	26·80	18	6	8	11	10	3	51	1 75-mm., 1 37-mm., 3 m.g.
12	Medium M.4	29·69	19	4	8	7	9	0	51	1 75-mm., 3 m.g.
13	Medium M.26	41·52	20	9	11	6	9	1	102	1 90-mm., 3 m.g.
14	Heavy M.6	56·48	24	9	10	2	9	10	82	1 3-in., 1 37-mm., 4 m.g.
9	75-mm. H.M.C. M.8	15·44	14	7	7	4	7	6	44	1 75-mm., 3 m.g.
15	105-mm. H.M.C. M.7	22·60	19	9	9	5	8	4	62	1 105-mm., 1 m.g.
16	3-in. G.M.C. M.10	29·46	19	7	10	0	8	1	63	1 3-in., 1 m.g.
16	76-mm. G.M.C. M.18	16·80	17	10	9	5	8	5	25	1 76-mm., 1 m.g.
17	L.V.T.(A)4	18·30	26	2	10	8	10	2	13	1 75-mm.
17	L.V.T. 4	16·25	26	1	10	8	8	1	—	1 m.g.
	U.K., Canada and Australia									
21	Tetrarch	7·50	13	6	7	7	6	11	16	1 2-pr, 1 m.g.
21	Harry Hopkins	8·50	14	3	8	10	6	11	38	1 2-pr, 1 m.g.
22	Crusader I	19·00	19	8	8	8	7	4	40	1 2-pr, 2 m.g.
22	Crusader III	19·75	19	8	8	8	7	4	51	1 6-pr, 1 m.g.
23	Centaur IV	27·50	20	10	9	6	8	2	76	1 95-mm. how, 1 m.g
23	Cromwell	28·00	20	10	10	0	8	2	76	1 75-mm. or 6-pr., 2 m.g.
24	Challenger	31·50	26	4	9	6	8	9	102	1 17-pr, 1 m.g.
25	Comet	32·50	21	6	10	0	8	9	101	1 77-mm., 2 m.g.
26	Ram II (Canada)	29·50	19	0	9	10	8	9	76	1 6-pr, 2 m.g.
27	Aust. Cruiser A.C.I	28·00	20	9	9	1	8	5	65	1 2-pr, 2 m.g.
28	Churchill III	39·00	24	5	10	8	9	0	102	1 6-pr, 2 m.g.
28	Churchill VII	40·00	24	5	11	4	9	0	152	1 75-mm., 2 m.g.
29	Bishop	17·20	18	2	8	7	9	1	60	1 25-pr
29	Archer	16·00	21	11	9	0	7	4	60	1 17-pr
30	Sexton (Canada)	25·4	19	3	8	11	8	0	32	1 25-pr
37	Carrier, Universal Mk II	3·95	12	4	6	11	5	3	12	1 m.g.
37	Aust. 2-pr Carrier	5·15	13	11	6	10	6	5	12	1 2-pr
	Italy									
50	M.15/42	15	16	7	7	4	7	9	42	1 47-mm., 2 m.g.
51	P.40	25	18	8	9	1	8	3	50	1 75-mm., 2 m.g.
52	Semovente 75/34	15	16	7	7	3	6	1	42	1 75-mm., 1 m.g.
52	Semovente 105/23	15·7	16	8	7	11	5	9	50	1 105-mm., 1 m.g.

proximations. Performance figures are also approximate—they can vary widely under different condi-
not lend themselves to tabular description. However, their basic characteristics are similar to those of
performance of the special equipment carried.
action of the weapon) when comparing guns of the same calibre (i.e. diameter of the bore). In the 'arma-
ound 12–15 mm., but below 20-mm.

RMOURED VEHICLES

Engine	b.h.p.	Speed m.p.h.	Range miles	Crew	Notes
egai diesel	65	26	155	2	
tsubishi diesel	110	28	155	3	
pe 97 diesel	170	24	130	4	
pe 100 diesel	240	25	130	5	
pe 4 diesel	400	28	155	5	
M.W. (petrol)	550	28	125	5	
tsubishi diesel	110	23	200	5	Water speed 6 m.p.h.
pe 100 diesel	240	20	200	7	Water speed 6 m.p.h.
sel	134	25	—	15	
dillac	220	40	100	4	
coming	162	35	110	3	
dillac	220	35	175	5	
atinental	340	26	120	6	Grant, height 9 ft 4 in.
ntinental	400	24	120	5	
rd	470	20	75	5	
ight	800	22	100	6	
dillac	220	40	100	4	
atinental	340	25	105	7	
neral Motors	375	30	200	5	
atinental	340/400	55	105	5	Length including gun 21 ft 10 in.
atinental	250	16	150	6	Water: speed 7 m.p.h., range 100 miles.
atinental	250	20	150	7	Water: speed 7·5 m.p.h., range 75 miles.
adows	165	40	140	3	2-pr gun = calibre 40-mm.
adows	148	30	125	3	
ffield Liberty	340	27	100	5	
ffield Liberty	340	27	100	3	6-pr gun = calibre 57-mm.
ffield Liberty	395	27	165	5	
ills-Royce	600	32	165	5	
lls-Royce	600	32	105	5	17-pr gun = calibre 76-mm.
lls-Royce	600	29	123	5	Length including gun 25 ft 1 in.
atinental	400	25	144	5	
dillac (×3)	330	30	200	5	
dford	350	15·5	90	5	
dford	350	12·5	90	5	
.C. diesel	131	15	90	4	
neral Motors diesel	192	20	140	4	
tinental	400	25	180	6	484 b.h.p. engine on some
d	85	32	160	4–5	
d	95	20	160	4	
A.	190	25	140	4	
A.	330	25	175	4	
A.	190	25	140	3	
A.	190	24	95	3	

167

Ref. No.	Type	Weight tons	Length ft in.		Width ft in.		Height ft in.		Armour max. mm.	Armament
	Germany									
53	PzKpfw. Luchs	11·8	14	6	8	2	7	0	30	1 2-cm., 1 m.g.
54	PzKpfw. III, Ausf. L-M	21·95	18	1	9	8	8	3	50+20	1 5-cm., 2 m.g.
55	PzKpfw IV, Ausf. H.	24·61	19	4	10	8	8	10	80	1 7·5-cm., 2 m.g.
56	PzKpfw Panther (Ausf. G)	44·10	22	7	11	3	9	10	80	1 7·5-cm., 2 m.g.
57	PzKpfw Tiger I	54·13	20	4	12	3	9	5	100	1 8·8-cm., 2 m.g.
58	PzKpfw Tiger II	68·6	23	10	12	4	10	2	150	1 8·8-cm., 2 m.g.
59	PzKpfw Maus	185	29	8	12	1	12	0	200	1 15-cm., 1 7·5-cm., 1 m.g.
59	PzKpfw E.100	137·79	28	6	14	8	10	11	200	1 15-cm., 1 7·5-cm., 1 m.g.
60	JgPz 38(t) Hetzer	15·75	16	0	8	8	6	11	60	1 7·5-cm., 1 m.g.
61	Stu. G. III/10·5 cm. Stu.H.	23·52	18	4	9	9	7	0	50+30	1 10·5-cm., 1 m.g.
62	Stu. Pz. IV, Brummbär	27·75	19	4	10	2	8	2	100	1 15-cm.
62	JgPz IV/70	25·8	19	9	10	6	6	1	80	1 7·5-cm., 1 m.g.
63	8·8-cm. PzJg Jagdpanther	44·78	22	7	10	9	8	11	80	1 8·8-cm., 1 m.g.
64	JgPz Elefant	66·93	22	4	11	3	9	9	200	1 8·8-cm.
65	JgPz VI, Jagdtiger	70·57	25	7	11	11	9	3	250	1 12·8-cm., 1 m.g.
66	7·5-cm. Pak auf Gw. 38(t) Marder III (Ausf. M)	10·80	14	9	7	1	7	11	25	1 7·5-cm., 1 m.g.
67	7·62-cm. Pak auf Gw. II, Ausf D.	11·50	15	3	7	7	6	8	30	1 7·62-cm.
68	8·8-cm. Pak auf Gw. III/IV, Nashorn	23·62	19	0	9	8	8	8	30	1 8·8-cm.
68	15-cm. PzfH auf Gw. III/IV, Hümmel	23·5	19	0	9	7	9	3	30	1 15-cm.
69	FlakpanzerWirbelwind	22·0	19	4	9	7	9	1	80	4 2-cm.
69	Flakpanzer Möbelwagen	25·0	19	4	9	7	10	2	80	1 3.7-cm.
	U.S.S.R.									
77	T-60	5·75	13	1	7	6	5	9	20	1 20-mm., 1 m.g.
73	T-34/76B	28·00	20	0	9	10	8	0	70	1 76-2 mm., 2 m.g.
73	T-34/85	31·5	19	8	9	10	7	10	75	1 85-mm., 2 m.g.
74	KV-85	46·00	22	4	10	8	9	6	110	1 85-mm., 3 m.g.
75	JS-II	45·00	21	9	10	3	8	11	120	1 122-mm., 3 m.g.
77	SU-76	11·55	15	3	8	9	6	8	35	1 76·2-mm.
74	SU-85	29·00	19	5	9	10	8	1	75	1 85-mm.
76	JSU-122	45·5	22	4	10	1	8	2	90	1 122-mm., 1 m.g.
76	JSU-152	46·00	22	4	9	10	8	3	90	1 152-mm., 1 m.g.
	Sweden									
80	Strv. m/42	22·50	20	0	8	0	8	6	80	1 75-mm., 3 m.g.
80	Sav. m/43	12·00	15	1	8	3	7	7	25	1 10·5-cm.

Engine	b.h.p.	Speed m.p.h.	Range miles	Crew	Notes
Maybach	178	40	155	4	
Maybach	300	25	124	5	Length including gun 21 ft
Maybach	300	24	124	5	Length including gun 23 ft
Maybach	700	28	110	5	Length including gun 29 ft 1 in., turret max. 120-mm.
Maybach	700	24	62	5	Length including gun 27 ft, turret 110-mm.
Maybach	700	24	68	5	Length including gun 33 ft 8 in., turret 185-mm.
Daimler-Benz	1200	12	118	6	Turret 240-mm.
Maybach	1200	24	130	6	700 b.h.p. engine fitted, turret 240-mm.
Praga	150	25	111	4	Length including gun 20 ft 7 in.
Maybach	300	25	98	4	Length including gun 20 ft 2 in.
Maybach	300	24	124	5	
Maybach	300	25	124	4	Length including gun 28 ft 3 in.
Maybach	700	28	130	5	Length including gun 32 ft 4 in.
Maybach (×2)	640	12·5	93	6	Length including gun 26 ft 9 in.
Maybach	700	23	105	6	Length including gun 35 ft
Praga	125	30	150	4	Length including gun 18 ft 8 in.
Maybach	140	34	93	4	Length including gun 18 ft 6 in.
Maybach	300	24	124	5	Length including gun 27 ft 8 in.
Maybach	300	24	124	6	Length including gun 21 ft 11 in.
Maybach	300	26	124	5	
Maybach	300	24	124	6	
AZ-202	70	27	380	2	
V-2-34 diesel	500	31	188	4	Length including gun 21 ft 7 in.
V-2-34 diesel	500	31	140	5	Length including gun 24 ft 7 in.
V-2K-S diesel	600	22	156	4	Length including gun 27 ft 10 in.
V-2-IS diesel	513	23	150	4	Length including gun 31 ft 6 in.
AZ-202 (×2)	140	28	280	4	
V-2-34 diesel	500	34	220	4	Length including gun 25 ft 9 in.
V-2-IS diesel	513	25	137	5	Length including gun 31 ft 4 in.
V-2-IS diesel	513	25	137	5	Length including gun 28 ft 9 in.
Volvo	380	29	—	4	
Scania-Vabis	140	27	—	4	

Ref. No.	Type	Weight tons	Length ft in.	Width ft in.	Height ft in.	Armour max. m.m.	Armament
	Japan						
8	Armoured Personnel Carrier, ½-tracked, Type 1	7·00	20 0	6 11	6 7	8	—
	U.S.A.						
19	T.17E1 (Staghound)	13·70	18 0	8 10	7 9	32	1 37-mm., 2 m.g.
19	T.18E2 (Boarhound)	23·70	20 6	10 1	8 7	51	1 6-pr, 2 m.g.
20	M.8	7·80	16 5	8 4	7 4	19	1 37-mm., 1 m.g.
20	M.20	5·27	16 5	8 4	7 7	19	1 h.m.g.
18	Car, ½-track M.2A1	7·90	19 7	6 5	7 5	13	1 h.m.g., 1 m.g.
18	75-mm. G.M.C., M.3	9·40	20 5	7 1	8 3	16	1 75 mm.
	U.K., Canada, India and S. Africa						
39	Humber Mks III–IV	7·1	15 0	7 2	7 10	15	1 h.m.g., 1 m.g.
40	Daimler Mks I–II	7·5	13 0	8 0	7 4	16	1 2-pr, 1 m.g.
41	A.E.C. Mks II–III	12·7	17 10	8 10	8 10	30	1 6-pr, 1 m.g.
38	S.A. Mk IV	6·12	15 0	6 0	7 6	12	1 2-pr, 1 m.g.
38	S.A. Mk VI	11·00	18 8	7 3	—	30	1 2-pr, 1 m.g.
42	Scout Car, Humber	3·39	12 7	6 2	6 11	14	1 m.g.
43	Scout Car, Lynx II	4·00	12 1	6 1	5 10	30	1 m.g.
44	Light Recce Car, Humber Mk IIIA	3·50	14 4	6 2	7 1	10	1a.t.r., 1 m.g.
44	Light Recce Car, Morris Mk II	3·70	13 3	6 8	6 2	14	1 a.t.r., 1 m.g.
43	Light Recce Car, Otter I	4·80	14 9	7 0	8 0	12	1 a.t.r., 1 m.g.
45	Carrier, I.P. Mk IIA	5·70	15 6	7 6	6 6	14	1 a.t.r., 1 m.g.
45	Carrier, I.P., A.O.V.	6·87	15 6	7 7	8 2	14	1 m.g.
47	Deacon	12·00	21 1	8 1	9 6	25	1 6-pr
47	Straussler S.P. 17-pr	8·00	26 5	9 5	5 4	25	1 17-pr
	Germany						
71	SdKfz 250/8	6·00	15 0	6 5	6 9	14·5	1 7·5-cm., 1 m.g.
71	SdKfz 250/9	6·00	15 0	6 5	6 11	14·5	1 2-cm., 1 m.g.
72	SdKfz 234/2 Puma	11·00	20 1	7 10	7 8	100	1 5-cm., 1 m.g.
72	SdKfz 234/3	10·50	20 1	7 10	7 0	30	1 7·5-cm., 1 m.g.
	U.S.S.R.						
78	BA-64	2·4	12 0	5 0	6 3	10	1 m.g. or 1 h.m.g.

Engine	b.h.p.	Speed m.p.h.	Range miles	Crew	Wheel arrange-ment	Notes
sel	134	31	190	15	½-track	
eral Motors (two)	194	55	450	5	4 × 4	
eral Motors (two)	250	50	250	5	8 × 8	
cules	110	55	350	4	6 × 6	
cules	110	55	350	6	6 × 6	
ite	147	45	200	10	½-track	
ite	147	45	220	5	½-track	
tes	90	45	250	4	4 × 4	Mk IV has crew of 3 and 37-mm. gun instead of h.m.g.
nler	95	50	205	3	4 × 4	
.C. diesel	158	41	250	4	4 × 4	Mk III: length 18 ft 5 in., 75-mm.
l	95	50	200	3	4 × 4	
l (two)	190	35	200	3	8 × 8	Width 8 ft 8 in. over spare wheels
iber	87	60	200	2–3	4 × 4	
l	95	57	200	2	4 × 4	
iber	87	50	250	3	4 × 4	a.t.r. = 0·55 in. Boys anti-tank
is	72	50	250	3	4 × 4	
eral Motors	104	45	260	3	4 × 4	
	95	50		3–6	4 × 4	Typical armament given
	95	50		—	4 × 4	
.C. diesel	95	19		5	4 × 4	
ord	72	30	200	5	4 × 2	Third wheel also driven for gun traverse
bach	100	37	186	3	½-track	SdKfz = Sonderkraftfahrzeug
bach	100	37	186	3	½-track	(Special Motor Vehicle)
a	220	53	375	4	8 × 8	—Prefix to ordnance
a	220	53	375	5	8 × 8	numerical designations.
	50	31	375	2	4 × 4	

Tanks and Other Tracked Vehicles
in Service

Mechanized Warfare in Colour

TANKS

and other Tracked Vehicles
in Service

by
B. T. WHITE

illustrated by
JOHN W. WOOD
B. Hiley
J. Pelling
E. Bruce

NEW ORCHARD EDITIONS

New Orchard Editions Ltd.
Stanley House
3 Fleets Lane
Poole, Dorset BH15 3AJ

Copyright © Blandford Press 1978
This edition published 1988

ISBN 1 85079 039 6

Colour printed by W. S. Cowell, Ipswich
Text printed and books bound in Great Britain by
Richard Clay Ltd, Bungay, Suffolk

PREFACE

A selection of the more important or interesting military tracked vehicles in service today (or shortly to enter service) is included in this book. The choice is entirely the author's and has to some extent been dictated by the availability of information and suitable illustrations: the inclusion of one vehicle or omission of another should in no way be taken as an index of their relative importance.

The arrangement is broadly by country of design of the basic vehicle, but where a modification is carried out in a different country to that of design so as to radically modify the original function or design, the second country is given credit in the page heading. Also, where a country is the major producer of a vehicle designed elsewhere, this may likewise be noted in the title. It should be mentioned here that Italy, for example, is a major producer of German and American equipment but not in greater numbers than in the countries of its origin.

Under each country, the general arrangement is under main battle tanks, light tanks, armoured personnel carriers, self-propelled guns, missile carriers and support vehicles. However, this strict arrangement cannot always be followed where, for wider coverage, two different types of vehicle are included in one plate.

Vehicles are shown in typical colours for the country represented. In order to emphasize the widespread export of fighting vehicles by some of the major countries, as well as to add interest to the illustrations, some user countries as well as those of design are included.

Camouflage colours are liable to be changed without notice, but some notes on schemes in use in different countries are included in an Appendix at the end of the book.

A few cross-sectional drawings of modern tracked fighting vehicles are also included to supplement the coloured views by giving a general idea of interiors. These section views cannot, however, necessarily be taken as being either fully up to date or complete in detail. Many modern fighting vehicles, which are very costly machines, are progressively up-dated during their time in service. Illustrations which are released for publication will have classified details omitted.

Tabulated data on the majority of vehicles in the book is included in a further Appendix. This should be taken as a rough comparative guide only. Methods of assessing performance vary between different countries, for example, and data on the vehicles of some countries cannot be guaranteed.

The information drawn on in preparing this book has come from many sources, varying from manufacturers, or military attachés to the author's friends, among whom in particular must be mentioned Colonel Robert J. Icks, who has an unrivalled collection on the subject of A.F.V.s. For published sources, however, the author would particularly like to mention the works of Richard M. Ogorkiewicz, the outstanding writer on A.F.V. design, and Christopher F. Foss, who is one of the leading writers in English on the development of current military vehicles. No one interested in the history and development of A.F.V.s should over-look the two excellent journals *A.F.V. News* (published in Ontario, Canada) and *Tankette* (published in England). The author gratefully acknowledges the help he has received from all sources.

If this book has aroused in the reader an interest for the first time in armoured fighting vehicles, he is recommended to visit some of the tank museums which now are established in many different countries, of which the Royal Armoured Corps Tank Museum at Bovington, Dorset, England is one of the earliest and certainly one of the best.

B. T. White
London, 1977

INTRODUCTION

The object of this Introduction is to draw attention to some of the problems encountered in the design of a modern armoured fighting vehicle—which is always a compromise between protection, mobility and armament—and the answers arrived at by different countries. Solutions to these problems have been influenced by differing tactical and operational criteria and—even for the richest countries—cost.

Tracks versus wheels

Only tracked fighting vehicles are covered in this book. Effectively, this category includes all main battle tanks today, nearly all self-propelled guns and heavy support vehicles, such as bridge-layers, all of which require a stable platform.

The lighter categories of armoured vehicle, such as for reconnaissance or personnel carrying, are by no means confined to tracks, however. The greater simplicity, cheapness, speed, reliability and lower noise factor of wheeled vehicles all have their attractions where size and stability allow wheels instead of tracks to be used and where a generally lower cross-country performance is acceptable.

Main Battle Tanks

Now that the practicable maximum size of a tank gun seems to have been reached and is tending to become almost standard (at around 120 mm. for rifled guns) so that the old categories of

medium and heavy tank have become merged, the self-explanatory term 'main battle tank' has become popular.

The layout of a centrally mounted turret containing a gun of between 100 mm. and 125 mm. on a hull with the engine mounted at the rear is almost universal, although preferences for drive to sprockets at the front of the track (an easier distribution of weight and components but at the penalty of a transmission shaft running through the floor of the fighting compartment) or rear of the track vary.

Guns

Guns, within the range of calibres mentioned, vary from conventional rifled construction to smooth bore weapons firing fin-stabilized projectiles. In between is the French method of a rifled gun firing a projectile in which the warhead inside has its rotation retarded. Automatic loading is not yet common but is likely to be more so, since heavy rounds of around 120-mm. calibre are difficult to handle manually unless, as in the British Chieftain, the charge and projectile are loaded separately: a system likely to slow down the rate of fire. Range-finders vary from optical to laser, with future development tending to concentrate on the latter. The use of a heavy machine-gun for ranging the main gun avoids the need for ballistic corrections (manually or by computer) but can be slower in operation and cannot be used up to the full range of the gun. Complete or partial stabilization of the gun is now almost universal. This enables the gun to be fired while the vehicle is moving, although aiming on the move, with a stop for final sighting adjustments before firing, would be more normal.

All main battle tanks carry a machine-gun mounted coaxially with the main gun and most also have another machine-gun on the turret roof, sometimes capable of being controlled from inside the tank. This is usually described as an anti-aircraft weapon, although it is also available for area defence. Practice varies between countries as to whether the tank commander has the task of being a part-time machine-gunner, or another member of the turret crew, usually the loader. Machine-guns in the front glacis plate, once so common, have lost favour because, apart from being only rarely useful, they reduce somewhat the effectiveness of the frontal armour and take up valuable stowage space.

Night vision devices, such as infra-red searchlights are fitted to, or available for, most modern battle tanks and other A.F.V.s.

A means of making smoke for self-protection is present in all main battle tanks. In Soviet tanks this is done by vaporized diesel fuel being injected into the exhaust system, but elsewhere multiple dischargers for smoke grenades are more usual. These are generally mounted on the turret.

Protection

This tends to vary in accordance with the relative importance attached to armour as opposed to mobility. Actual figures, for current main battle tanks,

are rarely published but the thickest armour continues to be concentrated on frontal surfaces of hull and turret. Steel armour is still used for most M.B.T.s, although laminated armour, such as the British 'Chobham Armour', which is claimed to give good protection against all types of projectiles from solid shot to hollow charge, may become widespread. Protection of another kind—against nuclear fallout, biological or chemical (N.B.C.) warfare is provided for in most modern main battle tanks. This usually consists of a means of maintaining the air pressure inside the vehicle at a slightly higher level than outside, preventing the entry of toxic matter.

Keeping the size of a tank (and particularly its height) down as far as possible, and so decreasing the size of the target it presents is a form of passive protection. A low turret is desirable, but this can have disadvantages—as in Soviet tanks—of limiting gun depression. Eliminating the turret altogether—as in the Swedish S-tank—is one solution, as is the use of variable suspension height. The Japanese have taken advantage of the fact that the average Japanese soldier is smaller than his Western counterpart and scaled down the size of their tanks accordingly.

Engines

Diesel engines (or multi-fuel engines, which are usually modified diesels) are now used in nearly all modern main battle tanks. At least 700 h.p. for a tank of around 50 tons is regarded as necessary to provide an acceptable power : weight ratio and the mobility which largely depends on it. The dual system, where a diesel engine is combined with a gas turbine—the diesel for normal economic running and the turbine for giving extra power when needed—has worked well in the Swedish S-tank but has not been copied elsewhere, although a gas turbine has now been adopted for the latest American battle tank, the XM-1.

Transmission systems are still manual or semi-manual in some cases, but automatic transmissions are also used. Steering systems often are linked with the transmission, so that turns of varying radii are associated with different gear ratios. There are many varieties of steering for tracked vehicles, ranging from the relatively simple clutch and brake type upwards and for a lucid discussion of these (and, indeed, all aspects of fighting vehicle design) the reader is recommended to refer to *Design and Development of Fighting Vehicles*, R. M. Ogorkiewicz, London, 1968.

Suspension

The most common system today is where each road-wheel is independently sprung on a torsion bar, which passes transversely under the belly of the tank. The main disadvantage of this well-tried and efficient system is that it takes up space inside the armour of the vehicle and/or tends to increase its height—an important feature in a tank. The Horstmann type—road-wheels, sprung in pairs, the two wheels on the bogey being controlled by horizontal springs—used on the British Centurion

and Chieftain is also reliable but probably does not equal the riding qualities of the better independent systems. It leaves the interior of the hull clear, however, as does the Belleville washer system used on Swiss battle tanks. Hydropneumatic suspension systems give a good ride, but may be less reliable and require more maintenance than simpler types.

Tracks are usually of cast steel and the use of rubber pads on the shoes to cut down damage to roads, as well as wear on the tracks themselves on hard surfaces, is now common in the tanks of most countries except those in the Soviet bloc.

Mobility

The German Leopard, with a maximum road speed of 65 km./hr is one of the fastest modern main battle tanks, while the British Chieftain at 48 km./hr is one of the slowest. It is claimed, however, that the cross-country performance of a tank is more important than high road speed and the latter does not necessarily mean that a tank is proportionately fast off roads, where performance will vary widely according to the type of terrain but, in any case, may well be limited by the endurance of the tank crew. It is impossible to quote comparable cross-country speeds, but types of tracks and their ground-bearing area; the ground pressure of the vehicle and the type of suspension are all-important factors.

The comparatively light 38-ton Vickers Main Battle Tank is fully amphibious with the use of nylon screens to increase its buoyancy: it is

9

propelled by its tracks in water. Other, heavier, battle tanks, in the absence of bridges, can usually negotiate water obstacles only by deep wading, with the vehicle fully sealed and using breathing tubes for the air supply, such as that shown for the French AMX30 in this book.

Light Tanks

Vehicles that can loosely be classified as light tanks may vary widely in the function for which they are used in different countries. The French AMX 13 and Austrian Kürassier, for example, are tank destroyers, whereas the Swedish Ikv-91 is classified as an 'Infantry Gun Vehicle'. Generally, however, the role of light tanks is for fighting reconnaissance or to be air-droppable (or at least capable of being carried by air) in support of airborne formations. Their armament can be as powerful as that of a main battle tank (such as the U.S. M-551's 152-mm. gun-launcher) but the ammunition supply and protection is usually very much less. The top speed is usually higher than that of most main battle tanks (U.S. M-551—70 km./hr, British Scorpion—81 km./hr) although, depending on size and other factors, the cross-country speed may in some cases be lower. Water mobility is nearly always provided for, either without preparation (except usually the raising of a surf board or trim vane and starting a bilge pump) or by the use of flotation screens carried as standard and capable of being erected in a few minutes. Propulsion in water is, nowadays, usually either by means of hydro-jets

or the vehicle's tracks. Soviet practice tends to favour amphibious tanks (such as PT-76) propelled by water jets, while Britain and the U.S.A. prefer smaller, more compact reconnaissance tanks which therefore have less inherent buoyancy and need aids to float. Tanks propelled by their tracks when afloat cannot attain the same water speeds as hydro jet-propelled vehicles.

The armament of light tanks may, in some cases, be augmented by anti-tank missile launchers to supplement the conventional gun, which may lack range and power for defence against heavier armour.

Light alloy metal construction is becoming increasingly used for light tanks, whose general layout may often correspond to that of main battle tanks, although in the British Scorpion, for example, a front location for the engine has been adopted. Although not necessarily a prime consideration, a front engine location enhances crew protection.

Armoured Personnel Carriers

These are in two categories today:

Armoured Personnel Carriers (as evolved from features of vehicles like the British Universal Carrier, the German armoured half-tracked infantry carriers and converted tanks of World War II); and Mechanized Infantry Combat Vehicles, from which infantry can fight without dismounting. The latter generally have a turret-mounted weapon of 20-mm. calibre upwards, which may be supplemented by anti-tank missile launchers, and are fully provided with ports from which the infantry carried can operate their personal weapons. The M.I.C.V. has evolved from the normal A.P.C., however, and distinction between the two types is not always clear-cut.

The American M-113 pioneered the use of light alloy construction in light armoured vehicles and this is becoming common for many A.P.C.s/M.I.C.V.s today.

The majority of armoured personnel carriers can swim without special preparation, but the development of the Landing Vehicle Tracked category of personnel/load carrier, capable of operation in the open sea, has continued mainly in the United States.

The internal layout of A.P.C.s varies between different countries, but location of the engine at the front of the vehicle, leaving an unobstructed compartment at the rear (with doors in the hull rear plate) for the infantry carried, is a very common feature. Size and protection can vary widely, from the German Marder of 28 tons for instance, carrying a total of ten men and able to accompany main battle tanks, to the French AMX10 P, half the Marder's weight but carrying eleven men.

In most countries, A.P.C.s/ M.I.C.V.s are used as the basis for specialized variants, such as mortar carriers, command vehicles, etc.

Self-Propelled Guns

Today, these fall into three broad categories:

Anti-tank; Field; Anti-Aircraft; although most S.P. guns carry a range of ammunition to enable them to carry out alternative functions.

The chassis used are adapted from those of battle tanks, light tanks or armoured personnel carriers in most cases or, at least, have many features in common with them. Some anti-aircraft tanks, such as the German Gepard, based on the Leopard, or the French twin 30 mm. mounting on the AMX 30 chassis, have layouts closest to their parent vehicles. Self-propelled anti-tank guns, like the German Jagdpanzer-kanone and the Soviet ASU-85 mostly trace their ancestry to the assault guns of World War II—low, well-armoured vehicles with weapons having a limited traverse, although the anti-tank guided missile vehicles which are tending to replace them, being able to fire from off line or concealed positions, are not subject to the same design considerations. The German Jagdpanzer Rakete, adapted from the Jagdpanzerkanone, may be contrasted with the lightly armoured British Striker, which is similar to the Spartan armoured personnel carrier.

Self-propelled field artillery, with weapons from 105 mm. up to medium calibres (the U.S. 175-mm. gun or 203-mm. howitzer, for example) as a class tends to use more specialized chassis. Although these may use engines and elements of suspension in common with other vehicles, a front engine layout, leaving the back end clear for the gun and easy access for its service, is almost universal. Except for the 105-mm. British Abbot, a calibre of 155 mm. is generally regarded as the minimum for field pieces. Apart from some vehicles required to be air portable, where weight has to be reduced, most modern guns are in revolving turrets which give the crew protection at least against small arms ammunition and shell splinters and can be sealed against N.B.C. attack. Automatic or semi-automatic loading is becoming common on heavier weapons for field or anti-tank use. On the American M–109, for instance, it can double the rate of fire.

Anti-aircraft self-propelled guns (or anti-aircraft tanks as some are categorized) vary in capability from fire over open sights only to all weather day or night operation, controlled by radar and computer. All tend nowadays, however, to be multiple mountings of automatic guns limited to calibres of up to 35 mm. for use against close low-level attack only. Guided weapons are more generally being used for medium to long-range air defence. Some or all of the associated radar equipment is carried in accompanying vehicles.

Missile Carriers

The Soviet Union is tending to turn to high-mobility wheeled vehicles as carriers and launchers for its medium to long-range surface to surface missiles. The United States, on the other hand, has moved from the truck-mounted Honest John tactical missile system to the Lance, which has a tracked carrier-launcher. The French Pluton system has been designed from the start to be carried on tracked vehicles, of the AMX 30 type, so there is no general consensus of thought on the type of mobility to be given to such weapons.

Support Vehicles

In most countries, there is a desire to achieve as high as possible a degree of commonality of chassis between support vehicles (such as for recovery, bridging and engineer tasks) and the main battle tanks or other vehicles with which they are to work. The advantages of having the same level of battlefield mobility, common mechanical spares etc. need no emphasis. Most countries have support vehicles in the main categories using the same chassis as their current main battle tank, only the Soviet Union apparently continuing to make wide use of the chassis of obsolescent tanks.

Armoured Recovery Vehicles are all equipped with a winch and towing gear and some, such as the German Leopard and French AMX 30D, have revolving cranes for such tasks as engine changes. Some countries, such as Sweden, base their main recovery vehicle on a lighter type of chassis, leaving actual battlefield recovery of main battle tanks to other tanks. Most countries also have light recovery vehicles capable of dealing with armoured vehicles of their own class, such as armoured personnel carriers, light tanks and some self-propelled guns.

Most tank bridge layers, or armoured vehicle launched bridges (A.V.L.B.), continue to carry either a rigid single span bridge or a folded bridge of the 'Scissors' type. The latter, because of its more compact travelling configuration, is the more popular although its height during the laying process makes it more conspicuous in the battle area. The German Biber on the Leopard chassis, by using a span in two halves sliding forward for launching, combines advantages of both the earlier types. The most common means of launching is hydraulic, with power take-off from the main engine of the vehicle.

Pioneer vehicles, for battlefield tasks such as the demolition of obstacles and preparation of gun positions etc. are either standard tanks with attachments, such as dozer blades, or adaptations of main battle-tank chassis. In some countries, such as France, the armoured recovery vehicle (AMX 30D) can also act as a pioneer vehicle, or the pioneer vehicle is very similar to the recovery vehicle, as in West Germany. Only in the United Kingdom has a completely new vehicle, the Combat Engineer Tractor, which is unlike any existing chassis, been produced for the pioneer role. Many of the World War II devices for minefield clearance, such as rollers, ploughs and explosive devices, are represented in various armies today. The United Kingdom, for example, has a rocket-propelled explosive device (carried in a trailer towed by the Combat Engineer Tractor) while the Warsaw Pact countries have an array of roller and plough devices for attachment to main battle tanks. Mines can be laid mechanically by devices towed or carried by such vehicles as the British FV 432 armoured personnel carrier.

Command, signal, radar and ambulance functions are carried out, in most countries today, by adaptations of armoured personnel carrier chassis.

THE COLOURED ILLUSTRATIONS

A description of each coloured
plate is given between pages
81 and 138

1   Tanque Argentino Mediano (TAM)

2 Carrier, Full
Tracked,
Armoured,
M-113A1,
Fire Support
Vehicle, with
Saladin turret
(*above*) and
Scorpion
turret

3 Panzerjäger Kürassier

4 Schützenpanzer 4K4FA-G (*above*) and Schützenpanzer 4K4FA

5 Type T-59 Main Battle Tank (*above*) and Type K-63
Armoured Personnel Carrier

Czechoslovakia

6 Obrneny Transporter – OT.62 (TOPAS)

7 Char de
Combat
AMX 30

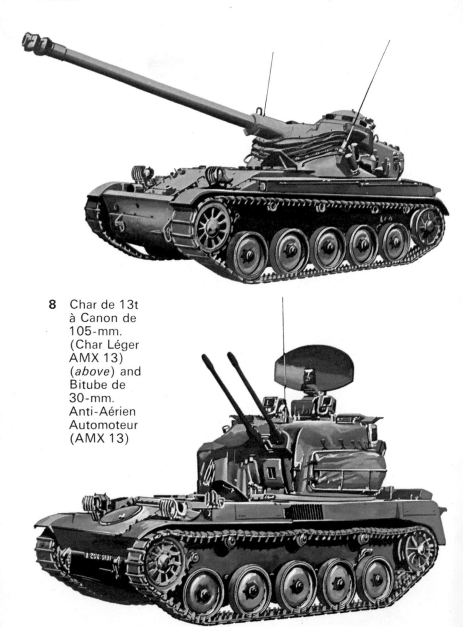

8 Char de 13t
à Canon de
105-mm.
(Char Léger
AMX 13)
(*above*) and
Bitube de
30-mm.
Anti-Aérien
Automoteur
(AMX 13)

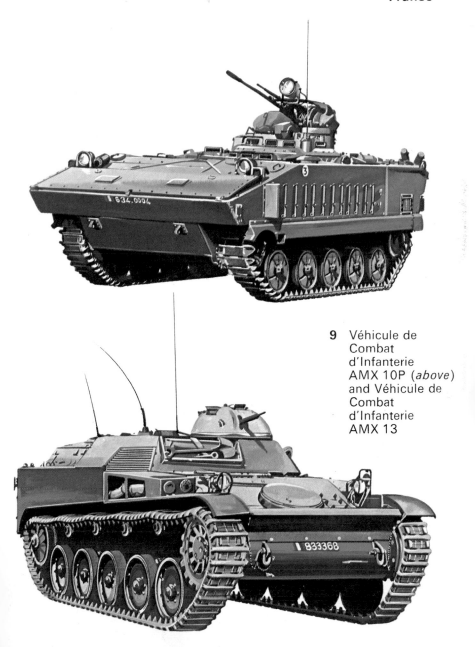

9 Véhicule de Combat d'Infanterie AMX 10P (*above*) and Véhicule de Combat d'Infanterie AMX 13

France

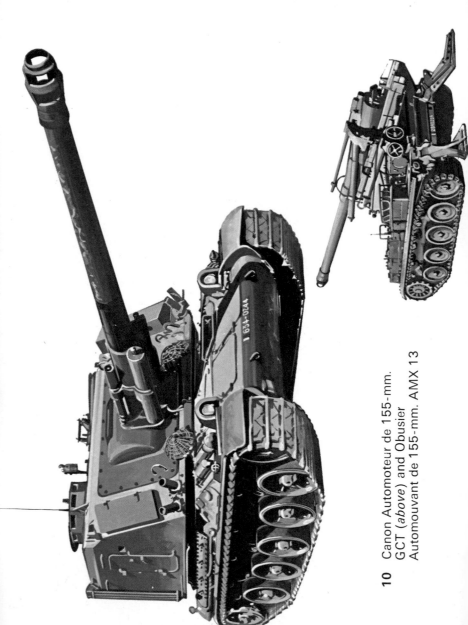

10 Canon Automoteur de 155-mm. GCT (*above*) and Obusier Automouvant de 155-mm. AMX 13

11 Véhicule de Tir Roland AMX 30
(*above*) and Véhicule de Tir Pluton
AMX 30

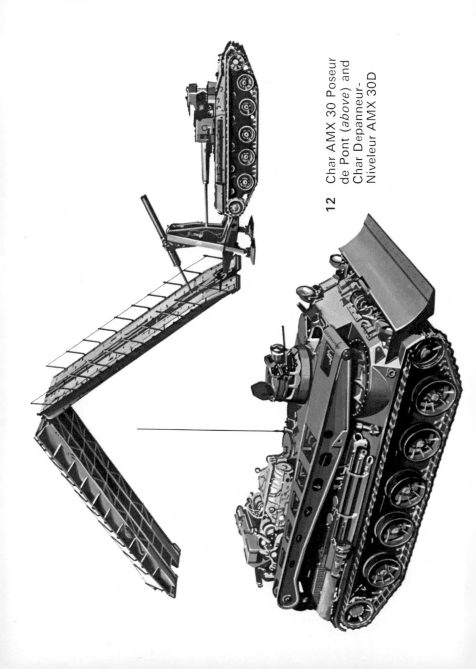

12 Char AMX 30 Poseur de Pont (*above*) and Char Depanneur-Niveleur AMX 30D

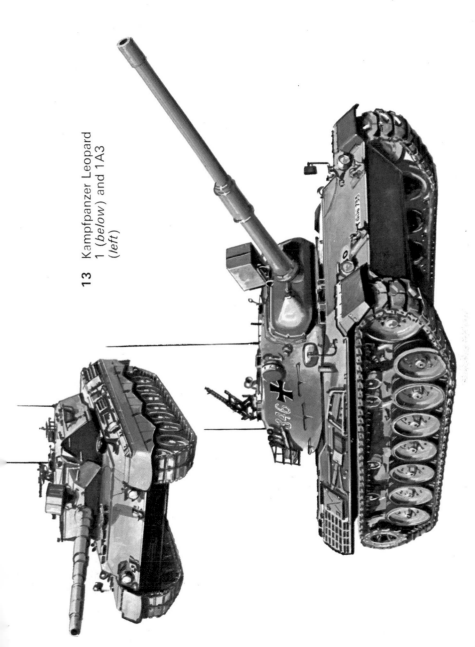

13 Kampfpanzer Leopard 1 (*below*) and 1A3 (*left*)

German Federal Republic

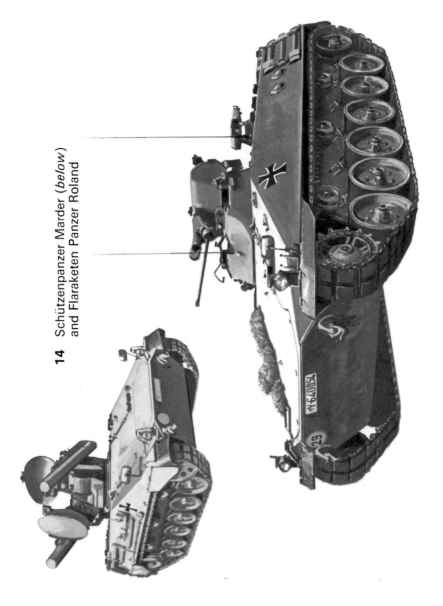

14 Schützenpanzer Marder (*below*) and Flaraketen Panzer Roland

German Federal Republic/Holland

15 Flakpanzer 1 Gepard (*below*) and Pantserrups LUA 35-mm.

16 Kanonenjagdpanzer KJPZ4-5 (*above*) and Raketenjagdpanzer RJPZ3

17 Bergepanzer 2 Leopard (*below*)
and Brückenlegepanzer 1 Biber

18 Self-Propelled 160-mm. Mortar (*below*) and Self-
propelled 155-mm. Gun-Howitzer

19 Tank, Type 74, 105-mm. Gun (*above*) and Tank, Type 61, 90-mm. Gun

Japan

20 Armoured Personnel Carrier, Type 73 (*above*) and
Armoured Personnel Carrier, Type 60

21 Self-Propelled 106-mm. Recoilless Gun, Type 60 (*above*) and 4.2 inch Mortar Carriage, Type 60

Japan

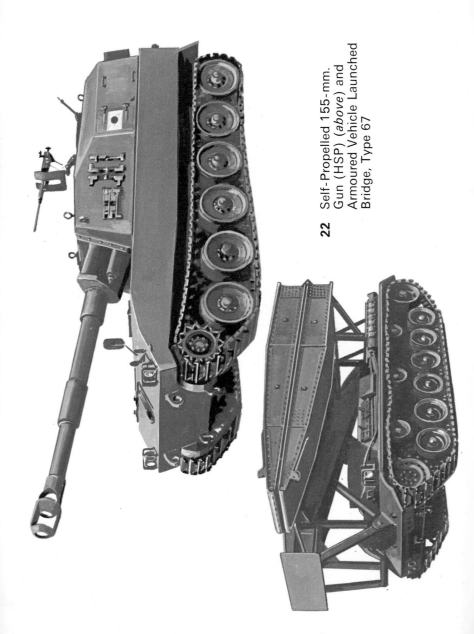

22 Self-Propelled 155-mm. Gun (HSP) (*above*) and Armoured Vehicle Launched Bridge, Type 67

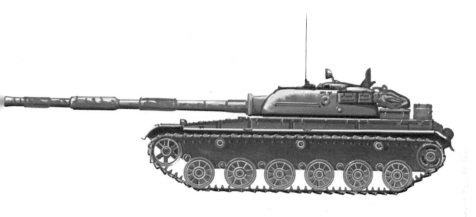

23   T-72 (Main Battle Tank)

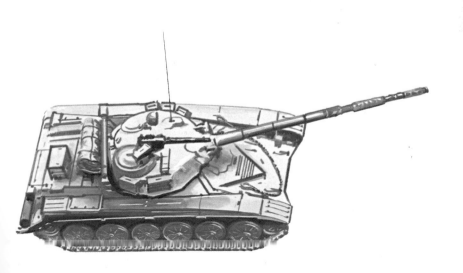

Soviet Union

24 T-62 (Main Battle Tank)

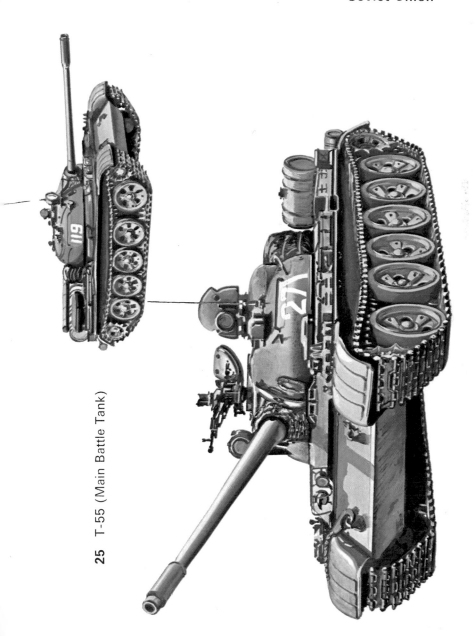

25 T-55 (Main Battle Tank)

26 ASU-85 (Airborne Assault Gun) (*above*) and PT-76 (Amphibious Tank)

27 BMP-1 (Infantry Combat Vehicle) (*above*) and
BMD (Airborne Combat Vehicle)

28 ZSU-23-4 (Anti-Aircraft S.P. Gun) (*above*) and ZSU-57-2 (Anti-Aircraft S.P. Gun)

29 SU-122 (Self-Propelled Gun)

30 SA.6 Gainful (Anti-Aircraft Missile Carrier) (*below*)
and Straight Flush (Armoured Fire Control Vehicle)

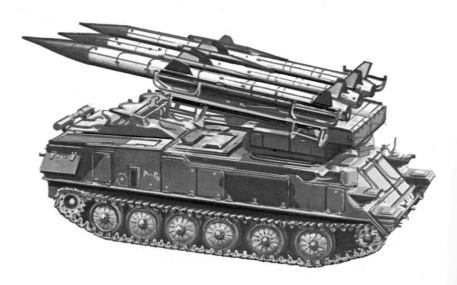

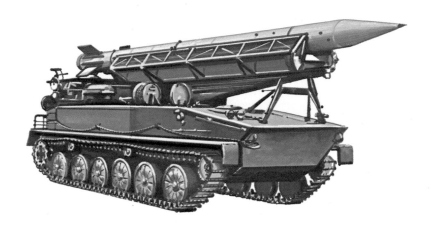

31 Frog 5 (Missile Carrier) (*above*) and SA-4 Ganef (Anti-Aircraft Missile Carrier)

Soviet Union

32 SS-15 (Scrooge) (Strategic Missile Carrier) (*above*)
and SS-14 Scamp (Scapegoat)

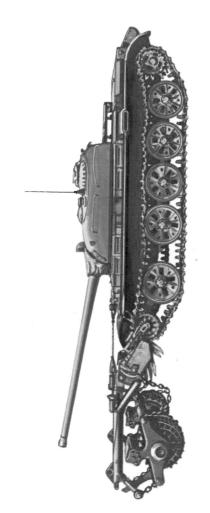

33 T-54/MTU (Tank Bridgelayer) (*above*) and T-54/PT (Tank Mineclearer)

Sweden

34 Stridsvagn Strv. 103B

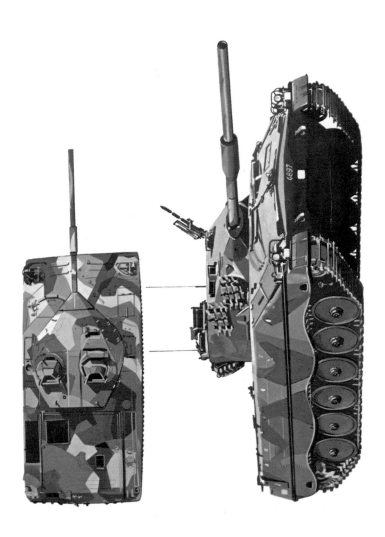

35 Infanterikanonvagn Ikv-91

Sweden

36 Pansarbandvagn
Pbv-302 (*below*) and
155-mm. Bandkanon
1A

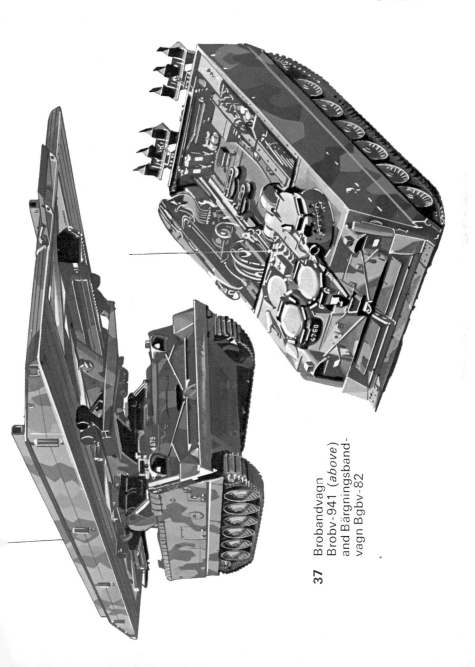

37 Brobandvagn
Brobv-941 (*above*)
and Bärgningsband-
vagn Bgbv-82

Switzerland

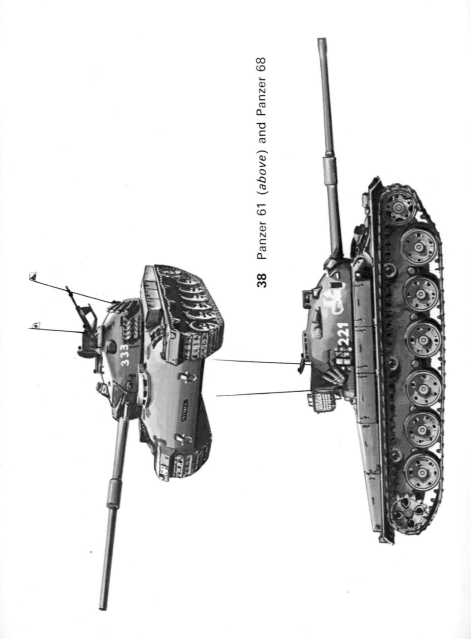

38 Panzer 61 (*above*) and Panzer 68

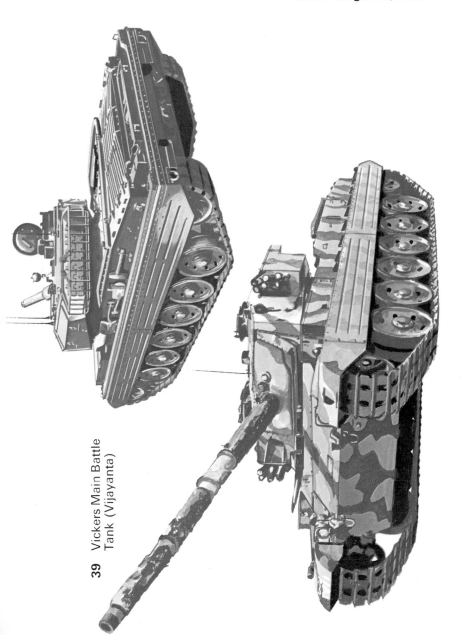

39 Vickers Main Battle Tank (Vijayanta)

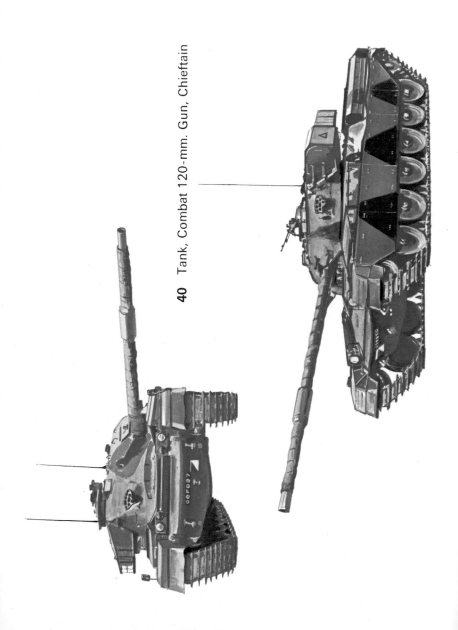

40 Tank, Combat 120-mm. Gun, Chieftain

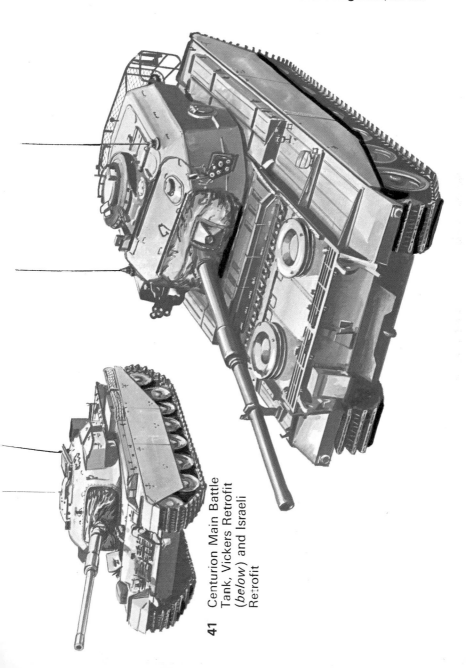

41 Centurion Main Battle Tank, Vickers Retrofit (*below*) and Israeli Retrofit

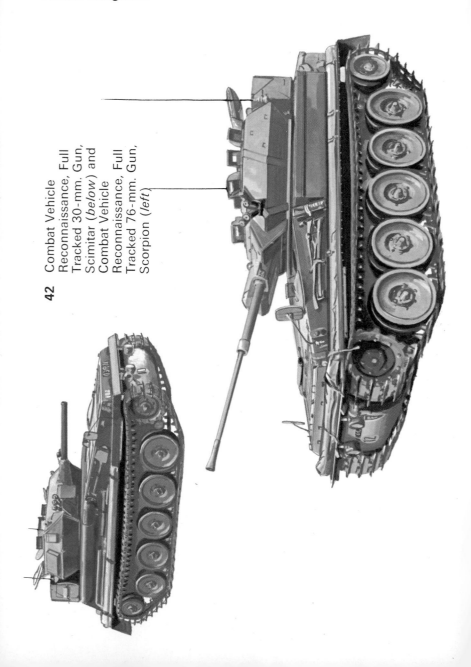

42 Combat Vehicle Reconnaissance, Full Tracked 30-mm. Gun, Scimitar (*below*) and Combat Vehicle Reconnaissance, Full Tracked 76-mm. Gun, Scorpion (*left*)

43 Combat Vehicle Reconnaissance, Full Tracked, G.W., Striker (*above*) and Combat Vehicle, Reconnaissance, Full Tracked, Personnel, Spartan

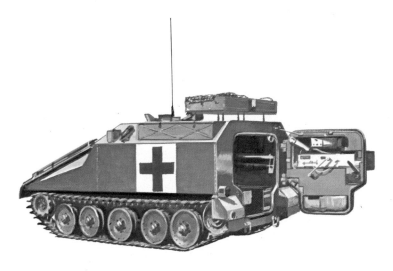

44 Combat Vehicle, Reconnaissance, Full Tracked, Command, Sultan (*below*) and Combat Vehicle, Ambulance, Full Tracked, Samaritan

45 Carrier, Personnel, Full Tracked, FV 432 (*below*) and Carrier, Maintenance, Full Tracked, FV 434

United Kingdom

46 Launcher, Guided
Missile, Carrier
Mounted, Full Tracked,
Swingfire, FV 438
(*above*) and Carrier,
FV 432 with Ranger

47 Gun, Self-Propelled, 105-mm. Fd Gun, Abbot (*above*) and Falcon, Self-Propelled, A.A. Gun

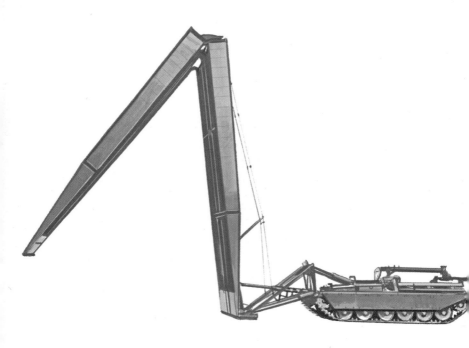

48 Tank, Bridgelayer, AVLB, Chieftain Mk. 5

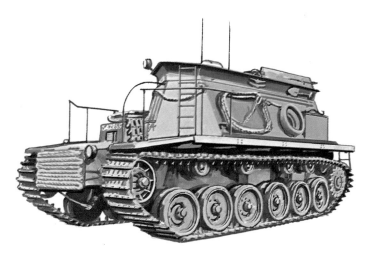

49 Armoured Recovery Vehicle, Beach, Centurion Mk. 5
(*above*) and Armoured Recovery Vehicle, Chieftain
Mk. 5

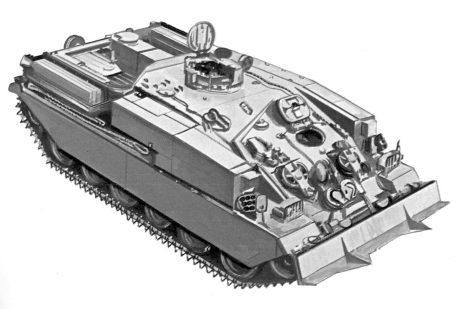

50 Combat Engineer Tractor, Full Tracked

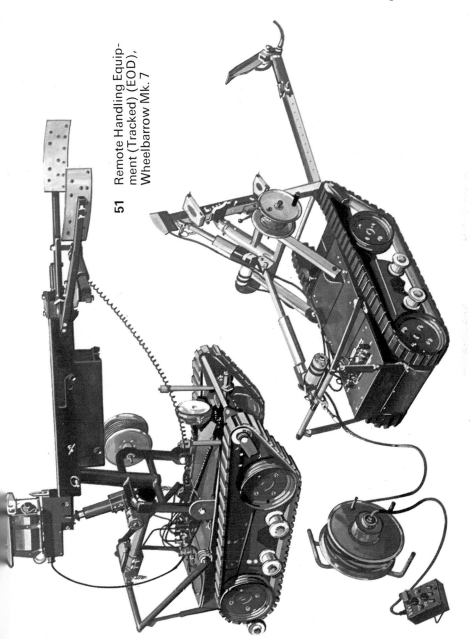

51 Remote Handling Equipment (Tracked) (EOD), Wheelbarrow Mk. 7

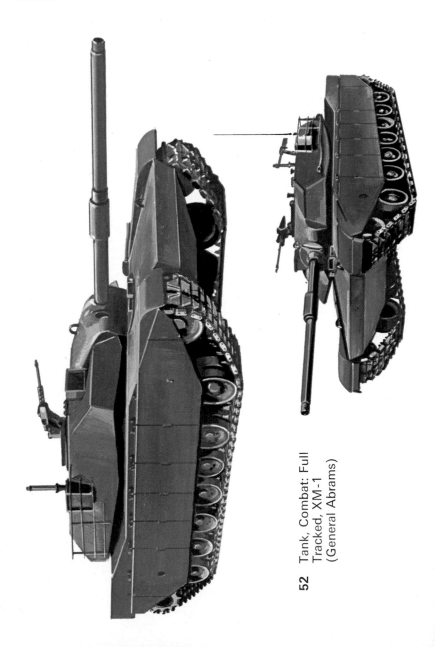

52 Tank, Combat: Full Tracked, XM-1 (General Abrams)

53 Tank, Combat: Full Tracked, 152-mm. Gun, M-60A2 (*above*) and Tank, Combat: Full Tracked, 105-mm. Gun, M-60A1

54 Armoured Reconnaissance/Airborne Assault Vehicle:
Full Tracked, 152-mm., M-551

55 Carrier, Personnel: Full Tracked, Armoured, M-113A1 Diesel (*above*) and Carrier, 107-mm. Mortar: Full Tracked, M-106A1

U.S.A.

56 Carrier, Command Post: Full Tracked, M-577A1
(*above*) and Carrier, M-113 with Radar

57 Command and Reconnaissance Vehicle (Lynx) (*above*) and Carrier, Command and Reconnaissance, Armoured, M-114A1

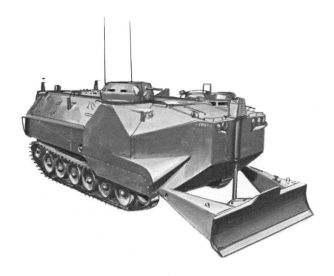

58 Landing Vehicle: Tracked-Engineer 7 (*above*) and Landing Vehicle: Tracked-Personnel 7

59 Gun, Field Artillery, Self-Propelled: 175-mm. M-107 (*above*) and Howitzer, Heavy, Self-Propelled: 8 inch, M-110

60 Lance Guided Missile System (*above*) and Howitzer, Medium, Self-Propelled: 155-mm. M-109G

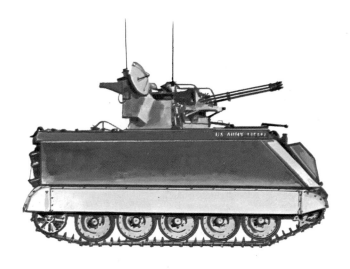

61 Gun, Anti-Aircraft Artillery, Self-Propelled: 20-mm., M-163 (*above*) and Guided Missile System Intercept — Aerial, Carrier Mounted (Chaparral)

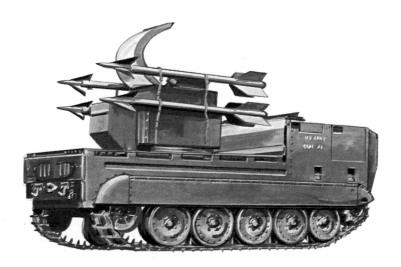

62 Recovery Vehicle, Full Tracked, Medium, M-88 (*above*) and Recovery Vehicle, Full Tracked, Light, Armoured, M-578

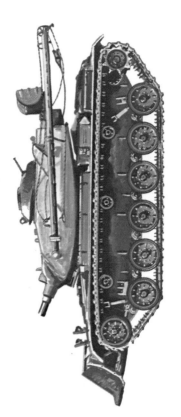

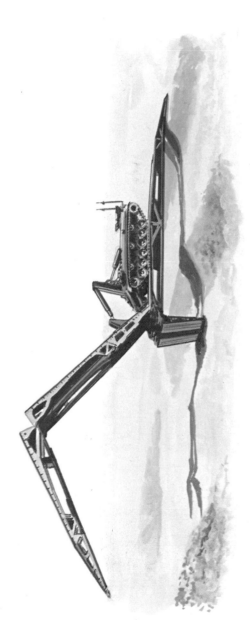

63 Combat Engineer Vehicle: Full Tracked, M-728 (*above*) and Armoured Vehicle Launched Bridge

Yugoslavia

64 Infantry Combat Vehicle, M-980

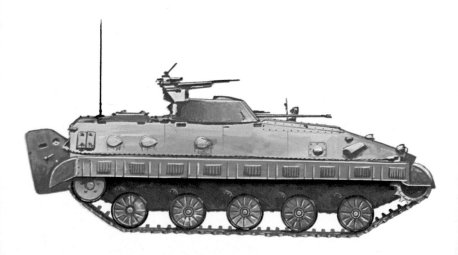

TANKS AND OTHER TRACKED VEHICLES IN SERVICE

1 Tanque Argentino Mediano Argentina (TAM), German Federal Republic.

This 30-ton battle tank has been developed by the West German Thyssen–Henschel company under a contract awarded in 1974 by the Defence Ministry of Argentina. The chassis of the Marder infantry combat vehicle has been used as a basis to which has been added a three-man turret mounting a 105-mm. gun. This gun has been developed in Argentina from the French 105-mm. gun used in the AMX 13 and built under licence in Argentina. As the fire control electronic system has also been developed in Argentina, there has been a considerable degree of collaboration between the two countries in the design of this tank, which is to be constructed in factories at Rio Tercero (turret and gun) and Buenos Aires (chassis and final assembly). The initial order is for 200 vehicles.

The maximum weight of 30 tons—similar to that of the World War II Shermans the TAM will replace—was fixed by the Argentine Army. Although it necessarily places limits on the amount of armour protection that can be offered, a vehicle of this weight can be accommodated by most bridges in the country and enables standard commercial heavy trucks to be used as transporters. It also helps to keep down initial and maintenance costs. The six-cylinder diesel engine of the Marder has been up-rated to 710 h.p. for the TAM and this gives a high degree of mobility, with a maximum speed of over 75 km./hr.

The 105-mm. gun is stabilized: it has a coaxial 7·62-mm. machine-gun with it in the turret and another machine-gun is mounted for anti-aircraft use. The machine-guns are also made in Argentina, under licence from the Belgian FN concern.

The prototype TAM which was completed early in 1977, and does not have the Argentinian gun, is shown in the illustrations.

Three hundred infantry combat vehicles are also to be built in Argentina. These are a simplified version of the Marder with different firing ports and turret from those of the standard Bundeswehr vehicles.

2 Carrier, Full Tracked, Armoured, M-113A1, Fire Support Vehicle, Australia/U.S.A.

The armoured vehicles with which the Australian Army is equipped are of American, British and German manufacture. However, these are modified to meet special Australian requirements, such as for climatic conditions, and in addition some adaptations have been carried out in Australia itself, partly on grounds of economy.

The American M-113A1 is the standard armoured personnel carrier of the Australian Army and this type has been used as the basis of a local conversion to produce a Fire Support Vehicle for Australian Armoured Cavalry units. The conversion consists of marrying an existing pattern of 76-mm. gun turret to a modified M-113A1.

The first type, which was used by the Australian Army in Vietnam, uses the turret of the British Saladin armoured car. As full depression of the main armament was required, the turret is mounted on a raised ring and, to enable the driver's hatch to be opened without respect to the turret position, the normal hinged type has been replaced with one of a sideways swinging pattern.

The addition of the turret has increased the M-113A1's all-up weight by about 2 tons and has adversely affected the vehicle's stability as well as track and suspension life. The M-113A1 FSV with Saladin turret cannot be air-lifted and care has to be taken in travelling over rough country to avoid overturning and, although the vehicle is amphibious, there would be a risk of capsizing if the turret were turned when in the water.

To overcome some of the above disadvantages, a second version of the M-113A1 F.S.V. has been developed which uses the British Scorpion light tank turret. This lowers the overall height to make the vehicle air-portable in the Lockheed C-130 Hercules and also improves stability on both land and water. The Scorpion turrets are made by Alvis Ltd in the United Kingdom and incorporate Australian detail requirements.

In both models, the armament consists of a 76-mm. gun, a coaxial 7·62-mm. machine-gun, and a second machine-gun mounted on the turret roof for anti-aircraft purposes.

3 Panzerjäger Kürassier, Austria.

The Jagdpanzer Kürassier, or Panzerjäger K, is a tank destroyer using the French FL-12 gun turret on a chassis developed from that of the Austrian Schützenpanzer 4K4FA, described separately.

Designated 4KH6FA, the 'H' probably stands for 'heckmotor' (rear engine) since the principal mechanical change in Kürassier from the Schützenpanzer's layout is that the engine has been moved to the back of the vehicle, and the drive sprockets are also at the rear. The turret, mounted almost in the centre of the vehicle, carries the commander and gunner and is of the oscillating type, with automatic loading for the 105-mm. gun. A rate of fire of approximately twelve rounds per minute can be achieved. An infra-red searchlight for night fighting is in a square container near the rear of the turret roof.

The 105-mm. gun, which has a performance not far short of that of the French AMX 30 battle tank, is a heavy weapon for a vehicle of only 17·5 tons and the armour protection is necessarily limited to little more than the Schützenpanzer's 8–20 mm., except on the turret face, where it is 40 mm. Mobility helps to compensate for light protection, however—the Saurer (Steyr) 6FA six-cylinder diesel engine gives the Jagdpanzer a maximum speed of 67 km./hr.

One hundred and fifteen or more Kürassiers (excluding prototypes) have been built for the Austrian Army by Steyr–Daimler–Puch AG (with guns and turrets supplied from France), and some have been sold to Tunisia. There is also an armoured recovery vehicle version, turretless and with heightened hull, bulldozer blade, crane and winches, known as Bergepanzer Greif, or Bergepanzer K.

4 Schützenpanzer 4K4FA and Schützenpanzer 4K4FA-G, Austria.

Like some of the other smaller neutral countries, not aligned with either the Eastern or Western power blocs, Austria has undertaken a programme of producing some of its own armoured fighting vehicles. It may continue to be more expedient to purchase the heavier A.F.V.s abroad (most of its tanks are either French or American) but the Austrian Army is now equipped with armoured personnel carriers of entirely Austrian design and manufacture.

The Österreichische Saurerwerke AG (which now forms part of the Steyr–Daimler–Puch organization) started work on the design of an armoured personnel carrier in 1956 and the first experimental prototypes were built from 1958 onwards. From these was evolved a vehicle fairly conventional in layout for an armoured personnel carrier, although perhaps owing more to German influence than, say, American practice. The general layout has been retained in successive prototype and production vehicles, which have included a number of improvements.

The Schützenpanzer is a fairly low vehicle, with the engine, transmission and final drive at the front, right of centre, with the driver at the left. The rear compartment (which has twin access doors in the back plate of the vehicle) has accommodation for eight infantry, in addition to the vehicle commander, who occupies a position behind the driver and operates the mounted armament. The basic version (4K4FA) has a 12·7-mm. machine-gun, normally on an open mounting al-though sometimes a shield is fitted. Alternatively, a turret containing a 20-mm. cannon may be fitted—this model is known as 4K4FA-G.

The suspension on all models consists of five medium-sized road-wheels carried on transverse torsion bars.

In the designation, 4K represents the chassis type and 4FA the engine model, which is a Saurer six-cylinder diesel, developing 250 h.p. Other models with slightly different engine models are 4K4F and 4K3F, and the basic Schützenpanzer is also produced in specialized ambulance, radio, command (three models), rocket launcher and 81-mm. mortar-carrying versions. External differences are not great (although the ambulance, radio and some other versions lack the turret or heavy machine-gun mounting), but some have only a 7·62-mm. MG-42, for which several alternative positions are available, in place of the heavier weapons.

Between 400 and 500 Schützenpanzer (of all models) have been built and are in service with the Austrian Army.

5 Type T-59 Main Battle Tank and Type K-63 Armoured Personnel Carrier, Chinese People's Republic.

Virtually no official information has been released about armoured fighting vehicles built by the Chinese People's Republic, although various types of tank and armoured personnel carrier have been exported by China to Albania and a number of African and Asian countries.

The most widely known Chinese A.F.V. is probably the Type T-59 main

83

battle tank, which is a close derivative and somewhat simplified version of the Soviet T-54. The main details are similar to those of the Soviet tank, although early Chinese versions, at any rate, did not have stabilization for the 100-mm. gun (as, indeed, neither did the earliest Soviet T-54s) and lacked the infra-red headlights and searchlight.

There are also at least three models of lighter tank in service. The Type T-60 is an amphibious tank similar to the Soviet PT-76, from which it has been developed, although the Chinese tank has an 85-mm. gun in a dome-shaped turret more like that of the Type T-59, and is probably heavier. The Type T-62 and Type-63 are also believed to be armed with 85-mm. guns and so all three models may be regarded as reconnaissance vehicles rather than main battle tanks.

The Chinese Armoured Personnel Carrier Type K-63 (or M-1967 or M-1970, as it was previously known for want of a more precise designation) appears to be an entirely original vehicle, as there is no known Soviet or other foreign prototype for it. A smallish vehicle of only about 10 tons with only four road-wheels each side, the Type K-63 has the engine at the front in the centre, and the transmission is to front drive sprockets, with the driver at the left and the commander at the right. A heavy 12·7-mm. machine-gun is mounted on the roof in the centre of the vehicle and appears to be operated from a hatch behind it. The compartment at the rear carries about eight infantrymen, who have access through doors in the rear plate.

A trim vane is carried on the nose plate of the Type K-63 for use in water

when erected. No other preparation is needed for swimming, the vehicle being propelled in water by its tracks.

In addition to the Type K-63, and in production before it, China also uses tracked armoured personnel carriers of the Soviet BTR-50P type.

6   Obrneny Transporter—OT.62 (TOPAS), Czechoslovakia.

The Czech OT.62 (also widely known by its Polish name Transporter Obojzivelny Pasovy Stredni or TOPAS) constitutes an important contribution from the long-standing Czechoslovakian armaments industry to the Warsaw Pact armoury. It is an armoured personnel carrier developed from the Russian BTR-50 PK, over which it is an improvement, having a better performance.

The suspension is similar to that of the PT-76 amphibious tank, to which both armoured personnel carriers owe their ancestry, with six road-wheels each side, sprung on torsion bars. The hull height, compared with that of the tank, is increased to give more headroom for the squad of eighteen infantrymen (plus a crew of two) that can be carried. Although there are various external differences between the Russian and Czech vehicles, the main difference lies in the power unit, which in the OT.62 is a 300-h.p. six-cylinder in-line water-cooled diesel engine.

With armour protection of 10 mm. maximum, the first model of OT.62 had no fixed armament. Model 2 has a small turret with a 7·62-mm. machine-gun mounted at the front right-hand side of the hull, and a later model, the result of Polish–Czech co-operation, the 2AP, has a turret like that of the SKOT eight-wheeled armoured personnel carrier. This turret mounts a 14·5-mm. heavy machine-gun and a 7·62-mm. machine-gun, and the space it takes up is no doubt responsible for the reduction in carrying capacity to twelve men in addition to the crew of three.

The OT.62 has a road speed of about 62 km./hr and is fully amphibious without preparation. Propulsion in the water is by means of two hydrojets at the rear of the hull. A pump, driven by a take-off from the main engine, draws in water through vents in the hull sides and ejects this through the apertures at the rear. A maximum speed of nearly 11 km./hr is possible in water and steering is effected by controlling the volume and direction of the flow from either hydrojet and associated vents.

The OT.62 TOPAS is used by the Czechoslovakian and Polish armies, as well as those of a number of African and Asian countries.

7 Char de Combat AMX 30, France.

The AMX 30 has been developed by France as her main battle tank after careful experiments over 10–15 years with differing layouts of hull and turret design and guns of calibres ranging from 90 mm. to 120 mm.

After the abandonment of the experimental AMX 50, which had a 120-mm. gun in an oscillating turret (like that of AMX 13) and weighed over 50 tons, efforts were concentrated on a much smaller, less conspicuous and more mobile tank of some 30 tons with a conventional turret armed with an unconventional gun of 105 mm. calibre. It was the original intention that this tank should compete for a common design to be adopted by both France and Germany, but ultimately the two countries went their separate ways.

The gun of the AMX 30 is a 105-mm. weapon of unusual design in that although rifled it fires a shaped-charge armour-piercing projectile in which inner rotation is retarded. This weapon thus combines the advantages of the accuracy of a rifled barrel with the high penetration for a relatively small projectile of the shaped charge, which for maximum effect should not be rotated. This projectile, the OCC 105F1, or Obus G, overcomes the problem of spin imparted by the rifled barrel of the gun by the charge itself being mounted on ball bearings, so that rotation inside the casing is so minimal as to have little effect on penetrative performance on impact.

The secondary armament of the AMX 30 consists of a 12·7-mm. heavy machine-gun coaxial with the 105-mm. gun (although it can be elevated 20 degrees beyond that of the 105 mm. for use against aerial targets), and a 7·62-mm. machine-gun mounted on the commander's cupola at the right-hand side, but controlled from inside the tank.

Apart from its armament, AMX 30 follows a layout fairly usual for many modern battle tanks, with medium-sized road-wheels, suspended on transverse torsion bars (although the wheels are, more unusually, of aluminium alloy) and a rear-mounted engine transmitting its power through a five-speed gear-box to track drive sprockets at the rear of the vehicle. The steering system is of the triple differential type, giving varying turning radii according to the gear used. The AMX 30's engine is the Hispano-Suiza HS-110 diesel, water-cooled, with twelve cylinders and develops 720 h.p.

Quantity production of the AMX 30 began about 1965 and over a thousand have been built for the French Army. It has also been supplied to Greece, Venezuela, Chile, Peru, Iraq, Libya, Saudi Arabia and Spain, where it is also being built under licence.

The standard AMX 30 can be fitted with a schnorkel breathing tube for deep wading (this is shown in one of the illustrations, both of which show French Army vehicles) and a simplified 'basic' model AMX 30 is available for export. A family of specialized vehicles is also based on the AMX 30 hull, and some of these are dealt with separately in this volume.

The AMX 30 is to be updated by the substitution of a 120-mm. smooth bore gun, which will use the same ammunition as the German Rheinmetall weapon intended for the Leopard.

8 **Char de 13t à Canon de 105 mm. (Char Léger AMX 13) and Bitube de 30 mm. Anti-Aérien Automoteur (AMX 13), France.**

One of the most successful light tanks ever built, the AMX 13 has been supplied to over two dozen countries from 1952 onwards and is still in service with the French Army.

The design weight of 13 tons and, to some extent its configuration, was dictated by the original requirement that this tank should be air portable for use by the French airborne forces. Design to meet the specification was carried out by the French fighting vehicle research and development centre Atelier de Construction d' Issyles-Moulineaux (and hence the initials AMX in the designation of tanks having their origin at this establishment).

A front engine layout, with the driver alongside on the left, with transmission to front-drive sprockets, allowed the turret to be mounted at the rear. This had the advantage of reducing the overhang at the front of the powerful 75-mm. gun that was adopted for AMX 13. The most interesting feature, however, was the use of an oscillating or trunnion-mounted turret. This kind of turret is constructed in two parts, the upper part carrying the gun, which is elevated and depressed with it. This upper part of the turret is mounted on trunnions on the lower part, which rotates on the hull. The oscillating turret simplified fire control equipment and made much easier the installation of automatic loading mechanism by eliminating relative movement between it and the gun mounting.

The AMX 13 entered service with the French Army armed with the long 75-mm. gun Mle. 50 although some tanks had a shorter gun mounted in a Panhard E.B.R. (armoured car) turret. During service with France and the many other countries that purchased the AMX 13 various detail improvements were introduced, and then the 90-mm. gun, firing hollow-charge projectiles, was made available. Conversion to the more powerful gun was carried out on many vehicles in service, including those of the French Army. A further enhancement of the armament, if not the performance of their somewhat heavily loaded chassis, was the addition to the turret of four SS-11 teleguided missiles. Finally, a model with the 105-mm. gun Mle. 57 was introduced. A batch of these have been supplied to the Dutch Army, although earlier models can, if required, be converted to the larger gun.

A specialized tank using the AMX 13 chassis is the 'Bitube de 30-mm. Anti-Aérien Automoteur'. This weapons system, evolved jointly by Direction Technique des Armements Terrestres; S.A.M.M. (responsible for the turret design); Hispano-Suiza (the guns) and Thomson-C.S.F. (radar), consists of a dome-shaped turret mounting the twin 30-mm. cannon, with a rate of fire of 600 rounds per minute each, together with the RD 515 Oeil Noir 1 radar system. The radar can acquire aerial targets up to 15 km. distance and 3,000 metres height and the analog computer of the system provides sight corrections. In addition, 'softskin' or light armoured vehicles can be engaged with direct fire.

This weapons system is in use with the French Army. The same system has been applied also to the AMX 30 chassis, which provides a steadier firing platform and can carry more ammunition.

9 Véhicule de Combat d'Infanterie AMX 13 and Véhicule de Combat d'Infanterie AMX 10P, France.

The chassis of the AMX 13 light tank was virtually standardized for a whole family of light support vehicles developed by the French Army in the 1950s and 1960s. The basic vehicle was an armoured personnel carrier (véhicule de transport de troupe—VTT), later redesignated infantry combat vehicle (VCI). This has an unobstructed compartment at the rear with a higher roof than that of the tank. This layout is easily adaptable to ambulance, command, cargo carrying and other functions and can be fitted for carrying and firing various calibres of mortar up to 120 mm., or equipped with a bulldozer blade and a jib as an engineer vehicle.

As an infantry carrier, the V.C.I. AMX 13 can transport a section of twelve men with their personal weapons, in addition to the driver. Totally enclosed, the vehicle was one of the first to provide firing ports to enable the infantry to use their weapons before disembarking. The V.C.I. itself carries a 7·62-mm. machine-gun mounted in a small turret on the top right-hand side of the hull, or a heavy 12·7-mm. machine-gun in an open ring mount in the same position. The Dutch Army has mounted the TOW anti-tank launcher in this location on some of its vehicles.

In addition to the French and Dutch armies, the V.C.I. AMX 13 has also been supplied to Argentina, Italy and Belgium (where it has also been built under licence).

The next generation of French Véhicules de Combat d'Infanterie and associated specialist types is represented by the AMX 10P family. This light armoured vehicle, designed by AMX and manufactured by Groupement Industriel des Armements Terrestres (G.I.A.T.) is able to carry out the functions of the AMX 13 series but has a superior all round performance. As an infantry vehicle, the V.C.I. AMX 10P carries only eleven men including the driver and gunner but, unlike the AMX 13 carrier, is fully amphibious, water propulsion being by means of hydro-jets and/or the tracks. The maximum speed on water is nearly 8 km./hr and on roads 65 km./hr. The use of a diesel engine—a Hispano-Suiza Type HS 115, rated at 280-h.p.—helps to give a much greater range of action than the petrol-engined V.C.I. AMX 13—600 km. compared with 400 km. The mounted armament of the AMX 10P consists of a 20-mm. gun and a 7·62-mm. machine-gun contained in a small turret.

The AMX 10P is replacing AMX 13 V.C.I.s in the French Army. Further models in the AMX 10 tracked vehicle range include command, recovery, mortar, 75-mm. gun and HOT anti-tank vehicles, either in production or under development.

10   Obusier Automouvant de 155-mm. AMX 13 and Canon Auto-moteur de 155 mm. GCT, France.

The high cost of modern military equipment means that many armies have two generations of weapons in service simultaneously, and the French 155-mm. self-propelled gun is a case in point.

The 155-mm. gun on the light AMX 13 chassis is classified as 'automouvant' because the crew in action is not fully protected and the weapon can only be fired when the spades at the rear are dug in to help absorb the recoil. The limited space in the vehicle means that only the driver and gun commander can be carried; the remainder of the gun crew and ammunition travel in a supporting vehicle. The gun-howitzer has a maximum range of 21,500 metres on standard ammunition; total traverse is 50 degrees; maximum elevation 67 degrees; and a rate of fire of four rounds per minute can be achieved. Vehicles of this type are in service in Argentina and Venezuela as well as with the French Army.

Although simple and generally effective, weapons of the kind described above are unsatisfactory on a modern battlefield where the ability to seal the vehicle and crew against the effects of nuclear fall out, biological and chemical warfare (N.B.C.) is needed and so development of the 'Canon Auto-moteur de 155 mm. à grande cadence de tir sur chassis AMX 30' (to give it its full title) began in 1970, the first proto-types being ready by early 1973. Apart from the protection against N.B.C. a weapon with longer range and with automatic loading was required, as well as improved vehicle performance.

The adoption of the AMX 30 chassis enables a fully rotating and fully enclosed armoured turret to be used and the automatic loading system enables a rate of fire of eight rounds per minute—double that of the manually served Automouvant de 155—to be achieved.

The 155-mm. gun has a barrel 40 calibres long; range is 23,500 metres; elevation is 66 degrees and depression 5 degrees; and forty-two rounds of ammunition are carried in the vehicle. A machine-gun is carried for the vehicle's close defence, mounted on the turret roof. The crew consists of commander, gunner and loader, who travel in the turret, and driver who occupies the same position as in the AMX 30 tank.

The Canon Automoteur de 155 GCT is gradually replacing in the French Army not only the Automouvants de 155 but also the 105-mm. weapons in AMX 13 chassis.

11 Véhicule de Tir Pluton AMX 30 and Véhicule de Tir Roland AMX 30, France.

The well-tried AMX 30 chassis has been used for the launcher vehicles of both the Pluton tactical nuclear missile system and the Roland anti-aircraft missile system.

The Système d'Arme Pluton is a means of launching and guiding the surface-to-surface Pluton nuclear missile, which weighs 2,400 kg and has a range of 120 kilometres. It has a simplified inertial guidance system and the missile, propelled by a solid fuel rocket motor, can be fitted with warheads ranging between 10 kilotons and 25 kilotons for ground support or interdiction missions.

The Pluton missile, 7·60 metres long, is carried in a launching container, in which it can be elevated and fired, mounted at the rear of a specially modified AMX 30 chassis, carrying a crew of four. The Command vehicle, also on an AMX 30 chassis, carries the data processing equipment centred on the IRIS 35M computer for identifying the target and firing and controlling the missile, as well as radio equipment for communications over long distances.

The first of five French artillery regiments, each equipped with six Pluton missiles and accompanying equipment became operational in 1974.

The Roland Euromissile as it is called, since it has been developed jointly by Germany and France, is a system intended to combat aerial attack, particularly at low levels and carried out at speeds up to Mach 1·3. The system has been developed in two forms—for all-weather use (Roland 2) and for optical guidance only (Roland 1). The German Bundeswehr uses only the Roland 2, whereas the French forces employ both Roland 1 and 2 in a ratio of about 2 to 1. The Roland 1s can, however, be converted within 48 hours to the all-weather type without difficulty, by addition of the tracking and guidance radar.

Mounted on an AMX 30 chassis, the French version of Roland 1 carries a fully rotating turret with a missile launcher each side and containing the Thomson–CST surveillance radar scanner on top.

In operation, the radar locates and identifies (as an enemy) the target, the vehicle commander centres it on the radar screen, whereupon the aimer (crew member) lines up the target when it comes into vision. The commander then, when the target is within range, activates the firing circuit. The aimer fires the missile and tracks this on to the target by keeping it centred in the optical sights, which include an infra-red tracker sensitive to infra-red emissions from the tail of the missile. This information is processed by a computer which passes corrections to the missile by a microwave transmitter: the signals received are converted into changes in course by the jet deflector in the cruise motor.

Two missiles in their container/launchers are normally carried ready for use, and inside the vehicle are two revolving drums, each carrying four reserve missiles from which they can be automatically loaded.

The AMX 30 Roland vehicle weighs 33 tons and has a crew of three—commander/radar operator, gunner and driver.

12 Char Dépanneur–Niveleur AMX 30D and Char AMX30 Poseur de Pont, France.

Two of the specialized vehicles using the chassis of the AMX 30 main battle tank are an armoured recovery vehicle and a bridge layer.

The recovery vehicle, or AMX 30D, has been designed to recover and/or service battle tanks in or near the battlefield and also to help clear the terrain for them, if necessary under fire. This vehicle, then, carries out functions for which, in the British and German armies, for instance, two different types of vehicle would normally be used.

Operated by a crew of four, the AMX 30D is equipped with a turntable-mounted crane, hydraulically operated, with a lift of 13 tons (or 20 tons when in the forward position only, supported by the stabilizer); a winch driven from the tank's main engine with a pull of 35 tons (also an auxiliary winch for lesser tasks with a 4-ton pull); and a front-mounted hydraulically operated bulldozer blade. This is for clearing obstacles, as a ground anchor for use with the winch,

or as a stabilizer if needed when the crane is in use.

One 7·62-mm. machine-gun for local defence is carried, mounted on a cupola like that of the battle tank; this position is occupied by the crew commander. The vehicle weighs 36 tons, except when (as shown in the illustration) a spare AMX 30 engine transmission assembly is carried on a special frame on the rear deck, when the total weight is 40 tons.

The AMX 30 bridge layer carries a 22-metre bridge, capable of spanning gaps of up to 20 metres wide. The bridge is of the scissors type, pivoted at the rear of the vehicle and rests, when folded, on a rectangular structure (armoured against small arms) on top of the hull, which contains the hydraulic operating jack as well as the commander and bridge operator. The third man, the driver, occupies the normal position in AMX 30 tanks in the left-hand side of the glacis plate.

In operation, the vehicle is backed up to the obstacle, two stabilizers are lowered to take the weight and the bridge is raised upwards and over, unfolding at the same time. The bridge trackway is 3·10 metres wide, but can be increased to 3·92 metres with widening panels.

On the road, the AMX 30 bridge layer weighs nearly 43 tons: its bridge can carry tanks up to 40 tons, or in emergency up to 46 tons.

13 Kampfpanzer Leopard, German Federal Republic.

The Leopard was designed, like the French AMX 30, to meet the requirements of a common main battle tank to replace ageing American equipment in the West German, French and Italian armies. Because of lack of agreement between France and Germany on the time scale of replacement as well as technical differences, the two tank projects went their different ways, Italy eventually adapting the German tank.

After preliminary tests beginning in 1961 between prototypes for the Standardpanzer, as it was called, submitted by two German consortia, the type designed under the leadership of Porsche KG was chosen for further development. Numerous changes and extensive evaluation tests of prototypes were carried out and Krauss–Maffei AG of Munich were appointed as main contractors for the production run. The first Leopard I emerged from the factory in September 1965.

Two fundamental features of the Leopard's design are the 105-mm. British L7A1 gun, chosen for its advantages of standardization with other NATO countries as well as its intrinsic merits, and the Daimler–Benz DB838 830-h.p. ten-cylinder diesel engine, which gives the tank an excellent performance. This transmits power to the tracks by means of a single stage torque converter offering four ratios. The maximum speed is 65 km./hr and the rate of acceleration is also very good: a more rare quality in main battle tanks. The suspension consists of seven road-wheels each side, carried on transverse torsion bars.

The Leopard's 105-mm. gun main armament is supplemented by a coaxial 7·62-mm. machine-gun and another mounted on the turret roof. The crew consists of gunner, loader and commander in the turret (where the commander has duplicate basic driving controls for emergency use) and driver, who sits at the right-hand side of the hull near the front.

Further development of the Leopard continued through production of the initial batches, although the first major change in external appearance occurred with the Leopard 1A3 which has a distinctive angular turret of welded construction, compared with the mainly cast pattern of earlier models.

The welded turret is used on subsequent models, including the A4, which has a fully automatic gear-box and an integrated fire control system, and the Leopard II, in which the hull form has been improved and armament changes, including the proposed 120 mm. Rheinmetall smooth-bore gun, experimented with.

Apart from those supplied to the Bundeswehr, Leopards have been ordered by or exported to Belgium, Norway, Holland, Turkey, Canada, Australia and Italy, where they are also being produced under licence.

14 **Schützenpanzer Marder and Flaraketen Panzer Roland,** German Federal Republic.

Following the traditions of the Panzer Grenadiers of World War II, the German Army began to develop an armoured infantry carrier in the 1950s, using both foreign and German-built vehicles.

Some of the earliest of these were French Hotchkiss carriers (Schützenpanzer kurz) and these were followed by a Swiss Hispano-Suiza design (HS-30, known as Schützenpanzer lang—Spz12–3), which for political and other reasons was produced by Leyland Motors in England, as well as by Henschel and Hanomag in Germany, and used a British Rolls-Royce engine. One of the first German post-war designs for an armoured personnel carrier was the Henschel HWK 11 of 1963, which formed part of a family of light armoured vehicles, which were not, however, used by the German Army although a few were exported.

Experience with the operation of the French and Swiss armoured personnel carriers helped to crystallize German ideas on the subject and the specification for an infantry combat vehicle—as A.P.C.s were to be considered—was drawn up in 1959. Mobility at least equal to that of the main battle tank, a good degree of protection, full use of infantry weapons from the vehicle and a mounted cannon were required. After the testing of three series of prototypes from three different manufacturers, a production contract was awarded to Rheinstahl (an organization which now includes the Henschel firm) in 1969. This long period of development has resulted in a very efficient, if somewhat heavy, infantry combat vehicle.

The Schützenpanzer Marder has an MTU six-cylinder diesel engine of 600 h.p., located at the front behind a long sloping glacis plate, with the driver beside it at the left. A turret containing a 20-mm. Rheinmetall cannon and a coaxial 7·62-mm. machine-gun is mounted on a plinth in the centre of the vehicle and the compartment for six infantrymen (in addition to the

driver, commander and two gunners) is at the rear. A ramp for entry and exit is at the back. Full nuclear, biological and chemical warfare protection is provided.

Besides the standard vehicle, there is a mortar-carrier version and the Marder has been adapted to carry the Roland 2 missile system. This anti-aircraft weapon is as described in the section dealing with the French AMX 30 Roland launcher, except that Roland 2, the only version used by the Germans, has the addition of tracking and guidance radar for all-weather operation. The Roland turret, with its two missile launchers is mounted in the position occupied by the 20-mm. turret in the standard Marder. Ten missiles are carried, two of them ready to fire.

15 Flakpanzer 1 Gepard and Pantserrups LUA 35 mm., German Federal Republic/Holland.

For mobile defence of armoured units in the field against low level air attack in all weathers, the German Army has developed and adopted a weapons system based on the 35-mm. Oerlikon gun and the Leopard tank chassis, and a special version of this, using Dutch radar equipment, has also been accepted by the Dutch Army.

The weapons are two 35-mm. automatic Oerlikon cannon with belt feed, mounted on either side of an armoured turret. The rate of fire is 550 rounds per minute per gun. The guns are allied to a surveillance radar system with a range of up to 15 km, which acquires the target (or targets) and then identifies it as friend or foe. The selected target is then transferred to the tracking radar which can hold it without any movement of the turret being necessary. Calculation of the points of impact is carried out by an analog computer, taking account of the attitude of the vehicle, muzzle velocity of the guns and all other relevant factors. The whole system is superior to many others in that it has the ability to switch rapidly from one target to another.

The version of Flakpanzer I being supplied to the Dutch Army (model 5PZF-C A1, known to the Dutch as Pantserrups LuA 35-mm.) differs chiefly from the purely German version in the radar equipment which, although of comparable performance, is manufactured by Hollandse Signaalapparaten (HSA) on the one hand and Siemens AG on the other. Externally, the Dutch radar system is distinguished by the search radar antenna of cylindrical appearance, while that of the German is rectangular and bowl-shaped. In both types the scanner can be folded for travelling.

The Flakpanzer is operated by a crew of three—commander, gunner and driver. Mechanically, the chassis is closely similar to that of the Leopard battle tank and shares its high degree of mobility.

16 **Kanonenjagdpanzer KJPZ 4-5 and Raketenjagdpanzer RJPZ3,** German Federal Republic.

Among the most effective German weapons of World War II were the Sturmgeschütz series of armoured artillery weapons, both field and anti-tank. A modern equivalent, the Kan-

onenjagdpanzer, was developed in the late 1950s when prototypes from three different manufacturers were ordered, followed by further prototypes from two of the same firms between 1963 and 1964 and yet again up to 1965, when production orders were finally given to the Henschel and Hanomag companies.

The KHpz 4-5 has a low, fully enclosed hull with a 90-mm. gun mounted in the front of the glacis plate, where it has a traverse of 30 degrees (15 degrees right and left) and elevation of only 15 degrees, since it is intended primarily for anti-tank use. Weighing 25·7 tons, the vehicle is powered by a Daimler–Benz MB 837 eight-cylinder diesel engine, giving it a maximum speed of 70 km./hr. The German Army received 750 of these vehicles and 80 were ordered for the Belgian Army in 1972. The Belgian vehicles are assembled in Belgium and although externally similar to the German version, have improved fire control equipment, transmission and suspension, using components of the Marder infantry combat vehicle.

The Raketenjagdpanzer 2 uses the same basic hull as the Kanonenjagdpanzer and has the same function—combating armour—but uses the alternative method of guided missiles. Production started in 1967 with a version equipped with two launchers mounted on top of the hull for the French-designed SS-11 missile. Fourteen of these rockets are carried: they have an effective range of 3,000 metres. A later version of the Raketenjagdpanzer, RJPz 3 is equipped to launch the later generation anti-tank missile HOT developed jointly by France and

Germany. This weapon has a range of 4,000 metres. Nineteen missiles are carried and there is a single launcher, mounted on the top left-hand side of the hull. Next to it is a periscope from which the missile is aimed and guided. Conversion from the SS-11 to the HOT system has been planned.

17 Bergepanzer 2 Leopard and Brückenlegepanzer 1, Biber, German Federal Republic.

Like most successful main battle tanks, the Leopard has formed the basis of a range of specialized armoured vehicles, including pioneer, recovery and bridgelayer tanks, and self-propelled mountings.

The armoured recovery vehicle, produced by Atlas–MaK Maschinenbau of Kiel, is basically a Leopard in which the turret has been replaced by a low rectangular superstructure and to which a revolving crane and a bulldozer blade have been added. The crane, mounted at the right-hand side of the hull, has a maximum lift of 20,000 kg and can be traversed through 270 degrees. One of its functions is to transfer a complete spare engine from the Bergepanzer's rear deck, where it can be carried, to a Leopard tank during an engine change (which can be effected in 30 minutes). The dozer blade is for stabilizing the vehicle when the crane is used in the forward arc when raising heavy loads, such as a complete battle tank, as well as in earth-moving operations. The other major item of equipment is a winch with a 35,000 kg pull. Many countries as well as Germany using Leopards have also ordered the Berge-

panzer version. The Pionierpanzer is similar in appearance to the Bergepanzer but its equipment includes additionally an auger, operated from the crane jib, for hole drilling.

Two different types of bridge layer on the Leopard chassis were built for experiment. Both models carried a 22-metre bridge mounted over the hull in two sections, the near half (i.e. when laid) on top of the other (distant) half. In the Type A bridge layer the bridge sections were mounted on a pivoted beam, the front of which could be extended over the gap. The bridge, the two halves joined, was then pushed forward along this beam for laying.

In the Type B Bridge Layer the lower (distant) half of the bridge was moved forward from under the upper (near) half to make the complete span, the front of the vehicle being supported on a stabilizing blade. The bridge was then fully extended from a carrying arm in front of the vehicle and laid.

The Type B was chosen for production and entered service with the Bundeswehr in 1973; it is known as Biber (Beaver).

18 Self-Propelled 160-mm. Mortar and Self-Propelled 155-mm. Gun/Howitzer, Israel.

Israel has, through economic necessity, had to get the maximum use out of the military resources available but the country's armaments industry has, nevertheless, managed to produce some effective weapons through the modification of obsolete or obsolescent chassis.

The two vehicles described here are

virtually new designs, although both use the lower hull and running gear of the World War II U.S. M-4A3E8 Medium Tank—Sherman. The armament in both cases is a weapon designed by the Finnish company Tampella and produced under licence by Soltam in Israel.

The self-propelled mounting for the 160-mm. mortar has the weapon mounted with the barrel projecting over the front plate of the hull, which has been increased in height over that of the original M-4A3E8 tank by means of light armour plate. In action, the side and front plates can be folded down to enable the crew to serve the weapon, which has a high rate of fire and a range of 9,600 metres.

The second and more important Israeli S.P. weapon on the M-4A3E8 chassis is the 155-mm. gun/howitzer, which saw action in the October 1973 war. Mounted inside a fixed, welded armour plate casemate with an enclosed roof, the M-68 gun has a barrel 33 calibres long. It has a range of about 20,500 metres and the semi-automatic breech mechanism and pneumatic rammer enables a good rate of fire to be achieved for a weapon of this size. This is four to five rounds per minute for short periods and two rounds per minute for up to one hour. For indirect fire—the normal mode of operation—a panoramic telescope is fitted, together with a normal telescope for direct fire against tanks, for example. Maximum elevation of the guns is 52 degrees, depression 3 degrees and total traverse 60 degrees.

Sixty rounds of ammunition are carried and the vehicle weighs 41·5 tons. One 7·62-mm. machine-gun is carried on the hull roof for defence against ground or air attack. On some vehicles this is mounted in a rotating cupola.

A further version of the 155-mm. gun/howitzer is mounted in a turret with 360 degrees traverse on the British Centurion hull or, alternatively, on American M-47, M-48 or M-60 hulls. This version uses a longer, 39-calibre barrel, which gives it a range of 23,500 metres.

19 **Tank, Type 61, 90-mm. Gun and Tank, Type 74, 105-mm. gun,** Japan.

The Type 61 Main Battle Tank's design was commenced in 1954 when the Japanese Self Defence Force was still almost exclusively equipped with American armoured vehicles, and the layout and general appearance of this tank shows the influence the United States M-47/M-48 tanks had on the Japanese designers.

Sixteen prototypes were built, of which the first pattern (STA-1), ready by early 1957, was lower and more compact than the final version, STA-4, which was standardized in 1961 for production.

The Type 61's gun is a 90-mm. weapon, built in Japan but similar in appearance and performance to that of the American M-48 series with the distinctive transverse tube muzzle brake. This is accompanied by a coaxial 7·62-mm. machine-gun, and a heavy 12·7-mm. machine-gun is mounted on the commander's turret hatch.

With a crew of four and weighing

35 tons, the Type 61 follows the long tradition in Japanese tanks of using an air-cooled diesel engine. This is a twelve-cylinder V unit built by Mitsubishi developing 600 h.p., which gives a maximum road speed of 45 km./hr.

Some 450 Type 61 Main Battle Tanks are estimated to be in service with the Japanese Self Defence Force.

The design of the Type 74 Main Battle Tank makes full use of the fact that the average Japanese soldier is less tall than his Western counterpart and so this tank is much lower and more compact than all other turreted main battle tanks, with the advantage of offering a smaller target and making concealment easier. This asset is further increased by the hydropneumatic suspension system, whereby the ground clearance can be adjusted from 60 cm down to 20 cm.

Designated STB, several different prototype versions were built, of which the first two vehicles, known as STB-1, were completed in September 1969. STB-1 featured a semi-automatic loading system for the British-designed 105-mm. L6 gun, although this feature was dropped in later prototypes on grounds of economy. The last prototype, STB-6, was finished in 1973 and this model incorporated all the final features of the Type 74 Main Battle Tank, production of the first 280 of which had already commenced in 1972 at the Tokyo Machinery works of Mitsubishi Heavy Industries.

The Type 74 uses a compact two-stroke ten-cylinder V-form diesel engine, developing 750 h.p. The maximum road speed is 53 km./hr, but the vehicle's overall mobility has been considered to be of the greatest importance. The hydropneumatic suspension enables a good cross-country performance to be sustained with the minimum crew fatigue, and water up to a depth of 1 metre can be forded without preparation. Complete submersibility is possible with the use of 'schnorkel' tubes for the engine exhaust and the tank commander.

Full stabilization for the 105-mm. gun is fitted and the weapon is controlled by a laser range-finder together with a ballistic computer, so increasing the probability of a first-shot hit on the target. Two machine-guns are carried: one 7·62 mm., coaxial with the main gun, and a 12·7-mm. anti-aircraft weapon mounted on the turret. There are also six launchers (three either side of the turret) for smoke or anti-personnel grenades, and the crew are protected against nuclear fall-out and biological and chemical warfare.

20 **Armoured Personnel Carrier, Type 60, and Armoured Personnel Carrier, Type 73,** Japan.

Among the earliest vehicles to be developed in Japan for the Japanese Self-Defence Force to replace American equipment were a range of armoured carriers: what might be called the 'standard' vehicle of the earlier series (although not the first to be developed) is the Type 60 Armoured Personnel Carrier.

Prototypes known as SU-1 and SU-2 were submitted by Komatsu and Mitsubishi respectively in 1957. The Mitsubishi vehicle was selected for further development and eventually went into production by Mitsubishi Heavy Industries and entered service as the Type 60 Armoured Personnel Carrier.

Fully enclosed and carrying eight men in addition to the crew of two, the Type 60 has an eight-cylinder diesel engine of 220 h.p. which gives it a maximum speed of 45 km./hr. A fixed armament of one 7·62-mm. machine-gun in a ball mount in the front glacis plate and a 12·7-mm. machine-gun on a ring mounting is carried.

The successor to the Type 60 is the Type 73 Armoured Personnel Carrier, which has the performance required of an infantry combat vehicle of the 1970s. Also designed and produced by Mitsubishi Heavy Industries, this vehicle makes use of aluminium armour so, although larger, with capacity for ten men in addition to the crew of two, and with a much better performance than the Type 60, it is only about 2 tons heavier.

A maximum road speed of 60 km./hr can be attained, powered by the air-cooled 300-h.p. two stroke diesel engine, which also propels the vehicle by its tracks in water. The Type 73 has full nuclear fallout, biological and chemical warfare protection and has infra-red equipment for night driving and combat. The armament consists of a ball-mounted 7·62-mm. machine-gun in the front glacis plate and a heavy, 12·7-mm. machine-gun mounted on the right-hand side of the hull roof, either in a turret or in an open ring mounting.

Type 73s are gradually replacing the Type 60s in infantry regiments of the Japanese Self-Defence Forces.

21 **Self-Propelled 106-mm. Recoilless Gun, Type 60, and 4.2-in. Mortar Carriage, Type 60,** Japan.

The first armoured vehicle developed for the Japanese Self-Defence Force was, appropriately, a self-propelled anti-tank weapon. Design work of the vehicle—the model SS—commenced in 1954; prototypes were submitted by Komatsu and Mitsubishi (SS-1 and SS-2 respectively) and after trials and some fusion of ideas further prototypes (SS-3 and SS-4) were built. The contract for the standardized vehicle, the Self-Propelled 106-mm. Recoilless Gun, Type 60, was awarded to the Komatsu company.

An interesting vehicle that has few parallels in other armies, other than the U.S. M-50 Ontos (now obsolete) and some experimental vehicles, the Type 60 is a small self-propelled mounting for two 106-mm. recoilless guns. These weapons are mounted on the right-hand side of the vehicle, with the crew at the left—the commander and loader behind the driver. The guns, in their mounting, can be raised, together with the commander's cupola, in which position they have a traverse of 30 degrees right and 30 degrees left of centre. They are breech loaded and a rate of fire of six rounds per minute can be achieved, although the projectiles are bulky and only ten are carried. The guns can also be fired from the low position, although the traverse is then limited to 10 degrees left and 10 degrees right. In this configuration, the vehicle is only 1·38 metres high and very inconspicuous, although in action this asset is offset by the prominent back-blast of the recoilless guns.

The thin-tubed guns are rifled and fire hollow charge anti-tank and high explosive rounds. The effective range is 1,100 metres and ranging is by means of a 12·7-mm. heavy machine-gun controlled by a range-finder and optical sight.

An air-cooled six-cylinder diesel engine of 120 h.p. mounted at the rear gives the Type 60 SPRG a maximum speed of 48 km./hr.

A specialized development of the Type 60 Armoured Personnel Carrier (described separately), the 4·2-in. Mortar Carriage, Type 60 (model SX), is closely similar to it, and uses the same engine, transmission and running gear and even the hull, apart from the rear portion, is basically the same.

At the rear of the mortar carrier is the compartment containing the 4·2-in. (107-mm.) mortar, from which it can be fired. For travelling, the roof of this compartment is covered by upward- and sideways-opening hatches.

For its own protection, the Mortar Carriage carries a 12·7-mm. machine-gun on the roof although, unlike the Type 60 Armoured Personnel Carrier, the machine-gun on the glacis plate has been eliminated.

22 Armoured Vehicle Launched Bridge, Type 67, and Self-Propelled 155-mm. Gun (HSP), Japan.

For the usual reasons of economy and rationalization, Japan has produced a range of support vehicles using the same chassis as, or many components of, current main battle tanks. These include armoured recovery and armoured engineer vehicles as well as the bridge layer and S.P. gun described here.

The bridge layer uses a turretless Type 61 battle-tank chassis with relatively slight modification. The bridge (some 12–13 metres long when extended) is of the scissors type, first introduced by the British during World War II. The laying process is similar to that of the U.S. M-60 AVLB: the folded bridge is raised, the weight taken up by a stabilizer in front of the tank, and then opened out and placed over the gap.

American-built self-propelled guns formed the first equipment of the post-war Japanese Self-Defence Force and in the 1950s there was a Japanese experimental S.P. 105-mm. howitzer which did not enter production. The model HSP is entirely Japanese in design—both vehicle and gun—although, like other S.P. guns of its class, it shares a general layout in common with the widely used American M-109 155-mm. S.P. gun.

Mounted in a fully enclosed turret at the rear of the vehicle, with 360 degrees traverse, the 155-mm. gun has an elevation of 65 degrees and depression of 5 degrees. This arrangement requires forward placing of the 420-h.p. two-stroke diesel engine and, although the same tracks, elements of the running gear and hull components of the Type 74 Main Battle Tank have been employed, the transmission is through front track sprockets. This is the reverse of that in the Type 74, although, more unusually for a modern Main Battle Tank, the earlier Japanese Type 61 used front drive. A heavy (12·7-mm.) machine-gun is mounted on the turret roof for the vehicle's defence.

Weighing 24 tons, the 155-mm. S.P. gun has a maximum road speed of 50 km./hr. The crew consists of six men, all of whom are in the turret except the driver, who is at the right-hand side of the hull in front of the turret.

The S.P. gun has been developed by by Japanese Ministry of Defence in conjunction with Mitsubishi Heavy Industries, by whom it is built, at their Tokyo Machinery Works.

23 T-72 (Main Battle Tank), Soviet Union.

Few details of the latest Soviet main battle tank have been made available despite the fact that over 800 are in service in East Germany and that over 2,000 are estimated to have been produced. Even the designation, variously reported as T-64 or T-72 (although more likely to be the latter) is not known with certainty at the time of writing.

An experimental tank, known as T-70, followed the T-62 and appears to have been used to test out ideas to be used in the definitive successor to the T-62. The T-70 has a 115-mm. gun, like that of T-62, but with the addition, it is believed, of an automatic loading device. The calibre of the T-72's very long gun is, however, between 122 mm. and 125 mm. and it fires fin-stabilized rounds. The small cast turret with near-vertical sides would seem to confirm reports that the gun has automatic loading, with four rounds ready for use and twenty-eight more in the loader. There is the usual 7·62-mm. coaxial machine-gun and a 12·7-mm. machine-gun on the commander's cupola.

A crew of only three is carried— driver, gunner and commander. The latter is at the right-hand side of the turret (contrary to earlier Soviet practice), the gunner at the left and the driver in the centre of the hull, just in front of the turret.

The suspension of the T-72 consists of six road-wheels each side, smaller than those of T-62, with track return rollers. The engine is thought to be a diesel of around 900–1,000-h.p. to give a maximum road speed, in the vehicle of around 40 tons, of 60 km./hr.

24 T-62, (Main Battle Tank), Soviet Union.

A further step in the systematic evolution of the Soviet main battle tank, the T-62 retains many of the main characteristics of the T-54/T-55 series, although it has a 115-mm. calibre gun for only a relatively slight increase in weight and overall dimensions.

The 115-mm. gun is a high velocity smooth-bore weapon, firing fin-stabilized projectiles, of which forty are carried, including high explosive as well as armour-piercing rounds. The gun is fully stabilized in both vertical and horizontal planes. The larger gun requires a larger turret ring than that of T-55 and this has led to an increase in width of just over a quarter of a metre and in length of just over half a metre, although the height (to turret top) has been kept down to the 2·4 metres of the earlier tank.

A twelve-cylinder V water-cooled diesel engine developing 700 h.p. is used in the T-62, which gives the same maximum speed as the T-55 of 50 km./hr, with probably an improved overall performance.

First seen in public in 1965, the T-62 has been built in large numbers and supplied to the Soviet Union and Warsaw Pact armies to supplement or replace T-54s and T-55s. It has also been provided for a number of African and Middle East Countries and is likely, in time, to replace earlier Soviet tanks at present employed by many other armies.

25 T-55 (Main Battle Tank), Soviet Union.

Although made obsolescent by further advances in design, the T-55 is still an effective fighting vehicle, and the sheer numbers of this tank still in service make it an important one.

Derived from the famous T-34 of World War II, through the interim models T-44 and T-54, which it closely resembles, the T-55 was first shown publicly in 1961 and possibly entered service a year or so earlier. The T-54, which first began to come off the production lines some twelve years before T-55, has been progressively improved through several models but the final changes in the basic design which resulted in the T-55 were principally in the engine and transmission and the gun stabilization equipment.

The power plant of the T-55 is an improved model twelve-cylinder V water-cooled diesel, developing 580 h.p. (compared with T-54's 520 h.p.), resulting in a slightly better performance. The transmission has been improved to match the increased output

and the fuel capacity has been raised to give a 25 per cent. better radius of operation. The T-54 (except for the earliest models) had the 100-mm. gun stabilized in elevation/depression only, but T-55 has stabilization in both vertical and horizontal planes, making accurate shooting on the move easier. The ammunition supply has been increased by nine rounds.

The layout of the T-54/T-55 series is fairly conventional for modern main battle tanks, with the engine and transmission at the rear of the hull (with rear track drive sprockets), the driver at the front left-hand side and the fighting compartment and turret, containing commander, gunner and loader, in the centre. The suspension consists of five largish road-wheels each side, carried on transverse torsion bars.

Common to both T-54 and T-55 is the armament of a 100-mm. gun with coaxial 7·62-mm. machine-gun and another fixed machine-gun (fired by the driver) in the front of the hull. The latter has, however, been omitted from the final models of T-55.

The turret of the T-55 has been evolved from that of T-54, which has a ventilation dome near the front of the roof and originally had cupolas for the loader as well as the commander. Late model T-54s have one cupola only—like the T-55, which also has no turret ventilator dome. An anti-aircraft machine-gun is carried on some, but not all, models of both T-54 and T-55.

A compact and reliable tank, the T-55, together with the T-54, has been produced in large quantities in the Soviet Union (and possibly also in Poland and Czechoslovakia) and supplied to over two dozen countries in addition to being used by the Warsaw Pact armies.

26 PT-76, Amphibious Tank, and ASU-85, Airborne Assault Gun, Soviet Union.

The PT-76 (PT = Plavayushchiy Tank, or amphibious tank) is a reconnaissance tank, air-portable and amphibious, that first appeared about 1950. Since then it has been supplied to some twenty countries outside the Soviet Union and is still widely used.

Weighing 14 tons, the PT-76 has full amphibious capability, the only preparation needed being the erection of a trim board, which is hinged at the junction of the glacis plate and the nose plate. In water, the tank is propelled by twin hydro-jets, the outlets for which are in the rear vertical plate of the hull. The hydro-jets are operated by a pump driven from the main engine. Steering in water is by means of the hydro-jets in conjunction with two extra vents, one on either side of the hull, towards the rear above the track guards. Ten km./hr can be attained in smooth water: on land the maximum road speed is 44 km./hr.

The driver in the PT-76 occupies a central position in the hull just forward of the turret. He is provided with three periscopes for closed-down vision on land and an extra extendable periscope for use on water, to enable him to see over the raised trim board. The commander and gunner are in the turret, which is set well towards the front of the vehicle and contains the armament of one 76·2-mm. gun and, coaxial with it, one 7·62-mm. machine-gun. Only on the final version of the PT-76 is the 76-mm. gun fully stabilized. The PT-76's engine is at the rear: it is a six-cylinder in-line water-cooled diesel of 240 h.p. and the drive is to rear track sprockets. The suspension consists of six medium-sized road-wheels carried on torsion bars.

A Polish-used PT-76 is shown in the illustration.

Successor to the much smaller and less powerful ASU-57, the ASU-85—which appeared in public for the first time in 1962—is the principal Soviet airborne assault vehicle. Based on the chassis of the PT-76 tank, the ASU-85 has the same engine, transmission and running gear and is approximately the same weight. It is not amphibious, however, and the hull form has been adapted to its different role as an assault gun and tank destroyer. The 85-mm. gun (which fires high explosive as well as armour-piercing rounds) is located just left of centre of the long-sloping glacis plate, where it has a total traverse of 12 degrees, elevation of 15 degrees and, like many Soviet A.F.V.s, a very limited depression of 4 degrees. The driver is to the right of the gun, the other three crew members (commander, gunner and loader) behind, and the engine at the rear.

Only 2·1 metres high, the ASU-85 can be transported by air and also parachute dropped. The illustration shows an ASU-85 bearing typical Soviet Airborne forces markings.

27 BMP-1, Infantry Combat Vehicle, and BMD, Airborne Combat Vehicle, Soviet Union.

The BMP-1 belongs to the second generation of armoured personnel carriers from which the infantry carried can use their small arms and have turret-mounted weapons effective against armour.

Perhaps one of the best vehicles of its kind in service, the BMP-1 is highly mobile, fully amphibious without preparation and has a low profile although (as in many Soviet A.F.V.s), this is to some extent at the expense of crew comfort. Built of light alloy armour and weighing only 12·5 tons (only half that of the German Marder), the BMP-1 has a crew of three and can carry eight infantrymen. The engine, a six-cylinder water-cooled diesel developing 280 h.p., is located at the front and can produce a maximum road speed of 55 km./hr, or 8 km./hr in water, when propulsion is by means of the tracks. Many components of the BMP-1 are in common with the PT-76 tank.

The mounted armament consists of a 73-mm. smooth-bore gun with automatic loading, firing fin-stabilized anti-tank or high explosive rounds, and a 7·62-mm. machine-gun in the turret and a launcher for the 'Sagger' (NATO name) anti-tank guided rocket on brackets, over the 73-mm. gun. Both gun and 'Sagger' are capable of penetrating heavy armour, the latter at longer ranges up to 3,000 metres.

The BMP-1 is in service with the major Warsaw Pact countries as well as several Arab countries. An East German vehicle is shown in the illustration.

Although the BMD (Boyevaya Mashina Desantnaya) looks like a miniature version of the BMP-1 it was, in fact, designed for a wider role with the airborne forces—as a light tank for mobile fire support and protection against enemy armour, as well as to carry a limited number of infantry. Weighing around 8·5 tons, this little vehicle is some 5·3 metres long and is only lightly armoured, but carries the same offensive armament as the BMP-1. In addition to the crew of three, up to six infantrymen can be carried—in very cramped accommodation. The vehicle shown is carrying the markings of the Soviet Airborne Forces as it appeared in a parade in Moscow.

28 ZSU-57-2, Anti-Aircraft S.P. Gun, and ZSU-23-4, Anti-Aircraft S.P. Gun, Soviet Union.

The Soviet Union, like other countries, has turned from guns to mobile missile systems to combat medium- to high-flying aircraft, while adhering to multiple quick-firing small-calibre cannon, usually radar controlled, to protect armoured columns from fast, low-flying machines.

The ZSU-57-2 is one of the older generation of S.P. A.A. guns, although it is still in service with fifteen countries, albeit probably only in second-line employment in the Soviet Union itself and its principal allies. Consisting of two 57-mm. guns in an open-topped turret on a shortened T-54 tank chassis, this vehicle was first shown to the public in 1957. The guns have an elevation of 85 degrees, and an effective range of 4,000 metres against aerial targets, although they are also usable against armoured vehicles or personnel, with appropriate ammunition. The commander and the four members of the gun crew are in the turret and the driver is situated at the left front of the hull. The engine is the same as that of the T-54 battle tank and the suspension and running gear is similar, but with one less road-wheel each side. The maximum road speed of the ZSU-57-2 is the same as the T-54's but the reduced weight of 28 tons results in a generally better overall performance.

As used by the Soviet Army, the ZSU-57-2 is a purely visual weapon and does not appear to have been updated by the addition of radar, although some of the other user countries may have done so.

The ZSU-23-4 on the other hand is fully operational in a wide range of visual and climatic conditions, being equipped with radar for both target acquisition and fire control, as well as normal optical sights. The quadruple 23-mm. cannon have a high rate of fire of up to 1,000 rounds per minute for each gun, although for normal use the rate is about 200 rounds per minute. The effective range against aircraft is up to about 2,500 metres. The radar can acquire targets up to 20 km. distant and the system enables the cannon to be armed and fired while the vehicle is moving.

The ZSU-23-4's layout and crew locations is roughly similar to that of the ZSU-57-2. The lower chassis and running gear is practically identical to the PT-76's and the engine and transmission are believed to be the same. The performance is also like that of the PT-76, although the ZSU-23-4 is not amphibious.

In service with about as many different countries as the ZSU-57-2, the ZSU-23-4 is replacing the earlier self-propelled weapon in the front line units of the major Warsaw Pact armies.

29 SU-122, Self-Propelled Gun, Soviet Union.

A comparatively late addition to the armoury of the Warsaw Pact nations, this armoured self-propelled field artillery piece was first shown in public in 1974, development having taken place over several years before this. The 122-mm. self-propelled mounting with a revolving turret is an innovation, as far as Soviet equipment is concerned—all earlier such guns having been in fixed mountings—but has a similar configuration to the American M-109, which may have inspired its design. There is also a 152-mm. howitzer mounting on a somewhat similar chassis.

Few details are available, but the suspension is similar to that of the Ganef missile carrier which, in turn, is derived from that of the PT-76 family. The engine of the SU-122 is at the front with the driver alongside it at the left. The turret, containing the commander and gun crew is at the rear; a position to facilitate loading of ammunition etc.

Both illustrations show vehicles of the Polish Army, one of the users of the SU-122.

30 SA.6 Gainful, Anti-Aircraft Missile Carrier, and Straight Flush, Armoured Fire Control Vehicle, Soviet Union.

The Surface to Air (SA) system known by the NATO code name of Gainful or SA-6 is a highly mobile and flexible weapon that has been given the credit for destroying over one-third of the

Israeli aircraft lost in the 1973 Arab–Israeli war.

A medium-range anti-aircraft weapon (the SA-4 Ganef covering greater ranges up to 70 km. and the SA-7 Grail (a hand-held or vehicle-mounted launcher) and ZSU-23-4 dealing with short distance and close up aircraft) intended for dealing with attacking aircraft at ranges between about 5 km. and 30 km., the Gainful consists of three rockets mounted on a fully rotating turntable carried on a chassis derived from that of the PT-76 tank.

The SA-6 is a 6·2 metres long, single-stage missile, launched by a solid fuel rocket engine and propelled in cruise (at approximately Mach 2·5) by a liquid fuel ram jet. Its warhead is of the high explosive fragmentation type. The command guidance system is in the centre section and there are receiver antennae and beacons on the tips of the two rear fins.

The carrier vehicle has the automotive characteristics and general performance (although it is not amphibious) of the PT-76, on which it is based.

The Gainful system has been supplied by the Soviet Union to other Warsaw Pact armies as well as those of several other countries, including Egypt and Syria. The illustration shows a vehicle in Egyptian colours: the supports for travelling under the forward part of the rockets have been lowered and the missiles have been elevated about 5 degrees in the first stage of preparation for action.

The Straight Flush (NATO name) fire control vehicle used in conjunction with the Gainful system has a similar chassis to that of the missile carrier. The target-tracking radar and the target acquisition radar are both mounted on a pedestal in the centre of the vehicle, the tracking radar on top. In action, the Straight Flush would usually receive the target information from a long-range radar (such as Flat Face (NATO name), mounted on a truck) and by means of its acquisition radar, after pinpointing it and identifying it as friend or foe, pass it to the tracking radar to lock the system on to the target so that a missile can be launched.

31 **Frog 5, Missile Carrier, and SA-4 Ganef, Anti-Aircraft Missile Carrier,** Soviet Union.

FROG is the NATO name for the Soviet battle-field support rocket, or Free Rocket over Ground. A tactical surface-to-surface (SS) weapon, Frog 5 is the final type of its series to have a tracked carrier-launcher, the later models being transported on eight-wheeled high-mobility trucks.

The earliest model, Frog 1, was mounted on a JS-3 tank chassis, but Frog 2 (first seen in 1957), Frog 3, Frog 4 and Frog 5 have all used a chassis based on that of the PT-76 reconnaissance tank, although differing from it in many ways. The Frog 2's chassis was the closest to its parent vehicle's design but later models have had track support rollers added, and a lowered front idler, as well as a different pattern of road-wheels. The engine and transmission are similar to that of PT-76 and Frog's performance (excluding amphibious capability) is still roughly comparable to that of the reconnaissance tank.

In all the tracked Frog series, the rocket is carried over the vehicle's hull, in a girder-structure launcher, pivoted towards the rear, with a bracket on the glacis plate for support when travelling.

The unguided artillery rockets are estimated to have ranges between about 20 and 50 km., according to model. They are of the two-stage solid propellant type (except for Frog 2, which was single stage) and can be fitted with nuclear, high explosive, chemical or bacteriological warheads. In length they range from about 10·5 metres for Frog 3 and 4 down to about 9·5 metres for Frog 5. The later type, Frog 7, is even shorter, but of increased diameter. The crew of the Frog 5 missile launcher and its carrier is three to four men.

The self-propelled anti-aircraft missile system bearing the NATO code name of Ganef, SA-4 or SAM-4 (Surface-to-Air-Missile) was first shown to the public in Moscow in 1964. Two missiles on a launcher are carried over the hull of a special tracked vehicle. This vehicle is unlike any other known earlier tank or armoured vehicle and, with engine and transmission concentrated at the front, leaving the rear end clear for the launching equipment, may have been specially designed for its task. It is air-portable.

The Ganef missile is about 9 metres long and is propelled by an internal ram jet after being lifted off by the four solid propellant boosters, mounted externally. It is operated in conjunction with a scanning radar, and the Pat Hand (NATO name) target acquisition and fire control radar are carried in separate vehicles. The system is intended for medium- to long-range targets up to about 70 km.

32 SS-14 Scamp (Scapegoat) and SS-15 (Scrooge), Strategic Missile Carriers, Soviet Union.

These monstrous Soviet long-range ballistic missiles are both carried on tracked chassis, although later carriers for this kind of weapon seem likely to be heavy wheeled vehicles.

The SS-14 missile is carried in a cylindrical container mounted on the carrier vehicle. Preparatory to launching, the container is raised hydraulically and placed in the vertical position on a launch pad lowered from the rear of the vehicle. The container is then opened, and moved away, leaving the missile ready for launching. An intermediate range missile with a nuclear warhead, the SS-14 is about 10·7 metres long, is propelled by a solid fuel rocket, and has an estimated range of 3,500 km.

The SS-15 intercontinental ballistic missile, which is about 18·3 metres long, is carried on the vehicle in a tube, from which its nuclear warhead projects. Erected in a similar way to the SS-14, the SS-15 is believed to be fired direct from the carrying tube. Propelled by a solid fuel rocket, it has a range believed to be about 5,600 km.

The carrier vehicles Scamp for the SS-14 or Scapegoat system and Scrooge for the SS-15 (all names and designations are those given by NATO, since the Soviet nomenclature has not been made public) are similar to each other mechanically, although the missile erecting systems differ in detail, and the very much longer and heavier SS-15 missile needs extra supporting brackets, which project from the front hull of its carrier. In both vehicles, the running gear is made up from components of the JS-III tank or, more likely, its later derivative the T-10 heavy tank. The carriers have eight smallish road-wheels each side (JS-III had six, T-10 had seven) sprung on torsion bars. The long upper track run is supported on five track rollers each side, unevenly spaced. Power transmission is via rear track sprockets and the engine is assumed to be a V-12 cylinder diesel similar to that of T-10, developing 700 h.p. In both types of vehicle the crew travel in a superstructure at the extreme front, which is unarmoured or only lightly armoured.

33 T-54/MTU, Tank Bridge Layer, and T-54/PT, Tank Mine Clearer, Soviet Union.

Relatively little use was made of specialized armoured vehicles—such as the range developed by the British Army—by the Soviet Union in World War II. The Russian Commanders were reputedly prepared to sacrifice if necessary a whole tank battalion to clear a minefield by the quick but costly method of sending the tanks straight across it. Since 1945, however, a variety of attachments and modified Soviet tanks for special tasks have appeared. It is perhaps significant that some of these vehicles have been developed in the Warsaw Pact countries, such as Czechoslovakia and the German Democratic Republic. Bulldozer and snowplough blades can be fitted to standard main battle tanks with slight modification and armoured recovery vehicles (including several models designed in the G.D.R.) are based on turretless T-54 or T-55 tanks.

The standard Soviet tank bridge layers all use T-54 or T-55 chassis (which, being turretless, are not readily distinguishable from each other) although T-62 chassis are likely to follow in the same role. One of the most widely employed versions of the MTU, or Mostoukladtschik Tankowje Ustrojstwo, is the T-54/MTU shown in one illustration. This vehicle carries a bridge with a span of 12 metres. A single rigid lattice structure, the bridge is supported on brackets over the hull of the tank. The front brackets project some 2–3 metres in front of the vehicle and the bridge is pushed forward over these supports when being launched.

Another type of bridge layer has a box-construction type of bridge carried in a similar way, but the two shorter end sections are folded over the main sections for transport. Opened out, the bridge has a span of about 19 metres: it is launched in a similar way to the type described above, but a stabilizing spade, mounted at the front of the tank is needed to take the much greater weight at launching.

A third type of bridge layer, developed in Czechoslovakia, has a bridge of about 18 metres. This is carried folded and is of the 'scissors' type, opening out for launching when the front supporting bracket is lowered to the ground to act as a stabilizer.

Both plough and roller devices for mine clearing are employed by the Warsaw Pact countries. A Czech-designed plough for use with T-54 or

T-55 tanks has a plough blade, capable of uprooting and turning aside mines in the vehicle's path. There are several patterns of anti-mine rollers in use, of both Soviet and Czechoslovakian design. The T-54/PT (Protivo Tankoviy) shown in the illustration, has two heavy spiked rollers, towed behind a frame projecting in front of the tank. Each roller is made up of three pinion wheels, side by side, and can roll a lane wider than the tank's tracks. It weight should be sufficient to detonate any normal anti-tank mine.

34 **Stridsvagn Strv. 103B**, Sweden.

Credit for the most completely original approach to the design of a modern main battle tank must be given to Sweden for the S-tank, or Stridsvagn 103 as it is known in service.

Three important—and often conflicting—criteria to be taken into account in a battle tank are an effective gun (in which the possibility of a first time hit on an enemy tank and a good rate of fire are highly important); the maximum practicable degree of protection (and overall size, minimizing the target offered, is relevant here); and mobility—notably speed in traversing the battlefield, changing position and, not least, getting out of action quickly when necessary.

These criteria have been met in a tank having the unusual combination of a low turretless hull with an automatically loaded, rigidly mounted gun, traversed and elevated by movements of the vehicle itself. Motive power is provided by the combination of a diesel engine with a gas turbine engine.

Independent experiments were conducted from the 1950s onwards with a range of different chassis, to test the viability of systems for elevating a gun by altering the attitude of the hull in which it was mounted; for means of traversing a tank chassis to a fine degree for gun aiming in the horizontal plane; and automatic loading systems to take advantage of a gun fixed in relation to the tank hull. Before the actual S-tank prototypes were built, test rigs for a hydro-pneumatic suspension and steering system were constructed.

The firm of AB Bofors was entrusted with the design of the new tank, in conjunction with the Swedish Army Ordnance tank design section. The first prototype, which appeared in 1961, contained all the essentials of the new design. A low compact vehicle, the gun —a 105-mm. weapon of British design but built in Sweden with an increased barrel length of 62 calibres—projects from the centre of a long sloping glacis plate. There are four roadwheels each side (these are of the Centurion type, to simplify spares problems), rear idler wheel and front driving sprocket. The two engines and transmission are under the glacis plate with the crew behind them, either side of the gun—the driver and radio operator back-to-back on the left and the commander on the right. The radio operator is provided with a basic set of driving controls to enable him to drive the tank backwards in emergency. Commander and driver both have a set of driving and gun controls (which are integrated) so either can drive the tank and fire the gun or exchange roles in case of necessity. The automatic loading equipment is at the rear of the tank where it can readily be reloaded through two hatches in the rear plate. The automatically loaded gun can achieve a rate of fire of fifteen rounds per minute—about twice that of a manually served gun of the same calibre. Fifty rounds are carried. The secondary armament consists of two fixed 7·62-mm. machine-guns located in an armoured box on the left side of the glacis plate, and there is also a machine-gun mounted externally on the commander's cupola.

The idea of a dual diesel and gas turbine engine system was derived from warship design where the diesel is used for cruising, with the gas turbine there to provide supplementary bursts of power for short periods when needed. In a tank the extra advantage of an alternative source of power, should one engine or the other be knocked out or fail in an emergency, is even more marked and, in Swedish winter conditions, the use of a gas turbine to start the diesel in low temperatures is an added advantage. The S-tank's diesel engine is the six-cylinder Rolls-Royce K-60 of 240 h.p. and the gas turbine was originally the Boeing 502-10MA of 330 h.p. on the Strv.-103 Type A, all of which have now been replaced by the Boeing 553 of 490 h.p. (produced in Belgium by F.N. under licence). Tanks with the 490-h.p. gas turbine are designated Strv. 103B. A maximum speed of 50 km./hr can be achieved.

A bulldozer blade to help the tank dig itself in can easily be added to the nose plate, and a flotation screen for swimming is carried folded in an armoured trough round the hull sides.

The S-tank is in service only with the Swedish Army. Some 300 have been built and although it has also been tested by other armies (perhaps because its design is so revolutionary), it has not so far been adopted elsewhere.

35 Infanterikanonvagn Ikv-91, Sweden.

Although having many of the characteristics of a light reconnaissance tank, the Ikv-91 has been specifically designed for infantry support—a role previously filled in Swedish service by vehicles of the German Sturmgesschütz variety. However, complete rethinking by the Swedish Army of its requirements for armoured fighting vehicles has resulted in a vehicle which can, in fact, carry out a much more versatile role than its immediate predecessors.

A design by AB Hägglund & Söner was chosen from among fourteen submitted and the first of three prototypes was completed by the end of 1969. Development proceeded fairly rapidly, so that the first production vehicles began to be delivered to the Swedish Army in 1975.

As the ability to operate in the difficult forest and lake country of north Sweden was required, amphibious capability without preparation was called for in the Ikv-91. This has been achieved by the adoption of a relatively wide and roomy hull in a vehicle weighing only 15·5 tons. Armour is necessarily light, but the maximum effective frontal protection is given by a long sloping glacis plate and a low, well-profiled turret. The tracks have been redesigned from an existing type to give longer wear in sandy soil and extra thrust when propelling the vehicle in water, where 7 km./hr can be attained.

The Ikv-91's gun is a Bofors-designed lightweight, low recoil 90-mm. weapon of the low pressure type, firing fin-stabilized projectiles, including armour-piercing and high explosive rounds. Although the gun can be fired on the move, it is perhaps more likely to be used from cover. It is not stabilized but has an advanced fire control system, including a laser range-finder, an automatic drift calculator, sensors to measure wind and atmospheric conditions, and a ballistic computer which processes all the information fed into it. Two 7·62-mm. machine-guns are carried—one coaxial with the 90-mm. gun and one externally on the loader's turret hatch.

A commercial-type Volvo Penta six-cylinder in-line diesel engine of 294-h.p. is used in the Ikv-91, mounted diagonally at the rear. This arrangement both decreases the space it takes up and simplifies the transmission. A maximum road speed of 64-km./hr can be attained. The vehicle has a crew of four—the driver at the front left-hand side and the commander, gunner and loader–radio operator in the turret.

36 Pansarbandvagn Pbv-302 and 155-mm. Bandkanon 1A, Sweden.

The Swedish Army relied for a number of years on a type of armoured personnel carrier rebuilt from the chassis of obsolete Strv M/41 tanks, which were the Czech TNH built under licence. Fitted with new engines and with an entirely different upper hull, these armoured personnel carriers, Pbv 301, were virtually new vehicles. An economical expedient, these carriers were highly successful in many ways. The limits imposed by the size of the original chassis, however, and the desire for a fully purpose-built armoured personnel carrier led to AB Hägglund & Söner, who had produced the Pbv 301, being asked in 1961 to design its successor.

The Pbv 302, which appeared in prototype form late in 1962 and as a production vehicle in 1966, has a layout very much like that of the American M-113. Unlike the U.S. vehicle, however, the Pbv 302 was designed to carry a 20-mm. gun turret: this is mounted on top of the hull at the left side near the front. The driver sits next to the turret in the centre and the vehicle commander is to the driver's right. The engine—a Volvo commercial six-cylinder diesel of 270 h.p.—and transmission are under the floor beneath the feet of the three front crew members. Up to nine infantrymen can be carried in the compartment at the rear, to which two doors in the vehicle's back plate give access. Roof hatches enable the infantry to use their personal weapons so, together with the turret, the Pbv 302 has the main characteristics of much later mechanized infantry combat vehicles.

An unusual feature is the double skin hull, which increases buoyancy, improves protection against hollow charge missiles and the opportunity has been taken of giving the outer skin a shape to lessen water resistance. The Pbv 302 can attain a speed of 8 km./hr in water, driven by its tracks and has a maximum road-speed of 65 70 km./hr.

The 155-mm. Bandkanon 1A is a weapon—both gun and its self-propelled mounting—designed and built by AB Bofors. Earlier known as VK-155, this self-propelled gun was developed during the 1950s, a production order was awarded in 1965 and all the vehicles (supplied only to the Swedish Army) were completed by 1968.

Mounted in a turret with limited traverse (a total of 30 degrees), the 155-mm. gun, 50 calibres long, has maximum elevation of 40 degrees. Loading is (apart from the first round) carried out automatically from a magazine holding 14 rounds. A jib mounted over the turret allows the magazine to be replaced from a supply vehicle in only two minutes. The rate of fire of the gun is 14 rounds (a full magazine) per minute, and the maximum range is 25,600 metres.

Many mechanical features used in the Bkv 1A are shared with the S-tank, including elements of the suspension and a similar transmission and dual engine arrangement. At 53 tons, however, the Bkv 1A is the heaviest Swedish armoured vehicle and with the relatively low speed of 24 km./hr and lacking amphibious capability it does not share the performance of most other Swedish A.F.V.s.

37 Bärgningsbandvagn Bgbv-82, and Brobandvagn Brobv-941, Sweden.

These two Swedish support vehicles share the same basic chassis, which also has many mechanical elements used in the earlier Pbv 302 armoured personnel carrier and the Ikv 91 infantry gun vehicle which followed them.

Intended to serve as an armoured recovery vehicle for units equipped with the Strv 103 battle tank ('S-tank') as well as the much lighter Pbv 302, the Bgbv 82 was designed by AB Hägglund & Söner, work started in 1966, the prototype appeared in 1968 and production commenced in 1970. In order to enjoy the advantage of greater mobility, including amphibious qualities for the standard armoured recovery vehicle, the decision was taken that actual battlefield recovery of S-tanks under fire should be undertaken by other S-tanks. This enabled the armour protection and weight of the Bgbv 82 to be kept down so that the desired mobility characteristics could be attained.

The Bgbc 82 has the front part of the hull fully enclosed, to give armour protection to the crew of four when travelling. For defence it has a turret, mounted at the left, containing a 20-mm. cannon. The rear compartment, which is open, contains the engine (a six-cylinder Volvo-Penta diesel of 310 h.p.) and transmission (at the left), the crew working area, the lifting crane (capable of a 5,500 kg lift with 1·5-metre jib or 1,500 kg when extended to 5·5 metres), the hydraulic winch motor, and other recovery equipment. Two ground anchor spades and two stabilizers on common brackets are positioned on the rear plate of the hull for use with the winch (the cable of which runs through a guide in the centre of the rear plate) and the crane respectively. The winch can exert a 20-ton pulling force or 60 tons in a triple-part pull. A bulldozer blade is carried on the front of the vehicle.

The armoured bridge layer Brobv 941 is likewise intended to serve vehicles up to and including the S-tank: in fact, the bridge's capacity is 50 tons, suitable also for Centurion tanks.

The hull of the bridge layer is closely similar to that of the armoured recovery vehicle, including enclosed protection for the crew of four men, although it lacks the 20-mm. gun turret, having a pintle-mounted machine-gun instead. The automotive characteristics and performance are also much the same as that of the Bgbv 82 including, more unusually in a bridge layer, the amphibious ability. For water crossing, the bridge, which is of box construction and buoyant, is towed by the laying vehicle.

The bridge is carried on the vehicle supported by a girder which is mounted on a bracket located just behind the crew compartment. For launching, the girder is extended by hydraulic means across the gap. The bridge, which is 15 metres long, is then run forward across the girder and lowered to touch ground on the other side of the gap. The girder is then withdrawn, placing the near end of the bridge on the ground, and returned to the horizontal position over the vehicle. A bulldozer blade is carried on the front of the bridge layer to help in preparing, if necessary, the approach ground for the bridge.

38 **Panzer 61 and Panzer 68,** Switzerland.

The Swiss Army has traditionally been provided with its small arms and light weapons largely from Switzerland's own armaments industry. The first tanks, however, were purchased abroad, but the difficulty during World War II of obtaining further supplies of armoured vehicles led to the first steps being taken to design and produce armoured vehicles in Switzerland. No great progress was made and foreign tanks were again purchased between 1951 and 1960—notably 200 French AMX 13 light tanks and a total of 300 British Centurions of various Marks. During this time, the desire for greater self-sufficiency in A.F.V.s and reduction of expenditure abroad, coupled with the Army's wish to have a main battle tank designed for Swiss conditions, led to the decision to undertake the development of a tank.

Before the armament was finally decided on, a small number of tanks was completed armed with a Swiss 90-mm. gun and these were known as Panzer 58. By the time of their completion in 1961, however, the British 105-mm. tank gun had been perfected and this was to be adopted not only for the Centurion—in both new and up-gunned versions—but also for the United States' M-60. This gun, then, was chosen for the Swiss tank, not only on its merits, but, no doubt, with the attractive possibility in mind of rearming the Swiss Centurions and so achieving standardization.

The new tank, named Panzer 61, exhibited several interesting features, the outstanding of which were its comparatively light weight of 38 tons and its compactness. These points aid mobility in a country in which well over half the terrain is mountainous but has an efficient rail network.

The hull of the Pz61, apart from its narrowness, achieved in part by the location of the diesel fuel tanks either side of the driver, with 105-mm. rounds stored between them, is unusual in being cast largely in one piece. As well as being a means of producing heavy armour within the capabilities of Swiss industry, this enables a good ballistic profile to be achieved. A second feature, and one contributing to the overall compactness, is the adoption of a Belleville washer suspension. The Pz 61 is one of the few tanks to use this system. Each of the six road-wheels each side is suspended independently on a nest of these conical springs, mounted outside the hull.

The turret, which is also cast, contains the 105-mm. gun. This gun is made in Switzerland under licence and has a modified breech block and its mounting allows for increased recoil, lessening the stresses in a tank much lighter than most others in which it is installed. Mounted with the gun in the turret is a 20-mm. Oerlikon cannon. A 7·5-mm. machine-gun is mounted on the loader's turret cupola, at the left-hand side.

As a suitable Swiss engine was not available, the German-built Daimler–Benz MB.837, a V-8 cylinder diesel of 630 h.p., was adopted. This is linked to a Swiss SLM gear-box and a double differential steering system with a hydrostatic steering drive. This power unit gives the tank a maximum speed of 55 km./hr.

One hundred and fifty Panzer 61s were built for the Swiss Army—to equip three tank battalions—and were delivered between 1964 and 1966. When it was decided in 1968 to order a further 170 tanks, the opportunity was taken of introducing improvements in the design. Designated Panzer 68, the new model is very similar in appearance and layout to its predecessor, the most obvious difference being in the substitution of a coaxial 7·5-mm. machine-gun for the 20-mm. cannon. Less obvious are modified idler wheels, redesigned tracks and aluminium, instead of steel, road-wheels. Much more important, though, is the addition of a hydroelectric stabilization system for the 105-mm. gun.

The engine of the Pz68 is an uprated version of the Daimler–Benz diesel, giving an extra 30-h.p. and increasing the maximum speed of the tank to 60 km./hr.

The Swiss have also developed a range of support vehicles (some only in prototype form) using components of the Pz61 and Pz68 battle tanks. These include the Panzerkanone 68 (a S.P. 155-mm. gun), Entpannungspanzer 65 (armoured recovery vehicle) and Brückenpanzer 68 (bridge layer).

39 Vickers Main Battle Tank, (Vijayanta), United Kingdom/India.

Designed as a private venture by Vickers Ltd, the Vickers Main Battle Tank, or 37-ton tank as it is sometimes called, was intended to incorporate the hitting power of the Centurion in a lighter, more simple, tank, suitable to the needs of some overseas countries.

Using the 105-mm. gun, by then current in the Centurion, the Vickers M.B.T. has roughly the Centurion's layout but is over 10 tons lighter, mainly through the acceptance of a lower degree of protection, both hull and turret being built up from welded rolled steel armour plates, rather than the more usual castings.

A good degree of mobility has been provided for by the use of the Leyland L.60 engine and transmission adapted from those designed for the 52 ton Chieftain. With output restricted to 650 h.p. the reliability is improved and the Vickers M.B.T. still has a top speed of 56 km./hr. The suspension of the Vickers tank differs from that of both Centurion and Chieftain in that the six road-wheels each side are carried on transverse torsion bars. Unusual additions to this system are secondary torsion bars for the first, second and last pairs of road-wheels, which come into action to absorb the greater wheel action encountered in these positions, where there are also hydraulic dampers.

To help compensate for its relatively light protection by British standards (80-mm. maximum on hull and turret, which is only between half and three-quarters of that on later Centurions), the Vickers M.B.T. has an advanced gun control and stabilization system, which enables its gun to be laid while on the move and fired very quickly after the tank halts or, in emergency, even fired while on the move. The 105-mm. gun is ranged by means of a heavy 12·7-mm. machine-gun, mounted next to it—a system which has advantages over optical range-finders in conditions of cross-winds or poor light, for example. Both the ranging machine-gun and a coaxial 7·62-mm. machine-gun for general use are mounted to the left of the main weapon and a second 7·62-mm. machine-gun can be mounted on the commander's cupola, which is at the left-hand side of the turret roof.

The Vickers Main Battle Tank went into production in India, where it is known as Vijayanta (Victor) in 1966. This followed tests of a Vickers-built tank in 1965 and delivery of many components for the Indian production line at Avadi, near Madras. The number of British-made components has subsequently been considerably reduced for the Indian Vijayantas, of which over 500 are believed to have been built.

An order for 50 Vickers Main Battle Tanks was placed by Kuwait in 1968 and the first tank was delivered early in 1971.

A Mark II version of the Vickers M.B.T. was armed with four Swingfire anti-tank guided missiles added to the turret sides in addition to the regular armament. This has not gone into production in England or India, as far as is known, but existing tank models could obviously be modified to this standard if required.

Various other improved versions of the Vickers M.B.T. have tentatively been called Mark III, the earlier of which (in scale model form only) had a new turret with a cast, rounded front part, and a cast hull glacis plate, greatly improving protection. Later, a version of the M.B.T. with basically standard hull and turret has been equipped with a General Motors 800-h.p. twelve-cylinder diesel engine in power pack form.

Provision is made in the design of the Vickers M.B.T. for a nylon flotation screen to be carried, folded, in a trough at upper track-guard level. This can be erected in 15 minutes: water speed, propelled by the tracks, is 7 km./hr. This equipment does not, however, appear to be carried as standard by either Indian or Kuwait M.B.T.s.

40 Tank, Combat 120-mm. Gun, Chieftain, United Kingdom.

The Chieftain was introduced to replace both the Centurion and the Conqueror as Britain's main battle tank. Conqueror was a support tank for Centurion and had a 120-mm. gun but weighed 65 tons (bridge group 80). It was, in fact, the heaviest tank then in service in the world and although heavily armoured, its mobility was low and the maximum speed was only 21 m.p.h. The Centurion was still a very good tank but it was desired to keep ahead of future Soviet tank developments by putting a 120-mm. gun in a tank at least as well protected as Centurion while keeping weight down to 45 tons, although early design studies for the new tank made it necessary to increase this figure to 51·8 tons.

The Chieftain's general layout is that common for most main battle tanks of the 1970s—the engine at the rear, the fighting compartment and turret in front of it and the driver in the hull at the front. One unusual feature in the Chieftain, however, is that the driver occupies a semi-reclining position when the tank is closed down. This enables the hull height to be kept down, reducing weight and, by decreasing the overall size of the target, improving invulnerability.

A new turret design was adopted for Chieftain in which the mantlet was eliminated. This also helped to reduce weight, to help compensate for the 120-mm. gun, which was and is more

powerful than those of the majority of main battle tanks in service which, in general, rely on guns of smaller calibre with hollow charge projectiles for their penetrative effect. Apart from the range and accuracy of the heavy rifled barrel, it can penetrate most forms of armour on current battle tanks, including the spaced plates which offer protection against hollow-charge projectiles. As the loading system is manual, for such heavy ammunition projectile and charge are separate but, nevertheless, a rate of fire of up to 10 rounds per minute (for short periods) can be attained. The gun is ranged by means of a 12·7-mm. (0·5-in.) heavy machine-gun in conjunction with optical sights, although a laser range-finder coupled with a digital computer is under development. A 7·62-mm. machine-gun, coaxial with the main gun, is also mounted in the turret, and another is carried on the turret cupola of the commander and can be aimed and fired by him from inside the turret.

A multi-fuel engine, basically a diesel but able to operate on a wide range of different liquid fuels in accordance with NATO requirements, was developed by Leyland Motors (now British Leyland) for the Chieftain. This engine, the Leyland L60, is a compact twelve-cylinder vertically opposed type, developing, in late versions, 750 h.p. The original models of this engine gave only 585 h.p. and were rather unreliable but successive improvements have been made, many of which have been incorporated retrospectively in earlier vehicles, to enhance reliability as well as increase performance.

The Chieftain's suspension is similar to that of Centurion, namely the modified Horstmann type consisting of road-wheels in three pairs each side, sprung on three horizontal springs to each pair of wheels. The maximum road speed of 48 km./hr is lower than that of most contemporary main battle tanks and is at the expense of the Chieftain's correspondingly better protection. It is claimed, however, that cross-country mobility—which in most tanks is often limited by the endurance of the crew—compares quite well with tanks of other countries. There is no provision for Chieftain to swim, but deep wading is possible with the use of schnorkel breathing equipment.

There are eight basic Marks of Chieftain, and numerous sub-types: few external differences are apparent, although many improvements have been made since the tank first went into service in 1966.

As well as forming the main tank equipment of the British Army the Chieftain has been ordered by Kuwait and is being produced in large numbers for the Government of Iran. The first Iranian orders were for a total of 857 tanks of a version known as Chieftain Mk. 5P. Later vehicles, to a reported total of 1,200, will be of an improved type of Chieftain called Shir Iran (Persian Lion) using the laminated protection known as Chobham armour and a new Rolls-Royce twelve-cylinder diesel engine of 1,200 h.p.

41 **Centurion Main Battle Tank,** United Kingdom.

Although its basic design goes back as far as 1944, the Centurion is a rugged and, even by today's standards, quite well-protected tank, which rearmed to modern standards has proved that it can still give a good account of itself. With further improvements, such as to increase mobility and range, it is superior to many tanks designed decades later.

The Centurion has a general layout which became common in World War II and has continued for the majority of main battle tanks ever since: driver at the front, fighting compartment and turret in the middle and engine compartment at the rear. The Centurion's track drive is to rear sprockets and the suspension is of the modified Horstmann type. This system, which consists of the road wheels being mounted in three sets of two each side, sprung on horizontal springs, lacks some of the advantages of the popular independent transverse torsion bars of today, but it does have the merit of not taking up floor space inside the hull.

The engine chosen for the Centurion was the twelve-cylinder Meteor of 600/650 h.p., which was derived from the famous Rolls-Royce Merlin aero-engine, used for R.A.F. fighters. The Centurion's original gun was the 17-pdr (76·2 mm.)—the most effective British tank gun of World War II. By the early 1950s the 20-pdr (83·4 mm.) gun had been introduced and this was, in turn, superseded in 1961 by the Vickers L7A1 105-mm. gun—a weapon that was to be adopted by the U.S.A., Germany and many other countries and is still one of the most widely used tank guns.

Centurions have been supplied to sixteen different countries and many are still in active employment. They were used on both sides in the Arab-Israeli wars and were still effective in the

1973 battles. This was perhaps the more so with the Israeli Centurions because of the modifications that had been carried out on them to improve their performance.

The Israeli Centurions were of different Marks and were obtained from different sources, but all are believed to have been standardized on armament with the Vickers 105 mm.—as, indeed, have Israeli U.S. M-48s of different models and captured Soviet T-54s and T-55s. Some Centurions, however, have been completely reworked with a new 750-h.p. Continental diesel engine, coupled with a new gear-box and steering system and other improvements. This has helped to increase the maximum speed from about 35 to 45 km./hr, as well as improving general mobility and range.

Vickers Ltd, the present 'design parents' of the Centurion, have offered their own rework scheme to bring older tanks up to the same or higher standard as the Israeli Centurions. The Vickers Centurion Retrofit Programme includes the following features: a General Motors V-12 cylinder diesel of 715 h.p. in power pack form to replace the Meteor petrol engine; modified final drives; TN 12 semi or fully automatic gear-box (as used in the Chieftain and Vickers Main Battle Tank); up-armouring of the glacis plate; fitting 105-mm. gun (on early models with 17-pdr or 25-pdr gun); modernized gun control equipment and/or adding laser range finder; improved commander's cupola; adding nuclear, biological and chemical warfare protection; fitting night vision equipment. Some or all of the above items can be supplied or fitted as required and, if necessary,

tanks can be completely overhauled and many detail improvements effected. The Swiss Army, which had 150 early Centurions equipped with the 20-pdr gun, has had some of its tanks refitted in accordance with this programme.

42 **Combat Vehicle Reconnaissance, Full Tracked 76-mm. Gun, Scorpion and Combat Vehicle Reconnaissance, Full Tracked 30-mm. Gun, Scimitar,** United Kingdom.

The Scorpion light tank was developed to meet a British Army requirement for a tracked air-portable reconnaissance vehicle. To enable it to tackle main battle tanks, if necessary, in fighting reconnaissance missions or for support in airborne operations a 76-mm. gun, firing a range of ammunition suitable against armour or infantry, is carried.

Developed by Alvis Limited (part of the British Leyland organization) in conjunction with the Military Vehicles and Engineering Establishment of the Ministry of Defence, the six-cylinder Jaguar car engine was adopted for Scorpion, giving the advantage of a well-tried and successful engine, coupled with economy in production and development. Derated from its normal output of 265 h.p. to 195 h.p., the Jaguar engine gives the Scorpion a maximum speed of 81 km./hr and a rate of acceleration that, for a tracked vehicle, can bear comparison with that of the Jaguar sports car.

A weight of just under 8 tons is achieved partly by the use of aluminium for the construction of the Scorpion's hull and turret. The engine is located near the front of the hull at the right-hand side, with the driver beside it at the left, and the seven-speed semi-automatic gear-box and final drive system is in front of them. The concentration of the automotive elements in this way, with front drive to the tracks, has left the rear of the vehicle completely clear for the fighting compartment, a layout that has enabled the Scorpion chassis to be used readily for a variety of other vehicles, some of which are described separately in this book. The suspension consists of five road-wheels—also made of aluminium—each side, sprung on transverse torsion bars. The turret, mounted over the fighting compartment, containing the commander and gunner, has the 76-mm. gun (with elevation of 35 degrees, depression 10 degrees) and a coaxial 7·62-mm. machine-gun, which can be used for ranging the main gun. Between forty and sixty rounds of 76-mm. ammunition are carried, the higher figure when the Nuclear, Biological and Chemical protection pack is not fitted in the rear of the fighting compartment. Scorpions supplied to countries with hot climates have a special air conditioning system fitted. Belgium shares in the production of the Scorpion and its family of vehicles and it is employed in her army as well as the British Army and those of several African and Asian countries.

The need was felt for a tracked vehicle to complement the Scorpion, with the same general characteristics, but with an automatic gun of smaller calibre and a much larger ammunition supply, effective against light armoured vehicles and 'soft skin' vehicles. This requirement has been met by the Scimitar, which has a 30-mm. Rarden

cannon, mounted (together with a 7·62-mm. machine-gun) in a modified Scorpion turret. The Rarden gun, named after the Royal Armament Research and Development Establishment and the Enfield (Middlesex, near London), Royal Small Arms Factory, where it was jointly developed, is an automatic weapon, capable of firing at a maximum rate of 100 rounds per minute, in bursts of up to six rounds. Single shots are also possible for 'sniper' fire. British-designed or Hispano 30-mm. ammunition can be used, and 165 rounds are carried. Although only lightly armoured or unarmoured targets are normally envisaged, the British APDS-T round is capable of penetrating the sides of main battle tanks. With an elevation of 40 degrees, the Rarden cannon, although not intended in Scimitar as an anti-aircraft weapon, can be used at least as a deterrent to helicopters.

Because of their compact hulls, although light in weight, Scorpion and Scimitar lack sufficient buoyancy for swimming, but both can be made amphibious by means of a flotation screen carried folded round the hull just above track level. This can be erected in under 5 minutes: water speed, propelled by the tracks, is approximately 6½ km./hr.

43 **Combat Vehicle, Reconnaissance, Full Tracked, Personnel, Spartan and Combat Vehicle Reconnaissance, Full Tracked, G.W., Striker,** United Kingdom.

The chassis of the Scorpion light tank proved readily adaptable as the basis of a family of light armoured vehicles, one of which is the Spartan armoured personnel carrier. Engine and driver are at the front, as in the Scorpion, but the hull at the rear is increased in height, providing accommodation for four men and their personal weapons and equipment, in addition to the commander whose position is on the right, immediately behind the engine. The rear compartment has a door at the back, observation periscopes at either side and hatches from which the crew can fire their personal weapons. The gunner (who also acts as radio operator) is behind the driver and operates a 7·62-mm. machine-gun, which is mounted externally on the gunner's cupola and can be aimed, fired and reloaded from under cover. Spartan is slightly heavier than Scorpion but has practically identical performance characteristics, including the amphibious capability with the use of screens.

The Spartan is highly mobile but as the number of men carried is relatively few, compared with the FV 432, it is not normally used as an infantry personnel carrier but rather for reconnaissance or engineer assault teams. It can also be used as a specialized load carrier, such as for demolition stores, or Swingfire missiles for Striker vehicles.

The Striker Anti-tank Guided Weapon carrier is basically the same vehicle as the Spartan but the rear compartment is occupied by the Swingfire equipment. The three front crew positions are the same as in the Spartan, except that the commander is behind the driver and operates the 7·62-mm. machine-gun. The man in the right-hand position is the missile controller, who has a split-field monocular sight with magnification of ×1 and ×10 which can be traversed 55 degrees either side of the vehicle's centre line.

The five Swingfire missiles are carried in a launcher box on the hull roof, which is pivoted at the rear and elevated by an hydraulic ram. Five spare missiles are carried inside the vehicle but the launcher can only be reloaded from outside the hull. With a range in excess of 3,000 metres, the Swingfire can destroy main battle tanks. When launched, it is automatically programmed into the controller's field of view and then controlled on to the target by means of a joystick, the commands being conveyed to the missile through the wire it dispenses. The Striker is commonly used as a back-up vehicle by reconnaissance units equipped with light tanks and other light armoured vehicles.

A further member of the Scorpion family (not illustrated here) is the Samson Combat Vehicle, Recovery (FV 106). This uses the same hull as Spartan, is equipped with a heavy duty winch and twin spades on the hull rear, and is intended for the battlefield recovery of Scorpion tanks or other light armoured vehicles.

44 **Combat, Vehicle, Reconnaissance, Full Tracked, Command, Sultan, and Combat Vehicle, Ambulance, Full Tracked, Samaritan,** United Kingdom.

The armoured command and armoured ambulance derivatives of the Scorpion reconnaissance vehicle share a similar hull, rather like that of the Spartan armoured personnel carrier but increased in height to 2·016 metres to give greater headroom inside.

Sultan, the command vehicle, has an operating crew of three—driver, commander (who can also act as a radio operator) and radio operator, together with accommodation for two to three officers of armoured or mechanized units or formations. There is internal provision for map boards and documents and command radio sets. Extra batteries are carried for lengthy operation of the communications equipment. For use when the vehicle is stationary, a penthouse can be extended at the rear of the hull, to give approximately double the covered area. This item is normally carried, concertinaed, on the vehicle's back plate. One 7·62-mm. machine-gun is carried for the vehicle's protection, for which a pintle mount is provided.

The armoured ambulance, known as Samaritan, has accommodation in the hull for four stretchers, or two stretchers plus three sitting cases, or six sitting cases. The rear door (like that of the command vehicle) is larger than that of the personnel carrier, to make for easier handling of the stretchers. These can be slid into or out of the vehicle on movable racks attached to the inside of the hull walls. The Samaritan is, of course, unarmed. The vehicle commander (who would usually be a medical officer) for travelling has a position at the front right-hand side of the rear compartment, behind the engine, and is provided with a hatch containing five periscopes.

45 Carrier, Personnel, Full Tracked, FV 432, and Carrier, Maintenance, Full Tracked, FV 434, United Kingdom.

The full-tracked carrier in World War II was largely a British development in both its main forms—a specially designed series of open-topped light vehicles, epitomized by the Bren and Universal Carriers, used for a wide variety of roles on the one hand, and slightly modified tank or S.P. gun chassis, used principally as armoured personnel carriers on the other. Postwar development in Britain moved towards a vehicle combining features of both the early carriers and modified tanks. Experiments in the U.S.A. led to the requirement for a fully tracked and fully enclosed armoured vehicle to carry infantry accompanying armour, resulting in the M-75, M-59 and M-113 series, while parallel experiments in Britain with different models produced as prototypes or in relatively small numbers resulted in the FV 432 series.

The first prototypes of the FV 432 were ready for trials in 1961. Because long experiments had already been carried out with earlier vehicles having many features of the FV 432, it was possible for series production to be commenced in 1962 and the first standard vehicles were running by the following year.

Welded steel construction is used for the hull of the FV 432, making it heavier than the aluminium alloy American M-113 and also (unlike the M-113) making it unable to swim without special preparation. The engine is a Rolls-Royce six-cylinder two stroke multi-fuel engine, developing 240 h.p. and the suspension is of the torsion bar variety, carrying five medium-sized road-wheels each side. The track drive is at the front, as is also the engine (at the left side) and transmission, leaving a clear compartment at the rear of the vehicle. The driver is seated at the right, beside the engine, and the vehicle commander (who has a rotating cupola with three periscopes and opening hatch) is immediately behind him. The infantry section of ten men are seated, five each side, on benches hinged to the side walls of the rear compartment. Normal ingress and egress is through a large door in the rear plate, but there is also a large circular hatch in the roof from which the crew's personal weapons or, for example, a 81-mm. mortar can be operated.

The FV 432 has a maximum road speed of 52 km./hr and in water between 6 and 7 km./hr. For swimming, a flotation screen has to be erected round the top edge of the hull—a fairly quick process—and a trim board raised on the glacis plate. The latter is carried permanently on some vehicles but not on others.

As well as its basic role of carrying a section of riflemen, the FV 432 in its more-or-less standard form can carry an 81-mm. mortar; or a 120-mm. Wombat recoilless anti-tank gun (mounted in the roof); or a Carl Gustav anti-tank launcher. There are also command and ambulance (four stretcher) versions, externally similar to the armoured personnel carrier.

The Carrier, Maintenance, Full Tracked, FV 434 is basically the same mechanically as the FV 432 but is a specialized adaptation to meet the needs of the Royal Electrical and Mechanical Engineers for a vehicle capable of carrying out repair and maintenance of A.F.V.s in the field. It is equipped with a HIAB hydraulically operated crane, mounted on a turntable on the right-hand side of the hull roof. This crane can lift 3·05 tons on a short radius of 7–8 ft or 1·25 tons at around 12 ft. It can be used for changing the power plants of Chieftain tanks, or gun barrels. A full range of tools including a vice is carried, some of which are stored in a compartment at the rear of the vehicle: the cover of this folds down to form a bench. The layout of the stowage differed in the earlier models.

The FV 434 has a crew of four men (driver, commander and two fitters) and approximately the same performance (including amphibious capability) as the FV 432.

46 Launcher, Guided Missile, Carrier Mounted, Full Tracked, Swingfire, FV 438 and Carrier, FV 432 with Ranger, United Kingdom.

As well as its employment in various infantry roles and as a repair vehicle, already described, the FV 432 series has a number of uses with the Royal Artillery and Royal Engineers. One model carries the Field Artillery Computer Equipment (F.A.C.E.) for controlling field guns, and several variants of FV 432 are equipped with radar, including the Green Archer mortar locating radar system (FV 436, with the scanner mounted on the rear of the hull, which has a lowered roof) and the Cymbeline radar, which is replacing Green Archer. FV 432's are also used to carry ground surveillance radar and sonic detection equipment.

In addition to these passive functions, a version of the FV 432 is used as an anti-tank vehicle—the FV 438 armed with the Swingfire wire-guided rocket system. Two launchers are mounted on the hull roof near the rear. When the target is sighted in the periscopic sight, the missile is launched and then automatically programmed on to the target sight line, when the controller applies corrections to ensure a hit. The missile has a range of 4,000 metres. Fourteen are carried and can be loaded from the protection of the vehicle's armour.

The FV 432 is used by the Royal Engineers as a carrier for the Ranger anti-personnel mine-laying device. The small Ranger mines are carried in a rotatable framework mounted on the roof of the FV 432. The frame holds 72 tubes in three banks of twenty-four, each tube containing twenty mines. Ejection of the mines up to a range of 100 metres is by an electrically fired cartridge and the rate can be controlled to suit the speed of the vehicle and the density of mine coverage needed. The Ranger-equipped FV 432 can also tow the Bar Mine Layer, which is a trailer for laying the anti-tank Bar Mines. The Bar Mines are 27 in. (685 mm.) long and 4¼ in. (108 mm.) wide, and are made almost entirely of non-metallic materials and thus difficult to detect. In the laying process the Bar Mines are fed into a chute attached to the trailer after having their safety pins removed by a man sitting in the rear of the towing vehicle. A plough on the trailer cuts a furrow into which the Bar Mine is laid (after having been made active by a catch) and the furrow is then covered. Some 600–700 mines an hour can be laid in this way.

Minefield clearance can also be carried out by an FV 432 towing the Giant Viper trailer, which is described with the Combat Engineer Tractor.

47 Gun, Self-Propelled, 105-mm. Fd. Gun, Abbot and Falcon Self-Propelled A.A. Gun, United Kingdom.

The Abbot (a title continuing a Royal Artillery tradition of naming its S.P. guns after ecclesiastics) is the principal British Army field artillery weapon; towed guns of this calibre now being used only in specialized functions, such as for airborne operations.

Although of comparatively light calibre (and likely to be supplanted eventually by the joint British–German–Italian 155-mm. gun), the Abbot's 105-mm. gun is claimed to have a greater range (at 17,000 metres) than comparable weapons of other countries and a high explosive shell of greater lethality, with a rate of fire of twelve rounds per minute.

The chassis of the Abbot (or F.V. 433) has many components in common with the F.V. 432 series of armoured carriers, including a version of the Rolls-Royce six-cylinder two-stroke multi-fuel engine, developing 240 h.p. and associated transmission, and a similar suspension system of five medium-sized road-wheels each side, carried on torsion bars. Also, the location of the engine at the front left-hand side, with the driver at the right, leaving the rear of the hull clear is common to both S.P. gun and armoured personnel carrier.

The 105-mm. gun is mounted in a

fully rotating turret, with powered traverse, where it has a maximum elevation of 70 degrees and depression of 5 degrees. The other three crew members occupy the turret; the ammunition stowage (in turret and rear hull) consisting of 32–34 high explosive rounds and HESH rounds, for use against armour. A 7·62-mm. machinegun can be mounted on the commander's cupola for the vehicle's defence.

A maximum road speed of 48 km./hr can be attained by the Abbot and the vehicle can be made amphibious by the erection of a screen normally carried, collapsed, round the top of the hull. Preparation takes about 13 minutes and the speed in water, propelled by the tracks, is 5 km/hr.

A version of the Abbot, built to the same engineering standards but stripped of all items not absolutely essential for the prime purpose of the vehicle, known as Value Engineered Abbot was designed primarily for the Indian Army between about 1965 and 1967 and subsequently approximately 100 were produced by Vickers Ltd for India. The most important differences from the standard Abbot are lack of the flotation screen; the engine modified for diesel fuel only; turret hand traverse instead of power traverse; simplified commander's cupola, non-rotating. Even the mesh guard over the exhaust pipe can be omitted to cut cost to the minimum in the Value Engineered Abbot; but, if required, modification of all features to bring the vehicle up to full British Army standard can be carried out subsequently. The alternative of a General Motors 214-h.p. diesel engine instead of the Rolls-Royce engine has been offered by the manufacturers.

The Falcon is a self-propelled antiaircraft gun system for combating low flying aircraft and also light armoured vehicles, developed by Vickers Ltd and British Marco Ltd in conjunction with the Hispano-Suiza Group. It consists of a Value Engineered Abbot chassis on which is mounted a special turret containing two 30-mm. Hispano-Suiza automatic guns, with a rate of fire (each) of 650 rounds per minute. The guns are power traversed and elevated, and are stabilized against vehicle movement so can be fired, if necessary, on the move. In action, target information, visually acquired, is fed into a computer which provides data for bracketing the target.

The Falcon's system, unlike that of the French Oeil Noir, for instance, does not incorporate target acquisition and tracking radar because it is felt that low level air attack is not a serious threat in darkness or poor visibility. External field radar surveillance systems can, however, be used to give advance warning of the imminence of attack and its likely direction, so as to give the Falcon's crew with their optical fire control system a good chance of hitting the targets.

48 Tank, Bridge Layer, AVLB, Chieftain Mk. 5, United Kingdom.

The Chieftain Bridge Layer, or Armoured Vehicle Launched Bridge, as successor to the Centurion Bridge Layer used by the British Army, has again reverted to the 'scissors' type of bridge which was first introduced during World War II with Valentine and Covenanter tank bridge layers.

Claimed to be the longest tank-laid

bridge in service, the Chieftain's No. 8 Tank Bridge is 24·4 metres long and can span a gap of 22·8 metres wide and is class 60—that is to say, it will take A.F.V.s of up to 60 tons. In order to keep weight down so that the loaded bridge layer itself is within class 60, the bridge girders are made of high strength nickel-alloy steel, with decking and kerbs of aluminium alloy. When travelling, the bridge is carried folded over the Chieftain's hull, with the hinges at the rear. For launching, a hydraulic pump, driven by a power take-off from the tank's main engine, brings the bridge forward on to stabilizers, raising it to the vertical position, opening it out and then, when fully extended, placing it over the gap. The launching process takes between three and five minutes. Recovery of the bridge, which may be picked up from either end, using the reverse process, takes about ten minutes. Tracked vehicles cross the bridge using both track ways (each 1·62 metres wide, with a 0·76-metre gap between them), but small wheeled vehicles, such as Land-Rovers, can use a single trackway, thus making two-way traffic possible for such vehicles.

The Chieftain Bridge Layer is operated by a crew of three and weighs, complete with bridge, 53 tons.

49 Armoured Recovery Vehicle, Chieftain Mk. 5, and Armoured Recovery Vehicle, Beach, Centurion Mk. 5, United Kingdom.

The Chieftain Armoured Recovery Vehicle is intended to replace the similarly equipped Centurion A.R.V. now that all Centurion main battle tanks have been superseded in the British Army by Chieftains.

Based on the Chieftain Mark 5, the armoured recovery vehicle version is turretless with a heightened hull roof, the commander's rotating cupola, mounting one remote-controlled 7·62-mm. machine-gun, occupying the highest point in the centre. The driver's position is at the left-hand side of the glacis plate and his seat lacks the reclining facility of the normal Chieftain battle tank. Besides commander and driver, the crew includes two fitters. Two winches are carried, the main one being of capstan type, driven mechanically by a power take-off from the tank's main engine. It has a maximum pull of 30 tons and has 120 metres of cable: as this is fed forward through a pulley on the glacis plate, control is easier than with the Centurion A.R.V.'s rear feed system. The secondary winch is of 3 tons capacity and has 300 metres of cable. It is hydraulically driven and is used for paying out the main winch cable and for light recovery duties. A range of pulley blocks is carried on the A.R.V. which can increase the purchase of the main winch to 90 tons when the bulldozer blade, mounted at the front of the A.R.V. and hydraulically operated, is used as an earth anchor.

The Chieftain A.R.V. can wade without preparation in water up to 1·07 metres deep and has a maximum speed of 42 km./hr. In the British Army, one A.R.V. is issued to each squadron of Chieftain main battle tanks. Chieftain A.R.V.s have been supplied to Iran.

The old Centurion continues in service in the British Army in a specialized version used for the recovery of vehicles and assisting landing craft in amphibious operations. A type of vehicle that has few parallels in other armies, the Centurion Beach Armoured Recovery vehicle is descended from British-operated Sherman tanks modified in 1943-44 particularly with the D-Day invasion in view. They did useful work in recovering 'drowned' vehicles and helping to keep the Normandy beaches clear.

The main features of the Centurion B.A.R.V. are the waterproofed engine, sealed hull and tall armoured super structure, which enable it to work in water up to 2·896 metres deep. Not primarily intended for heavy recovery operations, the vehicle carries only a light winch at the front and a range of towing cables, but the crew of four includes a diver to enable some equipment to be fitted underwater. A rectangular box extending slightly in front of the tracks and faced with a rope fender is to enable the B.A.R.V. to push off and help refloat damaged or stranded landing craft.

50 Combat Engineer Tractor, Full Tracked, United Kingdom

The latest manifestation of the British Army's close interest in and development of armoured engineer (or pioneer) vehicles, the FV 180 Combat Engineer Tractor is a purpose-built vehicle intended to carry out most of the roles previously performed by the Centurion A.V.R.E. (Armoured Vehicle, Royal Engineers). The FV 180 is not, however, designed for the direct assault role and does not carry a mortar for attacking concrete fortifications: its tasks are

normally in the preparation of the ground for tanks and other fighting vehicles, and other battlefield tasks under fire.

By adopting a specially designed vehicle instead of an existing tank chassis, it has been possible to keep the Combat Engineer Tractor's weight down to 17·1 tons fully loaded, with consequent advantages in mobility and the possibility of giving the vehicle a good amphibious performance. Powered by a Rolls-Royce six-cylinder water-cooled diesel engine of 320 h.p., the FV 180 has a maximum road speed of 60 km./hr, and in water, propelled and manoeuvered by twin Hydrojets, 9 km./hr. To aid it in surmounting exceptionally steep slopes, or to help it emerge from water up a soft earth bank, an earth anchor or grapnel is carried which can be fired by a rocket, carrying a winch cable. The vehicle can then help itself along by means of its winch.

The hull of the Combat Engineer Tractor is of aluminium alloy, helping to keep the weight down. The suspension consists of five road-wheels each side (the rear one acting as an idler) sprung on torsion bars. Internally, the layout consists of the engine near the rear at the right-hand side, with the crew of two seated in tandem on the left at the highest point of the hull, under a superstructure with ten vision blocks all round. Each man has a separate hatch. This high position for the crew both improves observation and makes them less vulnerable to mine explosion. The crew seats can be revolved for different operations. For normal running the front man drives, but the second man has full duplicate controls: there are four reverse as well as four forward gears and land performance is nominally the same in both directions. The gear-box is in front of the engine, with the hydraulic pump for winch and shovel located above it, and the final drive and steering units are at the front of the vehicle. The winch cable outlet is on the long-sloping front glacis plate which also carries a large trim board for swimming, folded back when not in use.

The bulldozer equipment is attached to the back of the vehicle: the shovel is made of aluminium alloy with steel teeth and has a capacity of 1·7 cubic metres. A small jib, for handling engineer stores, with a lift of 4 tons, can be attached to the shovel, which also performs a function when the Combat Engineer Tractor is swimming. A load of expanded polyurethane is lashed to the shovel and helps to keep the vehicle trimmed while in the water. At the same time, flotation bags, kept under the trim board, are inflated when the trim board is erected: these help to keep the FV 180's nose up when entering the water. The hydro jet outlets are just above track level at either side of the bulldozer hydraulic arms.

The Combat Engineer Tractor is unarmed but it has smoke-bomb launchers for its own protection. It can perform a wide range of duties, including the following: earth moving, clearing obstacles, preparation of river crossings, making gun emplacements, etc.; assisting in bridging operations, by moving pontoons in water, etc.; helping to recover bogged-down vehicles; laying portable carpets or roadways (carried rolled up in the bulldozer shovel); towing trailers carrying supplies; and minefield clearance. In the last opera-

tion, the vehicle tows the Giant Viper equipment in its two-wheeled trailer. (The FV 180's towing bar is at the front, so it normally operates 'backwards' when towing.) The Giant Viper consists of a hose filled with explosive, which is propelled by a rocket across the minefield and exploded, detonating a clear lane.

51 Remote Handling Equipment (Tracked) (EOD), Wheelbarrow Mk. 7, United Kingdom.

The development of a remote-controlled machine to help deal with terrorist devices being tackled by the British Army in Northern Ireland was begun in 1971. The idea was to produce a robot vehicle that could undertake work previously carried out in person by explosives ordnance disposal personnel and so cut down the risks involved.

Three different organizations produced prototypes, of which the one called 'Wheelbarrow' was judged the best. The three-wheeled chassis of this device was adapted from an existing model of powered wheelbarrow, hence its name.

The first production Wheelbarrow Mark I arrived in Northern Ireland in April 1972 and co-operation between the Army and the designers enabled improvements, in the light of practical experience in operation, to be made. The Mark 2 had a power-steering system instead of the lanyard-operated tiller system of the Mark 1 and Mark 3 was four-wheeled and had skid-steering.

Wheelbarrow Mark 4 was a tracked version of Mark 3; the tracks gave it more of a 'go-anywhere' performance, enabling it to climb steps or kerbs in urban areas, for instance. By 1973 the Mark 5 had appeared: this had a 24-volt electrical system, the driving wheels were relocated to reduce slippage, and a closed-circuit television monitoring system (first used in Mark 3) was adopted as standard. The Mark 6 had a new pattern of boom, operated by two 12-volt motor actuators, with a reach both higher and lower than earlier models and was fitted with a panning facility on its closed-circuit television system.

The latest version of Wheelbarrow, Mark 7, differs from Mark 6 in having geared rather than chain drive, with infinitely variable speed control, and a mechanical grab in place of the previous scissors grapnel attachment.

The Wheelbarrow Mark 7 is only 1·22 metres long (excluding attachments) and weighs 195 kg. Its reversible electric motors, powered by two 12-volt batteries, give it an infinite range of speeds up to 33·5 metres per minute, with an endurance of two hours. The operating range with the standard cable and drum is 100 metres. The range of equipment it can carry and the tasks it can perform are as follows: three types of boom, for holding and positioning the various accessories, at heights ranging from ground level up to about 2·5 metres; a panning-head television camera, for investigating suspicious objects, with a 9-in. (228-mm.) monitoring screen; a window-breaking device, which can be used in conjunction with a small disruptive charge (for dealing with a car loaded with explosives, for example); a grab for removing containers suspected of containing lethal devices; a car-towing hook, which can be placed by the Wheelbarrow, enabling a suspect car to be towed away (by means of a long tow rope) for subsequent investigation in a safe area; an automatic shot gun, holding five rounds, for destroying suspicious objects, for example, or for breaking door locks to force entry into buildings; and twin nail guns (mounted between the front 'horns' of the vehicle) to drive spikes into the floor when the Wheelbarrow enters buildings, to prevent the doors from closing and preventing easy retreat.

Manufactured by Morfax Ltd, the Wheelbarrow Mark 7 and its predecessors was developed by this company in conjunction with the British Ministry of Defence.

52 Tank, Combat, Full-Tracked, XM-1 (General Abrams), U.S.A.

Although the United States Army's efforts to develop a successor to the M-60 series have been costly, it is expected that the end result will be a main battle tank that will be substantially less expensive to maintain than its predecessors.

Following the abortive MBT-70 joint project with the German Federal Republic, new requirements were formulated in 1972 and contracts for prototypes were issued in June of the following year to the Defense Division of Chrysler Corporation and the Detroit Allison Division of General Motors Corporation. A considerable degree of latitude was allowed to the contractors in their designs.

Both Chrysler and General Motors delivered their prototypes to the Army for testing in February 1976. The possibility of standardizing components between the American tank and the German Leopard was also taken into consideration and the decision was taken to develop a turret for the XM-1 that would be capable of taking either the U.S. 105-mm. gun (originally of British design and common to many NATO countries) with a new, more effective, round, or a 120-mm. gun—the calibre favoured by the Germans.

The Chrysler project was chosen in November 1976 and Chrysler were awarded a Full Scale Engineering Development Contract for the construction of further prototypes and other development work, leading to full production of standard vehicles scheduled to commence in February 1980.

One of the principal factors leading to the choice of the Chrysler design was their use of the Avco Lycoming AGT-1500c gas turbine engine which, although somewhat less efficient than the diesel engine favoured by General Motors, and more expensive initially, it is claimed to be much more reliable and durable, with lower maintenance costs. The power output of 1,500 h.p. gives the Chrysler XM-1 the ability to accelerate from zero to 32 km./hr in 6·2 seconds and to reach a maximum of 70 km./hr. The engine is linked with an Allison automatic transmission and differential steering system.

The suspension consists of seven road-wheels each side, sprung on torsion bars—chosen instead of a hydropneumatic system because of their lower vulnerability and simpler maintenance requirements. The leading torsion bars are specially protected against mine damage.

The main armament of the XM-1 is the 105-mm. gun with improved ammunition but provision has been made for adapting the turret to take either the German 120-mm. smooth bore gun or a British 120-mm. rifled gun. There is also a 7·62-mm. coaxial machine-gun, a 12·7-mm. machine-gun on the turret roof, for operation by the tank commander, and a 7·62-mm. machine-gun on a pintle mounting for the loader. Stabilization in elevation is provided for the 105-mm. gun and for the turret in the horizontal axis. The fire control unit also includes a thermal imaging night vision system.

The protection on the XM-1 is based on spaced armour and includes side-skirting plates over the upper half of the suspension. A crew of four operates the XM-1—commander, gunner and loader (all in the turret) and driver, who is in the front centre of the hull in a semi-reclining position.

The illustrations show a prototype Chrysler XM-1, armed with the 105-mm. gun.

53 Tank, Combat, Full Tracked, 105-mm. Gun, M-60A1, and Tank, Combat, Full Tracked, 152-mm. Gun, M-60A2, U.S.A.

The American M-48 medium tank first went into service with the U.S. Army in 1952 and, like its predecessors, the M-46 Pershing, of late World War II vintage, and M-47, was armed with a

90-mm. gun. The M-48 had many faults due, in the main, to lack of adequate tests and failure to rectify the weaknesses that did show up, before full-scale production began. Production variants corrected some of these design faults. The advent of the Soviet 100-mm. tank gun made it necessary for the M-48's gun to be replaced and the M-48E1, and the M-48A1E1 which followed it in production, was equipped with the British-designed 105-mm. gun.

A new tank was then planned to be armed from the start with the 105-mm. gun, although the first version, M-60, was merely a M-48 with suitable modifications.

Parallel to consideration of the British 105-mm. gun, a design for a 152-mm. gun-howitzer capable of firing both conventional (rifled) shot as well as fin-stabilized rocket missiles, controlled on to the target by means of radio micro-waves, was examined. Known as Shillelagh, this weapons system was intended for the main battle tank MBT-70 being jointly developed by the U.S.A. and Germany. The MBT-70 project in the end came to nothing but the Shillelagh system was installed in the M-551 light tank and, later, in a version of the M-60, the M-60A2. Considerable development difficulties occurred with the 152-mm. gun, not so much with the missile ammunition as with the conventional ammunition, which has a combustible cartridge case. Testing of the system on M-551s in action in Vietnam and further trials led to the solution of the problems, however.

All the M-60 series are powered by a Continental diesel twelve-cylinder engine of 750 h.p. situated at the rear, with an Allison transmission system driving rear track sprockets. The suspension is of the torsion bar variety and there are six medium-sized road-wheels and three track guide rollers each side. The cast hull contains the driver near the front in the centre and the commander, gunner and loader are in the turret, which like the hull is of cast construction.

The M-60 and M-60A1 both have a 105-mm. gun as main armament, accompanied by a coaxial 7·62-mm. machine-gun in the turret and a heavy 12·7-mm. machine-gun mounted in the commander's cupola on the turret roof. The main difference between these two models is that the M-60 has, as mentioned earlier, a modified M-48 hull.

The mounting in the M-60 of the Shillelagh system with its 152-mm. gun/launcher in a special turret has resulted in the M-60A2. Most of the performance characteristics, including the maximum speed of 48 km./hr, are unchanged despite the increase in loaded weight of around 3,000 kg. The quantity of ammunition carried is, however, reduced to forty-six rounds, compared with sixty-three rounds of 105 mm. for the M-60A1 and sixty for the M-60.

Only 526 M-60A2s were built and they are used to support conventional gun tanks, as their missiles have an effective range of over 3,000 metres, compared with the 105-mm. gun of M-60/M-60A1 which has an effective range of 1,800 metres using APDS ammunition. The M-60 and M-60A1 have been supplied to nearly a dozen armies, including that of the United

States, and production of the M-60A1, and an improved version the M-60A3, continues. The process of continually updating the M-48 and M-60 series has resulted in a confusing variety of hybrids and M-60A3 is the designation for the M-60A1 including a number of specified improvements, such as full stabilization for the main armament, a new laser range-finder, night vision equipment and an improved engine.

54 Armored Reconnaissance/Airborne Assault Vehicle, Full Tracked, 152 mm., M-551, U.S.A.

An air-portable light tank, the M-551, or General Sheridan, weighs just under 16 tons loaded and has the same main armament as the M-60A2 main battle tank. Development of the Sheridan (as the XM-551) began in early 1959 as a vehicle to replace both the M-41 Walker Bulldog light tank for reconnaissance and the M-56 self-propelled 90-cm. anti-tank gun as an airborne support vehicle.

The Shillelagh 152-cm. gun/launcher system is similar to that used in the M-60A2 and the now-abandoned MBT-70 main battle tank. Secondary armament consists of a 7·62-mm. machine-gun mounted in the turret coaxially with the main weapon and a 12·7-mm. machine-gun on the commander's cupola.

Lightness in weight is achieved by the use of an aluminium alloy forged hull and extensive use of aluminium in the engine, transmission and radiator. Weight has also been saved by attention to detail in other components, such as hollow road-wheel arms used in the transverse torsion bar suspension system and aircraft-type cables for vehicle control linkages. The vehicle is amphibious—propelled in water by its tracks —by the use of a screen. The front of this screen is formed by a high surf board (with two see-through panels), which is normally carried folded on the front glacis plate, and the sides and back are of flexible fabric which is kept folded round the hull top when not in use. The side barriers are kept rigid when erected by means of support posts.

The M-551 is powered by a Detroit Diesel six-cylinder engine developing 300 h.p., which produces a maximum road speed of 70 km./hr and 5·6 km./hr in water.

A total of some 1,700 M-551s have been built and are in service only with the U.S. Army, which employs them for reconnaissance purposes in armoured units, including those in airborne formations. Some early production vehicles were used in action in Vietnam, as a result of which a number of faults were corrected and improvements made such as, for example, the addition of a shield to the machine-gun on top of the turret.

55 Carrier, Personnel, Full Tracked, Armored, M-113A1 Diesel, and Carrier, 107-mm. Mortar, Full Tracked, M-106A1, U.S.A.

The American M-113 Armored Personnel Carrier and its variants is one of the most widely used armoured vehicles in the world. Getting on for 70,000 have been built (including licensed production in Italy) and different versions of M-113 and M-113A1 are used by some thirty-six countries.

The first production vehicle to use aluminium armour, the M-113 was developed by the FMC Corporation from its earlier armoured personnel carrier, the M-59 which, together with the M-75, it eventually replaced. Although having the same carrying capacity (for ten infantrymen, plus vehicle crew) as the M-59 and M-75, the M-113 is some seven tons lighter in weight. It should be mentioned here that to offer the same degree of protection as steel armour, aluminium has to be approximately three times as thick. The thicker aluminium hull is, therefore, roughly the same weight but much more rigid than a steel hull of comparable protection. Overall weight savings in aluminium hull vehicles can be made by the elimination of many structural components).

The M-113 has a box hull with vertical sides, a steeply sloping glacis plate at the front and a ramp at the rear containing a single door. The infantry occupy longitudinal seats against each wall, five each side, facing inwards. A large circular three-piece hatch in the hull roof near the rear enables the men to use their personal weapons from the vehicle. The vehicle commander's position is roughly in the centre of the hull roof and is equipped with a 12·7-mm. machine-gun mounted on his revolving cupola. The driver is at the front left-hand side of the vehicle, next to the engine.

The engine on the M-113 is a Chrysler eight-cylinder petrol type, developing 209 h.p. The M-113A1, which followed the M-113 in production in 1964 and, constitutes the bulk of vehicles produced, has instead a GMC six-cylinder diesel of 215 h.p. Transmission is to front sprockets, leaving the rear compartment entirely free of automotive components. The suspension of the M-113/M-113A1 consists of five road-wheels each side, carried on transverse torsion bars. Fully amphibious without preparation, other than erection of the trim vane carried on the glacis plate, the M-113 is propelled in water by its tracks, performance being enhanced by a rubber skirt covering the top run of the tracks. The maximum speed in water is just under 6 km./hr and on land about 68 km./hr.

There are many variants of the M-113 and M-113A1, one of which is the M-106A1 mortar carrier. This vehicle is mechanically identical to the M-113A1 and differs in other respects mainly in that the rear compartment has been modified so that the 4·2-in. (107-cm.) mortar mounted on a turn-table can be fired through the roof hatch. A base-plate and bipod for the mortar when used outside the vehicle are carried on the side of the hull. This variant of the M-113A1 has a crew of six. A similar vehicle used by the Swiss Army is equipped with a 120-mm. mortar, and Rheinstahl in Germany have modified standard M-113A1s for use as 120-mm. mortar carriers. The M-125A1 has an 81-mm. mortar.

Some other variants of the M-113 series are described elsewhere in the U.S.A. section of this book and the Fire Support Vehicle based on the M-113A1 developed in Australia is dealt with under that country.

56 Carrier, Command Post, Full Tracked, M-577A1 and Carrier, M-113 with Radar, U.S.A.

Among the many variants of the M-113A1 Armored Personnel Carrier are command and radar vehicles. Many M-113s are used at battalion level and below only slightly modified as command vehicles but the M-577A1 has a special hull structurally adapted for its function. The height of the hull just behind the engine and driver in the M-577A1 has been raised by 0·64 metres to allow full standing height for the command staff in the rear compartment. Further space can be provided, when immobile, by the erection of a tent extension at the rear. Equipment includes between three and five radios for rear and forward links to headquarters and formations or units in the field and a 28-volt generator to operate them for long periods. Field telephone and fire direction control equipment is also carried.

The M-113 has been adapted as a carrier for various forms of radar equipment. This includes the Franco-German RATAC on German M-113s (Radarpanzer 2) and the British Green Archer mortar locating radar on German (Radarpanzer 3) as shown in the illustration, and Danish M-113s. The Green Archer radar can track a mortar bomb in flight and by means of a computer plot the location of the mortar itself. When adapted to carry Green Archer, the M-113 has the upper part of the rear of the hull cut away for the installation of the scanner on its turntable. Power is provided by a silent-running generator, suitable for use in forward areas.

57 Command and Reconnaissance Vehicle (Lynx), and Carrier, Command and Reconnaissance, Armored, M-114A1, U.S.A.

The M-113 was used as the starting point for the design of two different smaller vehicles produced, respectively, for the U.S. Army and as a private venture by the FMC Corporation. As both vehicles are intended for command as well as reconnaissance functions, they have relatively roomy aluminium hulls, although both normally operate with a crew of three (optionally four in the case of the M-114A1). One advantage of the resultant volume: weight ratio is that both vehicles are amphibious without special aids other than a trim vane carried at the front.

The first prototype of the FMC Corporation's project was completed in 1963, and although rejected by the U.S. Army was purchased by the Dutch Army (who received them from 1966 onwards to a total of 260) and the Canadian Army, supplied with 174, who have given it the name Lynx. Very much like a scaled-down M-113, with only four road-wheels each side, the internal layout differs from the M-113 in that the engine is at the rear, although the drive is still to sprockets at the front of the track. The engine is a Detroit Diesel, developing 215 h.p., similar to that of the M-113A1, so the 8½ ton vehicle has a high maximum speed of 71 km./hr.

Both Dutch and Canadian vehicles were originally armed with a 12·7-mm. heavy machine-gun mounted externally on a cupola on the hull roof and capable of being fired from within the vehicle. There is also a pintle mounting near the rear roof hatch for a 7·62-mm. machine-gun. The Dutch vehicles, however, are being converted to take Oerlikon turrets mounting 25-mm. cannon in place of the cupolas with 12·7-mm. machine-guns. One of these modified Dutch vehicles is shown in the illustration.

The M-114, developed by the Cadillac Division of the General Motors Corporation also has four road-wheels each side, but has an internal mechanical layout more closely akin to the FMC Corporation's M-113 in that both engine and drive to the tracks are at the front. The engine is a Chevrolet V-8 cylinder petrol type, developing 160 h.p. and giving a maximum road speed of 58 km./hr. All versions of the M-114 have a 7·62-mm. machine-gun with two alternative mountings but the main armament has varied. In the M-114 this is a 12·7-mm. machine-gun on a pintle mounting on the hull roof, operated by the commander. The M-114A1 has provision for the weapon to be operated from inside the vehicle, and a later version is equipped instead with a 25-mm. Hispano-Suiza cannon.

Over 3,700 M-114s and M-114A1s have been built. Some were employed in Vietnam, where their cross-country performance in the terrain there was not satisfactory, but numbers are still in service with the U.S. Army.

58 **Landing Vehicle, Tracked— Personnel 7 and Landing Vehicle, Tracked—Engineer 7, U.S.A.**

The United States has been in the fore-front in the development of amphibious personnel and cargo carriers since World War II and Landing Vehicles Tracked from this period are still in service with some armies. The LVT-P5 (personnel carrier), and the mechanically similar LVT-H5 (with 105-mm. howitzer), and specialized variants, developed from 1950, in service from 1951 and produced up to 1957, have now been replaced by the LVTP-7 series.

Designed by the FMC Corporation in 1966, the fifteen prototypes of the experimental model, known as LVTPX-12, were completed between 1967 and 1969. The vehicle in its final form, known as LVTP-7, was running in 1970.

The LVTP-7 has a fully enclosed hull with an upturned nose plate or bow of an unusual angular design, found by experiment to reduce water resistance and turbulence. The suspension consists of six road-wheels each side, carried on transverse torsion bars. The engine and transmission are located at the front and the drive sprockets are at the front of the track. A power take-off unit supplies engine power to water jets in the rear of the hull, just over the track idler wheels, for propulsion in water. The jet outlets are fitted with movable deflectors for steering and reversing. The engine is a Detroit Diesel of eight cylinders, developing 400 h.p. This produces a maximum speed on land of 63 km./hr and 13½ km./hr on water. An interesting point is that both tracks and waterjets can be driven simultaneously—a useful feature when travelling in shallow water or when leaving the water, for example.

The LVTP-7 can carry twenty-five infantrymen, seated in three longitudinal rows, in addition to the crew. The latter consists of three men—the driver, who sits near the front at the left, the commander, just behind the driver, and the gunner, who occupies a turret, armed with one 12·7-mm. machine-gun, on the right-hand side of the hull roof. There is a large square ramp at the rear for loading cargo and this contains a door for the infantry.

The other members of the LVTP-7 family include the LVTC-7 command vehicle; the LVTR-7 recovery vehicle; and the LVTE-7. The latter, Landing Vehicle, Tracked, Engineer, Mark 7, is designed primarily for mine clearance in amphibious operations. For this purpose, a triple rocket launcher is carried in the rear compartment. For employment, the hull roof doors are opened, the launcher raised, and the three rockets are fired in succession over the minefield. The rockets carry line charges which are exploded, detonating the mines. To help level a path through the cleared minefield, and for other engineering tasks, a hydraulically oper-ated bulldozer blade is mounted at the front of the vehicle. The LVTE-7 has a crew of six men—three, as for the LVTP-7, and three to operate the rocket launcher.

About 1,000 vehicles of the LVTP-7 series have been delivered to the United States Marine Corps, where they have replaced earlier L.V.T.s. Some LVTP-7s have also been supplied to other countries.

59 Gun, Field Artillery, Self-Pro-pelled, 175-mm., M-107, and How-itzer, Heavy, Self-Propelled, 8 in., M-110, U.S.A.

In 1956 the United States felt the need for a fresh range of artillery weapons that would be air portable, and also the desire to achieve a much greater com-monality of components over the whole field of light armoured vehicles. The advent of the promising T-113 alu-minium hull armoured personnel car-rier (prototype of the M-113 series) at this time led to components of the armoured personnel carrier being used for the family of S.P. guns that was developed. Two successful vehicles to emerge were the T-235 175-mm. S.P. gun, which eventually became the M-107, and the T-236 8-in. S.P. howitzer, which after modifications became the M-110.

Designed by the Pacific Car and Foundry Company, the M-107 and M-110 have identical chassis and even the gun mountings are similar. The suspension is like a shortened version of the M-113s, without a separate idler wheel, the rear road-wheel, in contact with the ground, performing this function. The driver, who sits at the front left-hand side of the hull, is the only member of the crew to be protected, seats for the other four crew members travelling on the vehicle being provided around the gun mount-ing. Eight further crew members travel in a supporting vehicle (usually an M-548 cargo carrier), which also carries ammunition. The engine, located at the front right-hand side of the hull, is an eight-cylinder Detroit Diesel of 405 h.p. This produces, in both M-107 and M-110, a maximum speed of 56 km./hr, although the overall perform-ance of the M-107, which is getting on for 2 tons heavier than M-110, is probably slightly inferior to the M-110s. The M-107/M-110 have no pro-vision for amphibious operations.

The artillery piece on the M-107 is the 175-mm. model M-113, 60 calibres long. This gun fires an H.E. shell weighing 66·6 kg. to a maximum range of 32 km. The M-110's weapon is the 8-in. (203-mm.) model M2A1E1 howitzer with a calibre length of 25. This has a maximum range of 17 km. and the H.E. shell weighs 90·7 kg.

A dozen different countries, including the U.S.A., use the M-107 or M-110, or both. The illustrations show an Italian-used M-107 and a British M-110.

A replacement for both the M-107 and M-110, known as M110E2, is under development. This will use existing chassis and mountings (with modifications), the 175-mm. and 203-mm. barrels being replaced by a new and much longer 203-mm. barrel. The new gun should have a range somewhere between those of the two present guns.

60 Howitzer, Medium, Self-Propelled, 155-mm. M-109G, and Lance Guided Missile System, U.S.A.

Two tactical field artillery systems currently in service with the U.S. Army, and others, are the M-109, which is a conventional self-propelled howitzer, and the Lance, a surface-to-surface guided missile.

The M-109 was developed at around the same time as the M-107 and M-110, but because of its lighter and smaller calibre gun offers full armour protection for the crew within the same, air-portable, weight and can also be provided with nuclear, biological and chemical warfare protection and can be made to swim.

Sharing a common chassis with the 105-mm. S.P. M-108, both vehicles use the same engine as the M-107 and M-110—the 405-h.p. eight-cylinder Detroit Diesel. This gives the M-109 a top speed of 56 km./hr. On water, propelled by its tracks and made amphibious by the addition of nine air bags attached to the sides and front of the hull, the speed is about 6½ km./hr.

The suspension of the M-109 consists of seven road-wheels each side, carried on transverse torsion bars. The drive sprockets are at the front and the engine is in the front right-hand side of the hull, with the driver beside it at the left. The rear half of the hull consists of the fighting compartment, surmounted by the large fully enclosed rotating turret, in which is mounted the M-126 155-mm. howitzer, with a length of 23 calibres. The weapon has a maximum elevation of 75 degrees and maximum range, with a 43·5 kg. H.E. round, of 14·7 km.

An improved model, known as M-109G, uses a Rheinmetall-designed weapon with several improvements, having a range of 18·5 km. The vehicles only are supplied from the U.S.A. and the guns are installed in Germany for the Bundeswehr, or in Italy (by OTO Melara) for the Italian Army. There are also longer barrelled (39 calibres) versions of the M-109, the M-109A1 with a range of 18 km. which is already in service, and an improved model of the Rheinmetall gun under development by OTO Melara with a range of 24 km. Some fifteen countries use M-109 in different versions. Those used by the Swiss Army (M-109U) have been modified in Switzerland to take a semi-automatic loader and have a rate of fire of six rounds per minute—double that of the standard M-109. A M-109G in Italian use is shown in the illustration.

The Lance tactical guided missile system is now in service with several countries. Development was commenced in 1962 as a replacement for the Honest John unguided rocket then used by leading NATO countries. Later, work was concentrated on an extended range Lance which could replace the Sergeant guided missile. The first flight test of the Extended Range Lance took place in 1969 and it was classified by the U.S. Army as Standard A when fitted with a nuclear warhead in May 1972.

The complete Lance system consists of the missile, two types of launcher and ancillary equipment. Two tracked carrier vehicles are usually employed— the self-propelled launcher vehicle (M-752) and the loader–transporter vehicle (M-688). Both are derivatives of the M-548 unarmoured cargo carrier. The Lance can be launched from the M-752 or from a two-wheeled 'zero length launcher', which can be towed by a truck if necessary. All the equipment is air-transportable.

The loader–transporter vehicle M-688 can carry two missiles and is equipped with an hydraulic crane for transferring them to the launcher, the tracked M-752 normally being used as the firing platform.

All launch functions for Lance are controlled by a monitor/programmer, consisting of a combined analog and digital computer. The missile is propelled by a single-stage pre-packaged liquid fuel rocket over a range of about 112 km. with a nuclear warhead of 210 kg. The new neutron missile can also be launched by Lance. Other, non-nuclear, warheads of around 450 kg. can, for example, disperse guided sub-missiles to seek and track enemy armour. A new version of Lance, Lance 2, uses a solid propellant fuel rocket.

61 **Gun, Anti-Aircraft Artillery, Self-Propelled, 20-mm., M-163, and Guided Missile System Intercept— Aerial, Carrier Mounted (Chaparral), U.S.A.**

The Vulcan and Chaparral equipments together make up a low level anti-aircraft system. Vulcan consists of a 20-mm. revolving multi-barrel gun mounted in a turret on the hull of a modified M-113A1 armoured personnel carrier. Equipped with range-finding radar, but aimed visually and fired when an electronic indicator tells the gunner that the target is within range, the six barrels of the Vulcan can achieve a total rate of 3,000 rounds per minute. A lower rate of 1,000 rounds per minute is also available for use against ground targets. Nineteen hundred rounds of ammunition are carried, including tracer, incendiary, armour-piercing and high explosive.

The Chaparral consists of four modified Sidewinder heat-seeking missiles mounted on a turntable launcher on the rear of the hull of a modified M-548 tracked cargo carrier. The missiles are optically sighted but the final phase of their flight on to the target is controlled by signals from their passive infra-red target-seeking heads. The missiles weigh about 84 kg. each and eight are carried in reserve on the vehicle as well as the four on the launcher.

Vulcan and Chaparral are the U.S. Army's current air defence against low-flying subsonic and supersonic aircraft. Both systems have also been supplied to Israel.

62 Recovery Vehicle, Full Tracked, Medium, M-88, and Recovery Vehicle, Full Tracked, Light, Armored, M-578, U.S.A.

These two armoured recovery vehicles are intended for the battlefield recovery of tanks and other armoured vehicles up to about 56,000 kg. (M-88) or 30,000 kg. (M-578) respectively.

The medium recovery vehicle uses many components of the M-48 tank series, including the twelve-cylinder Continental petrol engine and generally similar running gear, but has a specially designed hull. The suspension, like that of the M-48, is of the torsion bar type and has six road-wheels each side, but the track base is longer and the upper run of the track is lower than that of the medium tank. The equipment includes a non-rotating A-frame jib, pivoted near the front of the hull and having a maximum lift of 25,400 kg.; a main winch with a pull of 40,800 kg., for which 61 metres of cable is carried; and a secondary (hoist) winch with a capacity of 22,680 kg. A hydraulically operated bulldozer blade is mounted at the front of the vehicle and this is used as a stabilizer for the jib as well as for earth moving. A more unusual facility for an armoured recovery vehicle is an auxiliary fuel pump, which enables the M-88 to transfer fuel to other armoured vehicles.

About 1,000 M-88s have been built

and they are in service with several armies equipped with American tanks, besides the U.S. Army. It is likely that many of these will eventually be rebuilt to the same chassis mechanical standards as the M-60 tank series, including the substitution of a diesel for the petrol engine.

The light recovery vehicle M-578 uses the chassis of the self-propelled guns M-107 and M-110, which have a layout conducive to the installation at the rear of a fully revolving crane in an armoured turret. This crane has a maximum capacity of 13,620 kg.—to the rear only, when the stabilizing spade at the back is in position. The vehicle is operated by a crew of three —the driver at the front left-hand side, alongside the engine, and the other two men in the crane turret. One 12·7-mm. heavy machine-gun is carried for defence, pintle-mounted on the turret roof.

Design of the M-578 commenced (as the T-120) in 1957 and the first production vehicle was completed in 1962. The production line continues and vehicles have been supplied to eight countries (including the U.S.A.) using American M-107 and M-110 S.P. guns and other light armoured vehicles.

63 Combat Engineer Vehicle, Full Tracked, M-728, and Armored Vehicle Launched Bridge, U.S.A./ Italy.

The chassis of the M-60, as the current United States medium tank, has been used as the basis of a family of support vehicles having the advantage of roughly the same performance as well as many components in common. Two of the most important of these derivatives are an armoured engineer vehicle and a tank bridge layer.

The Combat Engineer Vehicle, M-728, is intended for a variety of engineering tasks in or near the battlefield, such as the destruction of concrete fortifications, the levelling or filling of earthwork defences and the preparation of positions for artillery or dug-in tanks. The basic chassis is that of the M-60A1, complete with turret including the commander's cupola with its machine-gun. The main armament is, however, a short-barrelled 165-mm. gun firing a 30-kg. demolition charge with a range of 1,000 metres, capable of destroying concrete emplacements. A coaxial machine-gun is also mounted in the turret.

A secondary function of the turret is to act as a turntable for an A-frame jib. This crane, which has a 15-ton lift, is pivoted near the front of the turret and is carried over the rear deck of the tank when not in use. The turret also has a two-speed winch mounted on the rear. For earth-moving tasks, an hydraulically operated bulldozer blaze is carried at the front of the vehicle's hull.

The development of the M-728 began with the T-118 experimental vehicle, using a T-95 tank chassis. This was followed by the T-118E1 and then the T-118E2 on the M-60A1 chassis, which was standardized as the M-728 by the time it entered production in 1965.

The M-60 A.V.L.B. (Armoured Vehicle Launched Bridge) consists of a scissors-type bridge mounted on a turretless M-60 tank chassis. The bridge itself is the same as that previously fitted on M-48 chassis. It is of aluminium alloy construction and is hydraulically operated. Opened out, it is 63 ft (19·202 metres) long and can bridge a gap of 60 ft (18·288 metres). Pivoted at the front of the vehicle, the bridge can be laid in three minutes and retrieved in a minimum of ten minutes. A new lightweight bridge for the M-60 chassis with a span of 95 ft (28·956 metres) for a gap of 90 ft (27·432 metres) is in the course of development.

The Italian company Astra SpA has designed an interesting armoured vehicle launched bridge which can be used with American M-47 (as shown in the illustration), M-48 or M-60 tank chassis, or (as employed by the Israeli Army) the British Centurion chassis. A scissors bridge of mixed steel and aluminium alloy construction, the A-26 is 22 metres long when extended and can carry up to 54 tons. The end ramps can be adjusted vertically downwards to form supports, enabling a second bridge to be launched from the first, to give a clear span with two bridges of between 36 and 38 metres. The launching mechanism is hydraulic, and the bridge can be recovered from either end. A time of six minutes is claimed for either launching or recovery of the bridge.

64 Infantry Combat Vehicle, M-980, Yugoslavia.

Not long after World War II, a Yugoslavian version of the Soviet T-34/85 tank appeared with a turret apparently made locally. The bulk of the A.F.V.s used by Yugoslavia until recently were, however, standard equipment of American or Soviet manufacture.

A new armoured personnel carrier entirely of Yugoslav design appeared in public for the first time in 1965. This vehicle, known as M-60 or M-590 is rather high and bulky and with a diesel engine of only 140 h.p. has a relatively low performance. It was succeeded in 1975 by a much more advanced vehicle, the M-980, fully equipped as an infantry combat vehicle. This has a well shaped hull with a long sloping glacis plate. The driver is at the front left-hand side, with the engine beside him at the right. The engine is a Hispano-Suiza/SNECMA eight-cylinder diesel of 280 h.p., as fitted in the French AMX-10P. The rear compartment has accommodation for six to eight infantrymen with their personal weapons, for the operation of which eight ports in the hull sides and rear are provided. The other two crew members are the commander and gunner.

The M-980 is particularly well armed for a M.I.C.V. The centrally located turret contains a 20-mm. Hispano-Suiza cannon and two 7·92-mm. machine-guns and a twin launcher for 'Sagger' (NATO name) SS anti-tank missiles.

The vehicle is amphibious, with a maximum water speed of 8 km./hr. On roads 70 km./hr can be attained.

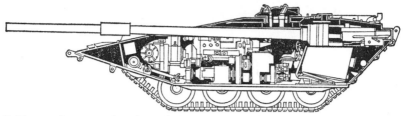

Stridsvagn Strv. 103—length (excluding gun) 7·0 metres (8·4 metres with stowage bins).

Bergepanzer 2, Leopard—length 7·57 metres.

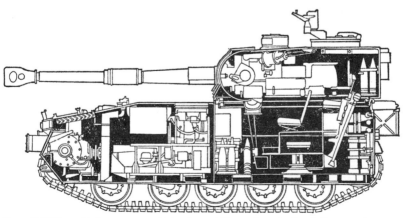

Gun, Self-Propelled, 105 mm. Fd. Gun, Abbot—length (excluding gun) 5·709 metres.

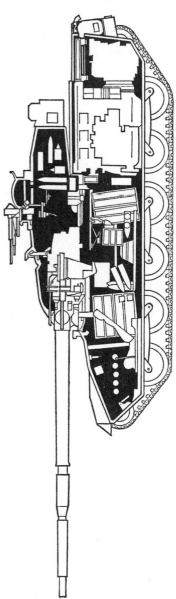

Tank, Combat, 120 mm. Gun, Chieftain Mk. 3—length (excluding gun) 7·52 metres.

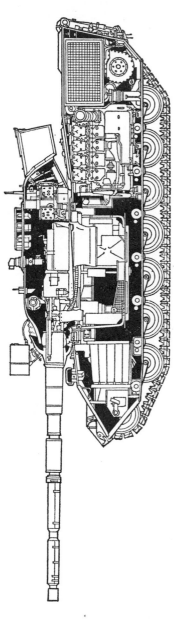

Kampfpanzer Leopard 1—length (excluding gun) 7·09 metres.

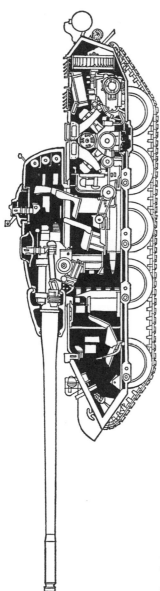

T-54A (Main Battle Tank)—length (excluding gun) 7·09 metres.

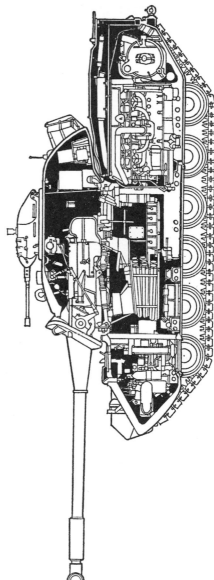

Tank, Combat; Full Tracked, 90 mm. Gun, M-48A2—length (excluding gun) 6·87 metres.

APPENDIX

Armoured Fighting Vehicle Camouflage Colours

The notes which follow give some guidance on the A.F.V. camouflage colours used by the countries—both of manufacturer and user—that are included in this book. It must be borne in mind, however, that to the eye the colour of a vehicle will differ widely with light and shade and that its paintwork will be changed in appearance, often quite drastically, by ageing, wear, or such additions as dust or mud.

Where one colour only is quoted, this is believed to be normal, but in any country at any time other schemes may be used to meet specific circumstances.

All NATO vehicles commonly show (at the front) the standard bridge group sign of a black figure on a yellow disc.

Argentina

Overall olive green, sometimes with other colours to make a disruptive pattern.

Australia

Overall olive drab colour. British-type tactical markings are used.

Austria

Overall dark green, similar to NATO green but with less of an olive shade. The National sign of a white hollow inverted triangle within a white ring is carried on A.F.V.s.

Belgium

Overall olive drab. Vehicle registration numbers are in black, preceded by a small rectangle in the national colours, on a white plate. Formation and tactical signs are usually carried.

Chinese Peoples Republic

Dark to medium green, overall. The national sign of a red star, outlined in yellow, is sometimes carried on A.F.V.s.

Czechoslovakia

Olive green overall. The national sign of a disc in blue, red and white segments is generally carried on A.F.V.s.

France

Olive drab colour overall. A tiny national tricolour flag precedes the vehicle number at the front and rear of the hull of A.F.V.s. Various regimental signs are used.

German Federal Republic (West Germany)

Normally, overall dark greyish-green, although sometimes a two- or three-colour disruptive scheme is used. The national marking is a black Iron Cross, outlined in white. Tactical numbers in white, or white outline, are commonly used on A.F.V.s, also, sometimes, small signs indicating the type of unit etc. The vehicle registration number in black, with prefix 'Y' and a small black/red/yellow sign (the national flag) is carried at front and rear on a white rectangle.

German Democratic Republic (East Germany)

Overall grey or olive green, with the D.D.R. national sign in black, yellow, red and gold in a small circle.

Holland

Overall olive green. Vehicle registration numbers are in black, prefixed by 'KN' or 'KZ' on a yellow rectangular plate, carried at front and rear of A.F.V.s.

India

Dark green overall. Disruptive pattern added sometimes. British-type tactical markings are used.

Israel

Overall yellowish sand colour. Vehicle registration numbers are in white on a black rectangle. Tactical signs (usually Hebrew characters in white) sometimes used. Also unit signs, mostly in white but sometimes using other colours.

Italy

Olive green overall. National sign (green/white/red rectangle) carried at front and rear. Vehicle number is in black, prefixed by 'EI' in red, on white rectangle.

Japan

Olive green overall. A multi-coloured disruptive pattern sometimes used. National sign—red disc sun on white rectangle is usually shown on A.F.V.s.

Poland

Olive green overall. National sign (diamond, quartered in red and white) carried on most A.F.V.s. Large white tactical numbers often used. Some unit or formation signs also appear sometimes.

Soviet Union

Overall dark olive green. Airborne forces have white parachute sign. Large white tactical numbers usually carried on tanks and armoured personnel carriers. The Red Star national sign appears, normally, to be used only on formal parades.

Sweden

A four colour scheme, using dark green, light green, light brown and black in a zig-zag pattern is to be applied to all A.F.V.s. Vehicle registration numbers are in yellow at front and rear.

Switzerland

Overall olive (brownish) drab colour. Vehicle numbers, prefixed by 'M' in white shown at front and rear of A.F.V.s White tactical signs—large numbers—used and (sometimes) unit insignia.

United Kingdom

Overall NATO green (dark olive green). Black disruptive patches added in Europe. In snow conditions, white is added, leaving some green. For desert conditions 'light stone' colour is used with black patches. Vehicle numbers (two digits, two letters, two digits, e.g. 13EA81) are in white at front and rear. Vehicle call signs are in white and follow a system such as 34=C Squadron (or 3rd fighting squadron), 4th Troop, Troop leader; 34A=2nd tank and so on. World War II tactical signs of a diamond for regimental (or battalion) H.Q., triangle—'A' Squadron; square—'B' Squadron; circle—'C' Squadron are often still used. Tanks and other A.F.V.s in B.A.O.R. only have a small national flag painted on front and rear.

U.S.A.

Olive drab or Forest Green overall, except where the four colour pattern scheme is used for tactical vehicles. The latter consists of four colours (including black) selected from a standard range of twelve colours. Typical combinations are (1) Sand (greyish, rather than yellow), Earth Red, Dark Green and Black, with the Sand and Earth Red predominating, Green and Black being used sparingly. This scheme has been used by the U.S. Army in West Germany. (2) Dark Green, Light Green, Earth Red and Black, with the two greens predominating and only small patches of the Earth Red and Black. This is suitable for wooded areas. The U.S. national sign used with the four colour schemes is a black five-pointed star and the U.S. Army vehicle number is also shown in black. Various geometric coloured tactical signs are sometimes used on armoured vehicles.

Yugoslavia

Greyish-green, overall. Tactical markings apparently not used.

Ref. No.	Type	Weight tons	Length (hull)	Length (inc. gun)	Width	Height	Armament
			Metres				
1	*Argentina:* TAM	29·5	6·775	8·23	3·25	2·42	1 105 mm., 1 7·62 mm m.g. (co-ax), 1 7·62 m (AA)
5	*Chinese P.R.:* T-59	40·6	6·45	9·0	3·27	2·4	1 100 mm., 1 7·62 mm m.g. (co-ax), 1 7·62 m (hull), 1 12·7 mm. m. (AA)
7	*France:* AMX-30	36	6·59	9·48	3·1	2·28	1 105 mm., 1 12·7 mm m.g. (co-ax), 1 7·62 m m.g. (AA)
13	*Germany:* Leopard I	40	7·09	9·54	3·25	2·62	1 105 mm., 1 7·62 mm m.g. (co-ax), 1 7 62 m (AA)
13	Leopard IA3	42·4	7·09	9·54	3·37	2·62	1 105 mm., 1 7·62 mm m.g. (co-ax), 1 7·62 m (AA)
19	*Japan:* Type 61	35	6·3	8·19	2·95	2·49	1 90 mm., 1 7·62 mm. m.g. (co-ax), 1 12·7 m m.g. (AA)
19	Type 74	38	6·85	9·09	3·18	2·48	1 105 mm., 1 7·62 mm m.g. (co-ax), 1 12·7 m m.g. (AA)
24	*Soviet Union:* T-55	36	6·45	9·0	3·27	2·4	1 100 mm., 1 7·62 mm m.g. (co-ax)
25	T-62	36·5	6·715	9·77	3·35	2·4	1 115 mm., 1 7·62 mm m.g. (co-ax), 1 12·7 mm. m (AA)
34	*Sweden:* Strv. 103B	39	8·4	9·8	3·6	2·5	1 105 mm., 2 7·62 mm m.g. (hull), 1 7·62 mm m.g. (AA)
38	*Switzerland:* Pz61	38	6·78	9·43	3·06	2·72	1 105 mm., 1 20 mm. (co-ax), 1 7·5 mm. m (AA)
38	Pz68	39·7	6·9	9·49	3·14	2·74	1 105 mm., 1 7·5 mm. m (co-ax), 1 7·5 mm. (A
40	*United Kingdom:* Chieftain Mk 3	54·1	7·52	10·79	3·504	2·895	1 120 mm., 1 12·7 mm ranging m.g., 1 7·62 m m.g. (co-ax), 1 7·62 m
40	Chieftain Mk 5	55	7·518	10·79	3·504	2·895	1 120 mm., 1 12·7 mm ranging m.g., 1 7·62 m m.g. (co-ax), 1 7·62 m
39	Vickers M.B.T.	38·6	7·92	9·73	3·168	2·64	1 105 mm., 1 12·7 mm ranging m.g., 1 7·62 m.g. (co-ax), 1 7·62 m (AA)
41	Centurion (Vickers retrofit)	52·0	7·823	9·85	3·39	3·00	1 105 mm., 1 7·62 mm m.g. (co-ax)
53	*U.S.A.:* M-60A1	49	6·946	9·31	3·631	3·257	1 105 mm., 1 7·62 mm m.g. (co-ax), 1 12·7 m m.g.
53	M60A2	52	6·946	7·28	3·631	3·108	1 152 mm., 1 7·62 mm m.g. (co-ax), 1 12·7 m m.g.
52	Xm-1	53·39	7·92	9·76	3·65	2·89	1 105 mm., 1 7·62 mm (co-ax), 1 12·7 mm., 7·62 mm. (on turret

Engine	h.p.	Speed km./hr road	Speed km./hr water	Range km	Crew	Notes
imler Benz 6 cyl. iesel	710	75		600	4	
esel 12 cyl.	520	50		500	4	
spano-Suiza 12 cyl. iesel	720	65		650	4	
imler–Benz 10 cyl. iesel	830	65		600	4	
imler–Benz 10 cyl. iesel	830	65		600	4	
tsubishi 12 cyl. iesel	600	45		200	4	
tsubishi 10 cyl. iesel	750	53		500	4	
del V-55 12 cyl. iesel	580	50		500	4	
cyl. diesel	700	50		500	4	
lls-Royce 6 cyl. iesel plus Boeing gas turbine	240} 490}	50	6	390	3	
imler–Benz 8 cyl. iesel	630	55		300	4	
imler–Benz 7 cyl. iesel	660	60		300	4	
yland 12 cyl. multi- el	750	48		500	4	
yland 12 cyl. multi- el	750	48		500	4	
yland 12 cyl. multi- el	650	56	6·5	480	4	
neral Motors 12 cyl. iesel	715	40			4	
ntinental 12 cyl. esel	750	48		500	4	
ntinental 12 cyl. esel	750	48		500	4	
CO Lycoming gas rbine	1500	70		450	4	With 120-mm. Rheinmetall gun: 54·44 ton, length inc. gun 9·80 m.

147

Ref. No.	Type	Weight tons	Length	Length (inc. gun)	Width	Height	Armament
	Austria:						
3	Panzerjäger	17·5	5·58	7·78	2·50	2·36	1 105 mm., 1 7·62 mm. m.g. (co-ax)
	France:						
8	AMX-13	15·0	4·88	6·36	2·51	2·23	1 105 mm., 1 7·62 mm. m.g. (co-ax)
8	AMX-13 (AA)	17·2	5·373		2·5	3·794	2 30 mm.
	Germany:						
15	Gepard	45·1	7·27	7·7	3·25	4·03	2 35 mm.
	Soviet Union:						
26	PT-76	14	6·91	7·63	3·14	2·25	1 76·2 mm., 1 7·62 mm m.g. (co-ax)
28	ZSU-57-2	28·0	6·22	8·48	3·27	2·75	2 57 mm.
28	ZSU-23-4	14	6·3		2·95	2·25	4 23 mm.
	Sweden:						
35	IKV-91	15·5	6·41	8·84	3·0	2·355	1 90 mm., 1 7·62 mm. m.g. (co-ax)
	United Kingdom:						
42	Scorpion	7·96	4·338		2·184	2·096	1 76 mm., 1 7·62 mm. m (co-ax)
42	Scimitar	7·89	4·388	4·74	2·184	2·115	1 30 mm., 1 7·62 mm m.g. (co-ax)
47	Falcon	15·85	5·333		2·641	2·514	2 30 mm.
54	*U.S.A.:*						
54	M-551	15·83	6·299		2·819	2·272	1 152 mm., 1 7·62 mm. m.g. (co-ax) 1 12·7 m

metres

Engine	h.p.	Speed km./hr road	Speed km./hr water	Range km.	Crew	Notes
aurer (Steyr) 6 cyl. diesel	300	67		520	3	
OFAM 8 cyl. petrol	250	60		350	3	
OFAM 8 cyl. petrol	250	60		300	3	Height includes radar.
TU 10 cyl. diesel	840	65		600	3	Height includes radar.
Model V-6 6 cyl. diesel	240	44	10	260	3	
Model V-54 12 cyl .diesel	520	48		400	6	
Model V-6 6 cyl. diesel	240	44		260	4	
Volvo 6 cyl. diesel	295	64	7	550	4	
aguar 6 cyl. petrol	195	81	6·5	644	3	
aguar 6 cyl. petrol	195	81	6·5	644	3	
Rolls-Royce 6 cyl. multi-fuel	240	48		390	3	
Detroit Diesel 6 cyl.	300	70	5·6	600	4	

Ref. No.	Type	Weight tons	metres			Armament
			Length	Width	Height	
2	*Australia:* M-113A1 FSV	26·3	4·86	2·68	2·87	1 76 mm., 1 7·62 mm. m.g. (co-a 1 m.g.
4	*Austria:* Schützenpanzer 4K4FA	12·5	5·40	2·50	1·65	1 12·7 mm. m.g.
5	*Chinese P.R.:*					
5	APC	10·0				1 12·7 mm. m.g.
6	*Czechoslovakia:* OT-62	15	7·08	3·14	2·038	1 7·62 mm. m.g.
9	*France:* AMX13VC1	14·0	5·544	2·51	1·92	1 7·62 mm. m.g. or 1 12·7 mm. m.g. (co-ax)
9	AMX10P	13·8	5·778	2·78	2·54	1 20 mm., 1 7·62 mm. m.g. (co-a
14	*Germany:* Marder	28·2	6·79	3·24	2·86	1 20 mm., 1 7·62 mm. (co-ax), 1 7·62 mm. m.g.
20	*Japan:* Type 60	11·8	4·85	2·4	1·70	1 7·62 mm. m.g., 1 12·7 mm. m.g
21	Type 60 (mortar)	12·0	4·85	2·4	1·7	1 107 mm. mortar, 1 12·7 mm. m
20	Type 73	14	5·6	2·8	1·7	1 7·62 mm. m.g., 1 12·7 mm. m.g
27	*Soviet Union:* BMP-1	12·5	6·75	3·0	2·0	1 73 mm., 1 7·62 mm. m.g. (co-a 1 ATGW launcher
27	BMD	8·5	5·3	2·65	1·85	1 73 mm., 1 7·62 mm. m.g. (co-a 1 ATGW launcher
36	*Sweden:* Pbv 302	13·5	5·35	2·86	2·5	1 20 mm.
37	Bgbv 82	26·3	7·2	3·25	2·63	1 20 mm.
45	*United Kingdom:* FV 432	15·28	5·251	2·8	1·879	1 7·62 mm. m.g.
43	Spartan	8·172	4·839	2·184	2·25	1 7·62 mm. m.g.
44	Sultan	7·918	4·991	2·184	2·016	1 7·62 mm. m.g.
	FV 434	17·75	5·72	2·844	2·794	
55	*U.S.A.:* M-113A1	11·156	4·863	2·686	2·5	1 12·7 mm. m.g.
55	M-106A1	11·996	4·926	2·863	2·5	1 107 mm. mortar
56	M-577A1	11·513	4·862	2·686	2·68	
57	M-114A1	6·928	4·463	2·33	2·155	1 25 mm. or 1 12·7 mm. m.g. 1 7·62 mm. m.g.
57	Lynx	8·5	4·597	2·413	2·171	1 12·7 mm. m.g.
58	LVTP-7	23·665	7·943	3·27	3·12	1 12·7 mm. m.g.
64	*Yugoslavia:* M-980	11·00	6·25	2·85	2·50	1 20 mm., 1 Sagger launcher, 2 m.g.

Engine	h.p.	Speed km./hr road	Speed km./hr water	Range km.	Crew	Notes
6 cyl. diesel	215	65	5·8	300	3	Height with Saladin turret.
rer 6 cyl. diesel	250	60		350	2+8	Model 4K4F AAG has 20 mm. gun.
-6 6 cyl. diesel	300	62	11	450	2+18	Height excludes turret. Data is for OT62B.
FAM 8 cyl. petrol	250	65		400	1+12	Height excludes turret.
pano-Suiza 8 cyl. esel	280	65	8	600	2+9	
U 6 cyl. diesel	600	75		520	4+6	
tsubishi 8 cyl. diesel	220	45		230	2+8	
tsubishi 8 cyl. diesel	220	45		230	5	
tsubishi 4 cyl. diesel	300	60			2+10	
del V-6 6 cyl. diesel	280	55	8	300	3+8	
		55	6		3+6	
vo 6 cyl. diesel	270	66	8	300	2+9	
vo 6 cyl. diesel	310	56	8	550	4	Armoured Recovery Vehicle.
lls-Royce 6 cyl. ulti-fuel	240	52	6	580	2+10	
uar 6 cyl. petrol	195	81	6·5	644	3+4	Height to hull top only 1·718 m.
uar 6 cyl. petrol	195	81	6·5	644	3+3	Samaritan ambulance: crew 2+4. stretcher cases or 6 sitting cases.
lls-Royce 6 cyl. ulti-fuel	240	52	6	480	4	Height includes crane.
neral Motors 6 cyl. esel	215	68	6	483	2+11	
neral Motors 6 cyl. esel	215	68	6	483	6	
neral Motors 6 cyl. esel		68	6	595	5	
evrolet 8 cyl. petrol	160	58	5·4	480	3+4	
roit Diesel 6 cyl.	215	71	6	523	3	1 25-mm. cannon in Dutch vehicles.
roit Diesel 8 cyl.	400	63	13·5	482	3+25	LVTE-7: crew 6.
pano-Suiza 8 cyl. esel	280	70	8	500	3+6/8	

Ref. No.	Type	Weight tons	Metres				Armament
			Length	Length (inc. gun/ missile)	Width	Height	
	France:						
10	155 mm. GCT	41	6·485	10·4	3·15	2·995	1 155 mm. gun, 1 7·62 mm. m.g.
10	155 mm. automouv.	17·4	6·22		2·72	2·1	1 155 mm., 1 m.g.
16	*Germany:* JgdPzK	27·5	6·238	8·75	2·98	2·085	1 90 mm., 1 7·62 mm. m.g. (co-ax) 1 7·62 mm. m.g. (AA)
16	JgdPzR	23	6·43		2·98	1·98	2 launchers SS-11, 1 7·62 mm. m.g., 1 7·62 mm. m.g. (AA)
22	*Japan:* 155 mm. SP	24	6·64		2·25	3·18	1 155 mm., 1 12·7 mm. m.g.
11	Type 60 (SS-4)	8	4·3		2·23	1·38	2 106 mm. (recoilless) ranging m.g., 1 12·7 m
26	*Soviet Union:* ASU-85	14	6·0	8·49	2·8	2·1	1 85 mm., 1 7·62 mm. m. (co-ax)
31	Frog 5	15	7·00		3·16	3·08	1 launcher
30	Gainful	15	6·80	7·39	3·18	3·33	3 SA6 launchers
32	Scamp	45		14·40	3·60	4·44	1 Scapegoat (SS-14) launcher
32	Scrooge	50		19·00	3·60	5·00	1 Scrooge (SS-15) launch
36	*Sweden:* Bkv 1A	53	6·55	11·0	3·37	3·35	1 155 mm.
47	*United Kingdom:* Abbot	16·5	5·709	5·84	2·641	2·489	1 105 mm., 1 7·62 mm.
46	FV 438	16·2	5·105		2·972	2·705	1 Swingfire launcher, 1 7·76 mm. m.g.
43	Striker	8·22	4·759		2·184	2·21	1 Swingfire launcher
59	*U.S.A.:* M-107	28·17	5·72	11·26	3·15	3·68	1 175 mm.
59	M-110	26·5	5·72	7·47	3·15	2·93	1 203 mm.
60	M-109G	24·5	6·25	6·61	3·58	2·80	1 155 mm., 1 7·62 mm. m.g.
61	Vulcan	12	4.86		2.69	2.60	1 20 mm (six barrels)
61	Chaparral	12·6	5·89		2·69	2·64	1 sidewinder launcher
60	Lance	10·7	6·55		2·69	2·72	1 Lance launcher

Engine	h.p.	Speed km./hr road	water	Range km.	Crew	Notes
Hispano-Suiza 12 cyl. diesel	700	60		450	4	
OFAM 8 cyl. petrol	250	65		300	2	
Daimler–Benz 8 cyl. diesel	500	70		400	4	
Daimler–Benz 8 cyl. diesel	500	70		400	4	Height is to hull top.
Mitsubishi diesel	420	50			6	
Komatsu 6 cyl. diesel	120	48		130	3	Height guns raised.
Model V-6 6 cyl. diesel	240	44		260	4	
Model V-6 6 cyl. diesel	240				3	
Model V-6 6 cyl. diesel	240	44		260	3	
diesel	690					
diesel	690					
Rolls-Royce 6 cyl. diesel / Boeing gas turbine	240} 300}	24		230	6	
Rolls-Royce 6 cyl. multi-fuel	240	48	5	390	4	
Rolls-Royce 6 cyl. multi-fuel	240	52	6·0	480	3	
Jaguar 6 cyl. petrol	195	81	6·5	644	3	
Detroit Diesel 8 cyl.	405	56		725	5	
Detroit Diesel 8 cyl.	405	56		725	5	
Detroit Diesel 8 cyl.	405	56	6·5	390	6	
General Motors 6 cyl. diesel	215	68	6		2	
General Motors 6 cyl. diesel	215	68			3	
General Motors 6 cyl. diesel	215	65			6	

Ref. No.	Type	Weight	Metres			Armament
			Length	Width	Height	
12	*France:* AMX 30 B/L	43	11·5	3·95	4·29	
11	AMX 30 ARV	36	7·20	3·15	2·65	1 7·62 mm. m.g.
17	*Germany:* Leopard B/L	45·3	11·40	4·;0	3·50	
17	Leopard ARV	39·8	7·57	3·25	2·46	
22	*Japan:* Type 67 AVLB	35	7·27	3·5	3·5	
33	*Soviet Union:* T.54 MTU	36	12·00	3·28	2·65	
37	*Sweden:* Broby 941	28·4	17·00	4·00	3·50	1 m.g.
48	*United Kingdom:* Chieftain AVLB	53·3	13·73	4·16	3·92	
49	Chieftain ARV	53·2	8·25	3·52	2·75	1 7·62 mm. m.g.
50	Combat Engineer Tractor	17·1	7·544	2·896	2·667	
49	Centurion BARV	40·63	8·08	3·40	3·45	
63	*U.S.A.:* M-728 CEV	52	7·88	3·70	3·20	1 165 mm., 1 7·62 mm. m.g. (co-ax) 1 12·7 mm. m.g. (AA)
63	M-60 AVLB	55·75	11·048	4·00	4·04	
62	M-88 ARV	50·8	8·25	3·43	2·92	1 12·7 mm. m.g.
62	M-578 ARV	24·47	5·94	3·15	2·92	1 12·7 mm. m.g.

Engine	h.p.	Speed km./hr road	Speed km./hr water	Range km.	Crew	Notes
pano-Suiza 12 cyl. sel	700	50			3	Bridge: 22 m. long. Dimensions of vehicle with bridge.
pano-Suiza 12 cyl. sel	700	60			4	
nler–Benz 10 cyl. sel	830	62				Bridge: 22 m. long. Dimensions of vehicle with bridge.
	830	65			4	
subishi 12 cyl. diesel	600	45		200	3	Bridge: 22 m. long. Dimensions of vehicle with bridge.
el V-54 12 cyl. disel	550	48				Bridge: 12 m.
vo-Penta 6 cyl. diesel	310	56	8	550	4	Bridge: 15 m. Dimensions of vehicle with bridge.
		42			3	Bridge: 24·4 m. Dimensions are with bridge.
land 12 cyl. multi- l	720	42		500	4	
s-Royce 6 cyl. diesel	320	60	9		2	
s-Royce 12 cyl. rol	650	34			4	
tinental 12 cyl. diesel	750	48		500	4	Length inc. jib 9·3 m.
tinental 12 cyl. diesel	750	48		500	2	Bridge: 19·2 m. Dimensions of vehicle with bridge.
tinental 12 cyl. rol	980	48		360	4	Length excludes dozer blade.
eral Motors 8 cyl. sel	425	60		725	3	Length 6·42 m. including crane.